NIETZSCHE
NIETZSCHE
NIETZSCHE

A Philosophical Biography

Gary Elsner

UNIVERSITY
PRESS OF
AMERICA

Lanham • New York • London

Copyright © 1992 by
University Press of America®, Inc.
4720 Boston Way
Lanham, Maryland 20706

3 Henrietta Street
London WC2E 8LU England

Library of Congress Cataloging-in-Publication Data

Elsner, Gary.
Nietzsche : a philosophical biography / Gary Elsner.
p.   cm.
Includes bibliographical references and index.
1. Nietzsche, Friedrich Wilhelm, 1844–1900.   2. Philosophers—
Germany—Biography.   I. Title.
B3316.E57   1992   193—dc20   92–5698 CIP
[B]

ISBN 0–8191–8696–1 (cloth : alk. paper)
ISBN 0–8191–8697–X (pbk. : alk. paper)

The paper used in this publication meets the minimum requirements of
American National Standard for Information Sciences—Permanence
of Paper for Printed Library Materials, ANSI Z39.48–1984.

Acknowledgements

Permission to publish excerpts from the following works were granted:

From The Birth of Tragedy and the Genealogy of Morals by Friedrich Nietzsche, translated by Francis Golffing. Reprinted by permission of Bantam, Doubleday, Dell Publishing, copyright 1956 by Doubleday & Co., Inc.

From Philosophy and Truth: selections from Nietzsche's notebooks of the early 1870's, translated and edited with an introduction and notes by Daniel Breazeale. Reprinted by permission of Humanities Press International, Inc., Atlantic Highlands, NJ, copyright 1979 by Humanities Press.

From Human, All Too Human: A Book for Free Spirits by Friedrich Nietzsche, translated by Marion Faber, with Stephen Lehman, introduction and notes by Marion Faber. Reprinted by permission of The University of Nebraska Press, copyright 1984 by University of Nebraska Press.

From Untimely Meditations by Friedrich Nietzsche, translated by R. J. Hollingdale with an introduction by J. P. Stern. Reprinted by permission of Cambridge University Press, copyright 1983 by Cambridge University Press.

From Daybreak: Thoughts on the Prejudices of Morality by Friedrich Nietzsche, translated by R. J. Hollingdale, introduction by Michael Tanner. Reprinted by permission of Cambridge University Press, copyright 1982 by Cambridge University Press.

From The Gay Science by Friedrich Nietzsche, translated by Walter Kaufmann. Copyright (c) 1974 by Random House, Inc. Reprinted by permission of Random House, Inc.

From On the Genealogy of Morals and Ecce Homo by Friedrich Nietzsche, translated by Walter Kaufmann & R. J. Hollingdale. Copyright (c) 1967 by Random House, Inc. Reprinted by permission of Random House, Inc.

From Beyond Good and Evil by Friedrich Nietzsche, translated by Walter Kaufmann. Copyright (c) 1966 by Random House, Inc. Reprinted by permission of Random House, Inc.

From Ecce Homo and The Birth of Tragedy by Friedrich Nietzsche, translated by Clifton Fadiman. Copyright (c) 1927 and renewed 1955 by The Modern Library, Inc. Reprinted by permission of Random House, Inc.

CONTENTS

Preface   vii

Foreward by Daniel O. Dahlstrom   ix

Introduction   1

Chapter One   The Path to Maturity   5

       Nietzsche's Early Life   5
       First Work: <u>The Birth of Tragedy</u>   8
       Two Gods: Schopenhauer and Wagner   12
       The <u>Untimely Meditations</u>   17

Chapter Two   The Transition   25

       False Starts and Philosophy   25
       A Third Force: Burckhardt   31
       Unpublished Thoughts   33
       Finding One's Self   36
       Finding a Method   41

Chapter Three   Philosopher in Development   45

       To Surpass His Background   45
       The Convalescent   50
       Finding Philosophy in Psychology   56

Chapter Four Joy and Love   61

        Work To Be Done   61
        The Joy of Wisdom   63
        Hope for Love   69

Chapter Five The Creation of a Free Spirit   73

        Poetic Philosophy   73
        Afterthoughts   80

Chapter Six Explaining His Gospel   85

        The Master Offers His Wisdom   85
        Renewed Hope Of Making a Difference   93
        The Lonely Wanderer   96
        "Will to Power" Explained   98

Chapter Seven The Final Rush   107

        Settling Accounts "with a Hammer"   107
        The Revaluation   112
        His Own Summation   116

Chapter Eight Conclusions   123

        The Dominace of Wagner   123
        The Transcendence of Schopenhauer   128
        To Transcend Philosophy   134
        Nihilism and Sustaining Illusions   144
        Inheritors of the Legacy   150

Epilogue The Intellectual Penalty   161

Appendix Timeline and Historical Bibliography   167

Bibliography   185

Index   191

Preface

One night in a bar on the North side of Chicago, I attempted to explain to a friend, but non-philosopher, the limits of philosophy as the disciples of the latter Wittgenstein set them down.   Analytical, or language analysis, philosophy, I explained, stated that philosophers were to clarify the uses of language. They were firm in their belief that philosophers were not to issue moral advice, discover metaphysical realities or, in general, lay claim to any special field where factual claims would be made, with the exception of facts about language usage. I had a great deal of trouble in deflating my friend's expectations toward such Wittgensteinian philosophers. He had an image of philosophers in the traditional mold, e.g., Plato, Descartes, etc. When he finally saw the light about the analytical philosopher, he was gravely disappointed. In so many words, he said, "Is that all there is to philosophy?" My "Yes" received words to the effect of "Why then bother to do philosophy?"

The constraints of a pragmatic anti-metaphysical philosophy on the philosopher are considerable, especially on one accustomed to old style philosophy. The heady air of the conversion experience to the Wittgensteinian perspective, with its liberation from moral and metaphysical claims, passes after a time. Do these constraints mean the death of philosophers in the mold of Nietzsche? Hopefully, no.

As a good Wittgensteinian, I should let you know my context, my ways to Nietzsche. My first contact with Nietzsche's thoughts came thru Will Durant's The Story of Philosophy which I read during my senior year in high school. There was an initial fascination then, and a continuing one now. In college, Nietzsche returned as a minor figure in Existentialism and the "death of God theology" before I had my first confrontation with the texts. This experience was in a course entitled "Modern Christian Challenges." I was mystified by Zarathustra, but remained interested. Graduate school brought no formal Nietzsche study. But while at the University of Chicago, I chanced upon a used copy of <u>Human, All Too Human</u>. I was forced to put it aside as I left the study of religion to take up philosophy at the University of Cincinnati.

After graduate school and my Wittgensteinian conversion, I slowly began reading Nietzsche's texts. I found <u>The Joyful Wisdom</u> to be a big turning point in my understanding of what Nietzsche was about. Gradually, I read more and more, and tried to explain him to a friend. Finally, I began a systematic examination of my notes over the years. This lead to exploring all his works and looking for hints in his sources. This lead to Schopenhauer and the removal of a veil of ignorance. That I had not taken on this obvious source before was unjustifiable, once I had seen what was there to be gained for understanding Nietzsche's philosophical context. Other veils fell from the reading Wagner and Burckhardt. I then read many of the excellent new books on Nietzsche published in the last ten years.

My essay for a friend grew into the book that this now prefaces. It would not have been a reality without Sheila Held's continuing faith in my creative products. I also must mention an informal philosophy discussion group I have attended for last ten years. This group, organized by Michael Marsh, read some early efforts and was always encouraging. Daniel O. Dahlstrom provided helpful corrections and suggestions for the final version, although its final form is my responsibility. Leatrice Jay proofed the manuscript. Lastly, my wife Emilie put up with my doing all this.

FOREWORD

In his inaugural lecture as R. G. Collingwood's successor at Oxford, Gilbert Ryle compared philosophical study of historical sources to a kind of "threshing" that, largely through the use of the *reductio ad absurdum* argument, "separates the grain from the chaff, discards the chaff and collects the grain." In a similar vein, P. F. Strawson contended that, for the descriptive metaphysician, there is "a massive central core of human thinking which has no history." The analytical temperament expressed in these remarks of Ryle and Strawson typifies a widespread sentiment among thinkers utterly taken by the liberating prospects for clarity and technical refinement afforded by the advancement of logical and linguistic studies during the past century. This contemporary development may, of course, also be viewed as an expression of a quite ancient philosophical self-conception that looks primarily, if not exclusively, to the model of science, and more particularly, to the eternal verities of mathematical science for the path to wisdom. For this tradition, history in general, including the history of a philosophy as well as the biography of a philosopher, is a peripheral matter, subject to personal and social idiosyncracies and contingencies of style that are only extrinsically related to timeless philosophical issues.

One of the motivations for Gary Elsner's Nietzsche: A Philosophical Biography is his sense of the need to rebut this "philosophical hubris" of examining a philosopher's ideas in isolation from their historical and biographical setting. Elsner's work is accordingly an attempt to articulate the uniqueness of Nietzsche's critical appropriation and revaluation of traditional philosophy within the context of the personal and public life of the philosopher from his Lutheran upbringing and school days at Pforta to his collapse on a Turin street in 1889.

Foreword

The opening chapters trace Nietzsche's early infatuation with Schopenhauer and Wagner, so much in evidence in The Birth of Tragedy, through his friendship with Burckhardt and studies of the Pre-Socratics, to his break with both his former "gods" as he molds--in Untimely Meditations, Human, All Too Human, and Dawn of Day--the notion of a will to truth unlimited by traditional morality, religion, and metaphysics. In the central chapters Elsner recounts how Nietzsche in The Joyful Wisdom, even as he suffers Lou Salome's rejections of his marriage proposals, dethrones science and knowledge in the complete affirmation of life afforded by the eternal recurrence doctrine, thus setting the stage for his "primary creative effort": the myth and poetic philosophy of Thus Spoke Zarathustra that heralds the transforming will to power of the *Übermensch* and the end of nihilism. The final chapters present Nietzsche, lonely and bitterly disappointed by the lack of disciples or even an understanding interlocutor, striving to refine and clarify the message of Zarathustra in Beyond Good and Evil and On the Genealogy of Morals, before the "final rush" of self-revelatory works--Nietzsche Contra Wagner, Twilight of the Idols, The Anti-Christ, and Ecce Homo--in the final four months before his collapse in January of 1889.

In his conclusion to Nietzsche: A Philosophical Biography Elsner provides a critical retrospective on the pervasive themes in the philosopher's development as well as their difficult legacy in the present. Elsner demonstrates not only the importance to Nietzsche of Wagner's early idealization of a pre-Christian, creative individuality, but also how this life-affirming vision led Nietzsche to develop what continued to pass for "philosophy" in some sense, even as it transcended Schopenhauer and traditional philosophy. Elsner then turns a critical eye on troubling features of this philosophy: the hopelessly vague character of the hypothesis of the will to power and the eternal recurrence, purportedly non-metaphysical proclamations; in contrast to the old ideal of metaphysical truth, the lack of a comparably compelling basis for his new ideal of perspectivism and his substitution of sustaining illusions for truth; the persistence of an individualism rooted in the Lutheran-Christian model and its metaphysical grounding in Kant and Schopenhauer, an individualism that, in Nietzsche's hands, is "out of control," leading ultimately to eschew the fundamental social reality and moral concerns of human beings. These charges are eminently controversial, to be sure, but by weaving them into the conclusion of his philosophical biography of Nietzsche Elsner renders them all the more worthy of consideration and debate. In a final segment, Elsner compares and contrasts the humbling legacies of the philosophical visions of both Wittgenstein and Nietzsche, finding in the latter an artistic, proto-Goethean celebration of life sorely lacking in the Viennese philosopher.

In his Principles of Art Collingwood demystifies the popular image of the artist as someone with a capacity to feel and suffer, far superior to that of ordinary human beings. Art in general, Collingwood argues, is the expression of emotion and artists are different, not by having emotions or feelings no one else has, but by being able to give more adequate expression to emotions shared by all human beings. In the Epilogue to <u>Nietzsche: A Philosophical Biography</u>, Elsner demystifies the figure of Nietzsche in a similar way. Granting that Nietzsche, like many an intellectual, perceived that he was different, indeed, someone, in his own words, "who never met one of his own kind," Elsner nonetheless sets forth the thesis that Nietzsche's philosophical activity can be explained as the expression of the quite human need for recognition and for some "justified meaning for his suffering." While its simplicity is certain to arouse a fair measure of controversy, this thesis has the compelling virtue of providing the very Nietzschean reminder that the dancing Dionysus himself was human, all too human.

Daniel O. Dahlstrom

Catholic University of America

INTRODUCTION

Why a "philosophical biography"? Or even, what is a "philosophical biography"? We all know that a biography is the historical narration of an individual's life. A few have been written on Nietzsche. The standard biography dwells on the timeline of events in an individual's life while including fairly specific details of the events. A "philosophical biography" is meant to shift the focus from the specific detail of events to the thoughts of the individual in their developmental environment.

If you are familiar with the American way of teaching and writing philosophy (for the most part), you are aware that philosophic discussions are far removed from biographical concerns, or even biographical or historical facts. The "philosophical biography" is meant to be a corrective dose of historical context setting to aid in a thorough understanding of a philosopher's ideas. Thus biography, though not overly detailed, is joined with the history of ideas as it is revealed in an individual's life. Philosophic ideas are the center of focus, but other ideas cannot be ignored.

My experience in studying history and philosophy has brought me to see the need for the philosophical biography. History courses, and most history books, present too little philosophy to make the philosophers mentioned at all understandable on even the most elementary philosophical level. I still recall the swirl of famous philosophers' names from my freshman Western Civilization course. But it wasn't until I started studying philosophy that I made any coherent sense out of their ideas. Yet philosophy in America seems to disown history. In philosophy courses I endured a presentation of texts without the slightest offering of their historical context. In a graduate course this parochialism was manifested in our studying a philosopher without the mention of any secondary materials at all. Just one text was supposed to come alive and create understanding on its own. This particular philosopher had written many books and his life spanned many years. Yet no concern was given to what the whole context of his other works and life might offer for understanding his ideas. My first contact with Nietzsche as a course text was through Thus Spoke Zarathustra without any background (and I was thoroughly mystified by much of it).

In this post-Wittgensteinian era of philosophizing, philosophers should be ashamed to ignore the context of the philosophic ideas they wish to teach about or write about. The traditional philosophic hubris exhibited in the isolated study of philosophic texts should be tempered by a realization that all meaning is contextual. And I mean this in a Wittgensteinian perspective which seeks to tie meanings back to human activities. Philosophers are human beings, and have always been human beings. They have no special access to a non-contextual source of great ideas. Their thought is bounded by their biographical environment. Not to be so bounded, would be to be non-human.

Common sense dictates that what one thinks about is intertwined with one's life events. Philosophers, and other intellectuals, are unique in our cultural history because the major events in their lives revolve around what they have read, have written, or have been taught. Reasons for their philosophic production therefore center on the intellectual influences in their lives. These intellectual influences are not given in a vacuum. Personal, emotional events are merged with these influences. The result is a unique amalgam of ideas, presented with an individual style. Usually this style changes over time as do the ideas. Continuity is usually maintained--because that is the way man is. The historical individual cannot walk away from his history. He can develop his ideas, but even in repudiating his earlier ideas, what he attacks is set by what he supported earlier.

If one ignores the total historical environment of thinkers one can find easy similarities or contrasts. When one zeros in on a thinker, the uniqueness of his appropriation of the influences on his development is revealed. Those who would place Nietzsche and Plato together as elitists, though they both somewhat fit this category, have failed to confront historically Nietzsche's intense rejection of Platonic philosophizing. Understanding requires re-living the developmental thought sequence as much as possible. With Plato, this can be done only by speculation. With Nietzsche, we are blest with many sources of data. Not only his extensive published output exists, but unpublished notes and letters abound. But here another trap awaits the seeker of understanding. The unpublished notes, for most part, were put aside by the author as not ready, or unfit, for publication. They can throw light on what the published author considered, but they cannot replace the focus of his finest efforts which he published.

Hopefully, the following philosophical biography will lead one toward understanding Nietzsche as a man and a philosopher. It may also expose the

Introduction

unique difficulties in the philosophic life, especially wherein one is driven to do philosophy rather than teach philosophy courses.

CHAPTER 1 THE PATH TO MATURITY

Nietzsche's Early Life

Nietzsche was born in 1844 in Saxony, the same year that an assassination attempt was made on the king of Prussia for whom Nietzsche was named. Also born in this year in Vienna was Ludwig Boltzmann, a physicist who would become a major influence on the young Wittgenstein. Karl Marx met Engels for the first time in Paris in this year. Revolution of the workers in Silesia and Bohemia was underway. August Comte's "Discourse on the Positive Spirit" was published in Paris. Evolution also showed its beginnings with "Vestiges of the Natural History of Creation". Modern communications was born with the first telegraph between Baltimore and Washington, DC. Finally, Arnold Schopenhauer's second edition of The World as Will and Representation came out--a book which would revolutionize Nietzsche's quest.

The revolutions of 1848 which swept Europe and finished Richard Wagner's life as a political revolutionary meant little to four year old Friedrich. However, 1849 brought sure trauma to his life as his father died, followed by his little brother Joseph a few months later. He grew up with his mother and younger sister Elizabeth. His father had been a Lutheran pastor and instructor. Although brought up in a proper Protestant household, his world was filled with music. His father played the piano, and Nietzsche would also master this instrument. Guests of the household brought current music and recent literature into Nietzsche's life at a young age. Besides biblical knowledge, Nietzsche strove for all knowledge he could consume. When this passion to conquer through knowledge focused on music he began composing: music, songs and poems. Other arts were attempted as well. He later said he was interested in everything except mathematics.

However, he decided to limit himself to certain subjects and approach these in depth.

Only five miles from Nietzsche's home in Naumberg was one of the most famous preparatory schools in Germany. The "little pastor" was an exemplary student and earned a scholarship to the Schulpforta. This academy with rigorous methods instilled a Spartan life filled with a solidly classical education. Life in this scholarly monastery and in Naumberg with its medieval walls was a retreat from the real world of the mid-Nineteenth Century. Nietzsche loved the long walks to his home on vacations, but he truly was trained to be a scholar.

This academy proved too narrow for Nietzsche's interests and he expanded his artistic passions in free associations outside of school. With "Germania", Nietzsche continued his Naumberg student friendships, yet even here it was quasi-educational events which dominated the group and Nietzsche's role therein. A freer forum was available for current political topics, poetry, contemporary culture, especially music. His first contact with Richard Wagner's music came from Germania. Robert Schumann remained his early favorite however. His heros were drawn from Hölderlin, Shakespeare, Byron, Norse Mythology, Schiller, Goethe, and Lessing.

Of course, at Pforta education meant learning the Greek and Latin classics in their original languages. This last bastion of the educated European was intact in Nietzsche's molding. Lutheran doctrine and Christian mythology were essentially welded to this classical base. A danger lurked in this approach as the study of non-Christian cultures clearly presented the option of a life without the Christian perspective. At least the intellectual mind will come to see this and question its convictional attachment to the Christian perspective. Some time during his education at Pforta Nietzsche gradually slipped away from Christianity. He never recounted any climactic event or associated experience with his loss of normal religious faith.

Another new love arose in response to Hölderlin's poetry, themes of which Nietzsche would revive in his own writings in later years. Hölderlin represented a Romantic appropriation of the Classical Greek world. The center of Romanticism was a return to nature: a feeling of oneness with nature. Hölderlin's writings were filled with this theme. The Romantic pantheism was a replacement for religious piety in the Christian mode. Hölderlin's version stressed an ideal vision of harmony in nature's larger processes. Nature was abstracted into the permanent reality, with metaphysical overtones. All strife and despair were reconciled in nature. This primary valuation of nature was imbibed by the young Nietzsche--it would be proclaimed in his mature works.

This budding romantic entered the University of Bonn in 1864. He set his goal of becoming a philologist. He chose this goal in order to discipline his activities. This does not appear to be easily understood from the outside. It seems counter to his passionate loves, to what would be his greatness. Anyway, Nietzsche immersed himself in Greek philology. Unlike majoring in Classics today, this was not an unusual choice in 1864. His Pforta training had given him an excellent preparation for Greek scholarship.

The freedom from Pforta was indulged while Nietzsche was at Bonn. He tried to be a current fellow: dueling, drinking, and partying with fellow college buddies. But the scholar who had resisted this while on vacation from Pforta could not turn his life around at 20 years of age. His character and life style were set in ways he did not see. He later had remorse for this wild period in his life. Nietzsche's Lutheran ethical perspective was fixed deep in his person, despite outward atheism. Nietzsche's intellectual quests would remain moral despite many claims to destroy morality.

Ritschl, Nietzsche's favorite teacher, went to Leipzig in 1865 and Nietzsche followed him. He was Ritschl's serious disciple and Ritschl's praise sealed Nietzsche's career path. While at Leipzig, Nietzsche discovered Schopenhauer. Schopenhauer's philosophy became Nietzsche's first serious philosophic study outside of the ancient Greek and Latin philosophers he had contacted through his Classics background. Nietzsche would come to see Wagner as the fulfillment of Schopenhauer's message and he would idolize the two as of one spirit. Wagner and Schopenhauer spoke to Nietzsche's artistic element, the repressed self of a would be scholarly philologist.

The budding philologist continued to read contemporary German philosophy after his Schopenhauer absorption. He read Lange's History of Materialism and Critique of Its Meaning in the Present and found it supportive of Schopenhauer. This book was a forerunner of the Neo-Kantian movement in German philosophy and a Kantian influence is readily visible in all of Nietzsche's later philosophy. Schopenhauer's works, of course, were also based on a Kantian philosophical foundation. Retrospectively, it appears that the base of Nietzsche's entire thought was centered in these crucial college influences:

1. Ancient Greek culture and philosophy
2. Richard Wagner's music and ideas
3. Arnold Schopenhauer's philosophy
4. F. A. Lange's Neo-Kantianism.

Nietzsche went on to be a practicing instructor in Greek philology, but the passions of philosophic and artistic activity did not die. They brewed, developed and finally transcended the philological training. Nietzsche's first book was not a scholarly treatise, but rather a compound of training and deeper loves. His later works would only betray his philological origins once in a while. He explained his turn to philosophy in an 1870 letter to a friend: "Each day I penetrate more and more into my kingdom of philosophy . . . I know not, I cannot know whither my destiny leads."[1]

First Work: <u>The Birth of Tragedy</u>

During the period from 1869 to 1871, Nietzsche finished his first book and volunteered to help Prussia in the war against France. This seems totally incongruous when looking back from the character of the older Nietzsche. The safe conclusion is that the Nietzsche of <u>The Birth of Tragedy from the Spirit of Music</u> was not nearly the same as the Nietzsche of <u>The Joyful Wisdom</u> (1882). This first book, although on ancient Greek culture, documented Nietzsche's break with the dry formalism of philology. The true subject was art as a metaphysical activity. The book was dedicated to Wagner, the most fervent love of the next few years of his life.

<u>The Birth</u> was a distillation of Nietzsche's study of ancient Greek history and culture. But this was presented from a quasi-Schopenhauerian perspective combined with Wagner's influence. His interest was the origin of Greek drama, or tragedy. He made famous the distinction of two themes in Greek culture: the Apollonian theme related to the mastery of form, especially in the plastic arts, and the Dionysian theme related to the irrational force expressed in mythic music. His thesis was that Greek drama represented the marriage of these two themes.

In both cases, aesthetic qualities were stressed. The Apollonian art was responsible for the beauty produced when a form was expressed in its true excellence. Reality was not copied, but enhanced. As Nietzsche said, the artist produced an "illusion", or untrue copy of life which radiated delight to man. The Dionysian element was related to that which was beyond man's power to enhance by "illusion." Rather it referred to man being caught up in the rapture of being in nature. The Dionysian follower was intoxicated while participating in human endeavors of great joy. The religious celebrant was probably the best example. Through Dionysian participation man was wrought together with his community and with all life. The Apollonian man was an artist, the Dionysian man was a participant in an artistic celebration.

The Apollonian artist achieved a distance from his work, as he had to contemplate in creation and appreciation. The Dionysian artist was the ecstatic, who created through participation, in a sense, through losing all distance from reality. Nietzsche saw Greek cultural history as a dynamic story of Apollonian versus Dionysian perspectives. The Apollonian perspective achieved a temporary victory in the Olympian religion while the Orphic cults counter-balanced this achievement. Tragedy was to represent the artistic synthesis of the two rival themes. Therein, an "illusion" was crafted that brought the appreciators into participation. And this necessary participation made the art form the greater "illusion."

Thus drama achieved the primary "illusion" of great art: the irrational actuality of life was appreciated, lived through, and transfigured in joyful participation. Drama represented an achievement beyond the mythic tales of the Olympians because of the greater participation offered and the more accurate portrayal of life, i.e., its absurd tragedy. As Nietzsche claimed, art made living bearable: "the arts, which make life possible and worth living."[2] The key to the success of the Greek drama was the role of the chorus. This borrowing from vocal music of the rites was necessary to convert the audience into participants. The stage with masked performers needed a transformational power. This the rhythmic chorus provided. In this manner the tragedy melded the Apollonian and Dionysian themes.

Historical interpretation was not Nietzsche's only concern. He had a philosophy and critique of culture he wanted to provide. He later called his philosophy a "metaphysics of art".[3] In this philosophy the influence of Schopenhauer was unmistakable. However, Nietzsche did provide a new twist. Unlike Schopenhauer, the artist was on center stage in preference to the art appreciator: "the artist . . . already delivered from the individual will. . . . His redemption in illusion."[4] It was thus not contemplation, but rather active, creative participation which released the individual from the woes of the world. The solitary individual without such engrossing activity was "the source of all suffering."[5] Natural man, without culture, was not able to bear life. Art was "not imitation of nature but its metaphysical supplement, raised up beside it in order to overcome it."[6]

Tragedy was art which gave the audience the engrossing participation together with a revelation of the truths of existence. Myths were used to depict "reality more truthfully and more completely than does civilized man."[7] The truths of natural life were brought back to civilized man: Tragedy cries, "We believe that life is eternal!" This message was being renewed by Nietzsche for his own generation. His Schopenhauerian metaphysics of nature was explicit: "the omnipotent will behind individuation, eternal life continuing beyond all appearance and in spite of destruction."[8]

Nietzsche's goal was to use this philosophical perspective to justify man's suffering in life:

> Now we see the struggle, the pain, the destruction of appearances, as necessary, because of the constant proliferation of forms pushing into life, because of the extravagant fecundity of the world will.[9]

The Dionysian celebrant, the creative artist and dramatic audience were to:

> become one with the immense lust for life and . . . made aware of the
> eternity and indestructibility of that lust . . . not as individuals, but as a
> part of the life force.[10]

Life was to be worshiped. Nietzsche animated it like a god: "life is at bottom
indestructibly joyful and powerful."[11]

The flux of appearance was not a world of change to be avoided, rather it
was to be seen as "a continuous chain of creations, each enhancing the other."[12]
At the cultural level, life, or will, found the "means to maintain its creatures in life
by spreading over existence the blandishments of illusion."[13]   Thus, the
Apollonian creation of illusions to defeat suffering represented a primary cultural
product.   Nietzsche called this the Hellenic or artistic solution: "complete
identification with the beauty of appearance." [14] Homer's Olympians triumphed
over "the terrors and horrors of existence . . . the shining fantasy of the Olympians
. . . justified human life."[15]

In the dynamics of cultural history, the artistic phase was followed by the
Socratic or theoretical phase according to Nietzsche. He decried the change in
drama represented by Euripides and in philosophy as represented by Socrates.
Nietzsche dwelled on the Socratic as a new cultural theme which abandoned the
Dionysian and Apollonian synthesis.   Neither "illusion" nor rapture were
acceptable to the Socratic quest. Knowledge and conscious criticism were the new
methods to reach the true. Nietzsche would retain this less than favorable view
of the Socratic revolution throughout his mature writings. The loss of both
interest in the unconscious and religious participation in the Dionysian perspective
would always appear to him as great mistakes.

Plato raised a new Apollonian "illusion", but it was without the Dionysian
complement. Plato believed, like Socrates, that knowledge was the avenue to
correct action. Whereas Socrates seemed content to expose the ignorance of his
fellow Athenians and to recommend ways to achieve clear definitions of moral
concepts, Plato went further. He declared that there was an "ideal" realm where
all truths resided and that man could come to know these truths through proper
training. Part of Plato's metaphysics stipulated that the reason in man was a
divine aspect of man, the aspect that allowed man access to the "ideal" realm.
The Platonic "illusion" therefore stressed methods of reasoning and found no
significant value in ritual or artistic creativity.

The Socratic and artistic cultural movements battled throughout Western
history according to Nietzsche. Occasionally the tragic synthesis was achieved
wherein the sufferings of existence were not banished through excesses of the

Apollonian or Dionysian element and instead accepted without debilitating effects. In Nietzsche's own time, it was science which carried the Socratic banner and romanticism which carried the artistic banner. Nietzsche was trying to present a new tragic synthesis based on Schopenhauerian philosophy and Wagnerian music drama.

The power of the Socratic perspective derived from its metaphysical "illusion" which made "existence appear intelligible and thereby justified."[16] The fear of the unknown and the meaninglessness of suffering were banished in the perception of timeless Truths. The life style itself was captivating. The seeker "finds his highest satisfaction in the unveiling process itself, which proves to him his own power."[17] Nietzsche felt this quest of science in his own life as many did in the explosion of Nineteenth Century scientific advances: "to encompass the whole world of phenomena . . . no sharper incentive to life than his desire to complete the conquest".[18] But Nietzsche came to realize the impossibility of completing the quest:

> When the inquirer, having pushed to the circumference, realizes how logic in that place curls about itself and bites its own tail, he is stuck with . . . a tragic perception, which requires, to make it tolerable, the remedy of art.[19]

Kant and Schopenhauer were accepted by Nietzsche as having defeated the prospect of achieving Truths about ultimate reality. Such metaphysical pretensions were just that. Now the Socratic "illusion" was shown to be a failure.

The scientist's quest was hopeless. He had hoped to "dissolve the power of myth" and to correct the world's ills "through knowledge."[20] The solace of art and knowledge blended in a new tragic vision was to be the goal of the new synthetic achievement. Nietzsche saw himself in this role and saw other "noble natures" as requiring this new renaissance. Once again art was needed to make life bearable. Nietzsche's answer: the music of the modern symphony, and especially the "new" music of Richard Wagner. Once again the "illusion" was created by the musician artist, but it was not redeeming art until performed for the audience participants, and they were enraptured and brought to joy in the transformation of the powerful musical experience. A triumph, neither conscious nor unconscious, was experienced as a new synthesis.

Nietzsche described his experience of Wagner's operas as myth, art, and philosophy made compelling. The participant was given "Dionysian wisdom made concrete through Apollonian artifice."[21] The synthesis of Wagnerian music drama created "the alternation of Apollonian and Dionysian excitation in the spectator."[22] In Apollonian moments one seemed to see beyond appearances to

11

the Truth. In Dionysian moments one lost oneself and merged joyfully into the eternal powers of life. Thus Nietzsche poured out the over-powering experiences which Wagner had given him. These were not the experiences of a philologist.

The Birth outraged his philological colleagues who may have seen through this thinly veiled passage, supposedly about the Alexandrian Greeks (the heirs of the Socratic):

> He remains eternally hungry, the critic without strength or joy, the Alexandrian man who is at bottom a librarian and scholiast, blinding himself miserably over dusty books and typographical errors.[23]

Nietzsche seemed to be aiming at himself and his limited colleagues. It was a confession that philology was a mistake for Nietzsche. He did not have the spirit for dusty books and the quiet of the library. He reached out for the participation which would offer Dionysian satisfaction. He found it in the Wagnerian experience. And as love overflowed its primary object, namely, Wagner's music, Nietzsche was drawn to Wagner and his circle.

Two Gods: Schopenhauer and Wagner

Nietzsche's discovery of Schopenhauer's The World as Will and Representation in a Leipzig used book shop in 1865 had changed his life profoundly. It had personally given him a new outlook on life and had provided him with the perfect background to ignite his Wagner friendship. Schopenhauer and Wagner dominated Nietzsche's ideas in the 1865-1871 years. The dominance was strong enough to have caused Nietzsche to modify his first published work. As he turned to new publishing ventures in 1871, Wagner was rising to his zenith and preparing for his triumphant return to Germany. In 1872, The Birth was published and the Wagners left Nietzsche's vicinity for Bayreuth in Bavaria. Wagner was moving physically away from Nietzsche and Nietzsche was intellectually moving away from Wagner and Schopenhauer, though slowly.

In his first Untimely Meditation, David Strauss, The Confessor and Writer (1873), Nietzsche reaffirmed his Schopenhauerian conversion, in a point blank fashion, as he laid out his view of the common man's Christianity: "The Christian point of view of an immortal heavenly life, along with all the other comforts of the Christian religion, has collapsed irretrievably."[24] In even earlier unpublished notes he had summed up his relation to Christianity:

Great revolutions are in the offing, once the masses understand that all Christianity is based on assumptions; the <u>existence of God</u>, the authority of the Bible, immortality, and inspiration will remain problems forever.[25]

Nietzsche had replaced his original Christianity with a Schopenhauerian faith. He explained his own conversion later:

> At that time I was hanging in the air with a number of painful experiences and disappointments, without help, without fundamental principles, without hope, and without friendly memory. To fashion for myself a suitable life of my own was my effort from morning till night . . . Imagine now what effect the reading of Schopenhauer's main work must produce in such circumstances.[26]

If there could be intellectual love, he obtained it:

> I belong to those readers of Schopenhauer who know perfectly well, after they have turned the first page, that they will read all the others. My trust in him sprang to life at once.[27]

Schopenhauer offered a synthesis of Christian and Eastern religious thought and presented this synthesis as an extention of Kantian philosophy. Nietzsche later said he had received Schopehnauer's message "as though he had written for me."[28]

Following Hinduism and Buddhism, Schopenhauer portrayed a man's life as suffering which was caused by the individual's inability to satisfy his desires. From the West came a new metaphysics: Kant's phenomenal world, the world of our senses, was the creation of the will's striving, the will to live. Therefore, the phenomenal world was not real, but merely apparent. The real world is <u>one</u>, is Will. Ignorance of this results in the constant struggle of individuals in pursuit of their egoistic desires. Yet man does occasionally glimpse the other world: a world beyond striving and suffering. Self and other, in this beyond, no longer compete against each other. Instead they realize their "oneness" and love each other as they formerly loved only themselves. This realization produces pity for all that still live with suffering. The vision of "oneness" leads past working to alleviate the sufferings of the world to seeing that only total suppression of willing in any form must be the final destination. Individuals must abstain from every physical pleasure, including sexual pleasures, and psychological pleasures, including the pleasure from good works. Such ascetic saints were the ideal of every high religion according to Schopenhauer. But Schopenhauer went on to demythologize the religious tradition: he removed God.

Nietzsche, who was burdened with a longing for a goal in his life, found in Schopenhauer an available role which was outside of Christianity. Schopenhauer's description of the genius fulfilled Nietzsche's longing. Schopenhauer set out the key criteria of the genius in comparison to the ordinary people: "The person in whom genius is to be found suffers must of all."[29] Nietzsche's frustrations and loneliness were also badges of genius. The genius also reflected Nietzsche's drive:

> instinct drives the genius to carry out his work to completion, with thinking of reward or applause or sympathy; to leave all care for personal welfare; to make his life one of industrious solitude, and to strain his faculties to the utmost.[30]

And what role did Schopenhauer lay out for the young Nietzsche? For the genius, who was the intuitive artist, lay the path of transcending his own individuality. His creations would have the power of moving the spectator to artistic contemplation. Participation in the art of genius brought transcendence of the will. True art of the genius captured the sublime in reality and disclosed beauty even in the finality of death.

Because the sublime situations engage our interest, the will's concern, they usually are the opposite of situations for disinterested contemplation, or transcendence. Tragedy, the artful portrayal of such situations, is thus the highest literary art. Schopenhauer went further and claimed music as the highest art. He claimed the real itself was revealed in great music. Music transcended the subject-object limitation of other art forms. The contemplator could become one with the music.

One can see the compatibility of Schopenhauer's ethics, aesthetics and metaphysics with the young Nietzsche. As Lea said, "At one stroke Schopenhauer welded him into a unitary being."[31] Much of this Schopenhauerian conversion appeared in The Birth where Nietzsche saw himself as a prophet for self-annihilation as means to creative achievement. Nietzsche blended his metaphysical belief in "everything is one" into his desire to found a new culture. Such a culture would lead his fellow men to a reintegration of their lives. The demands of morality and science would be balanced with the longing for Greek ideals in synthetic whole bound together with Schopenhauerian truths. Nietzsche and his followers would satisfy their longing for meaning in this new community. This very longing revealed a void which the Christian tradition, and all religions, had filled. Nietzsche thought he had found the right orientation in Schopenhauer

14

to begin his task: to develop a new world view for post-Christians. He could turn his creative abilities away from the bareness of philology. He would also write for his contemporaries.

It was under the spell of this fascination that he encountered Wagnerian music and then Wagner himself. Nietzsche had been overpowered by music from Wagner's Tristan and Meistersinger. He described his concert experience to a friend: "every nerve of my being is set tingling. . . . [I] experienced a feeling of such sustained enjoyment."[32] In The Birth, Nietzsche had captured this as the experience of "the very heart beat of the world-will" and "the unruly lust for life."[33] Nietzsche perceived it as Dionysian art, as Schopenhauerian transcendence. This was not unusual given that Wagner was also an admirer of Schopenhauer's thoughts and of Greek culture. Wagner had called for a rebirth of the spirit of Athenian drama. He specifically designed the role of the chorus in Lohengrin to be like that of the Greek dramatic chorus. In Tristan, the orchestra took over the role of the chorus. Wagner sought "a subtle integration of word and tone, the conceptual was to be conveyed in terms of the musical."[34] Wagner also sought to revitalize the mythical, as the source of the spirit of the new culture.

It was not only the Greek renaissance in Wagner's Tristan that seemed to call out to Nietzsche. Jacques Barzun described this epic work as follows:

> Tristan enshrines, celebrates . . . the biological act. . . . the passion is external to the lovers. It is a force of nature. . . . Everything is fated, and the fatalism is gladly accepted. . . . desire is the driving force behind every character.[35]

Wagner's attempt to weld poetry, song and drama with musical power was a compelling experience, an experience that captivated the young Nietzsche:

> Tristan and Isolde, the real *opus metaphysicum* of all art. . . . insatiable and sweet craving for the secrets of night and death. . . . overpowering in its simple granduer.[36]

Nietzsche's later works would recapitulate these themes of natural force, fate and celebration.

After meeting Wagner in Leipzig, Nietzsche visited the Wagner's near Basel, where Nietzsche was teaching, 23 times between 1869 and 1872.[37] Wagner was the same age as Nietzsche's deceased father would have been and Nietzsche enjoyed his visits as if he were at home. All the time he could spare away from his professorial duties was invested in his Wagner relationship.

Nietzsche referred to his days at the Wagners' as "days of confidence, of serenity, of sublime flashes, of profound moments."[38]   He had found an environment meeting his deepest needs as a human being. Richard was a replacement for a missing father and a "true" spiritual friend. Richard's wife became a love object, though this was never a consummated attachment.

Nietzsche and Wagner revitalized each other. Wagner found a willing young disciple with a penetrating mind. Nietzsche found a real Schopenhauerian who was very interested in ancient Greek culture. As Nietzsche was becoming a loyal follower, he was drafting his first major work on Greek tragedy. Eventually, The Birth became Nietzsche's offering to the "movement." The final product merged classical scholarship with Wagnerite themes. Once again he was reaching out, trying to escape the narrow confines of philology, this time under the spell of a great musical artist. Wagner called out to this desire in a letter to Nietzsche:

> Now you have a chance to show the usefulness of philology, by assisting me to achieve the great renaissance wherein Plato will embrace Homer, and Homer, full of Plato's spirit, will become more than ever the utterly supreme Homer.[39]

For Nietzsche, Wagnerian music was a reenactment of the Dionysian spirit. Wagner's Siegfried was the new Dionysian man.

Intellectually, they were concerned with similar topics: classical Greece and Schopenhauerian thought. Wagner's writings attacked Christianity and praised a new culturally revolutionary movement with Schopenhauerian themes. Wagner, as a Romantic, harkened back to the olden times, that is, classical Greece, of the time before philosophers had destroyed the harmony of that culture. Wagner, once an active revolutionary, was looking forward to a rebirth of new harmonious culture with a Dionysian spirit. The political revolution of 1848 had failed. Nietzsche seemed to reappropriate the sense of mission that Wagner had embodied.

Most importantly, Wagner embodied the ideal of the Schopenhauerian genius. Nietzsche as a cult follower said this in a letter to a friend:

> I have found a man who reveals to me, as no other does, the image of what Schopenhauer called the "genius" and who is penetrated through and through by that wonderfully deep philosophy.[40]

He went on to describe life with Wagner as like taking "a practical course in Schopenhauerian philosophy."[41] Nietzsche read all of Wagner's early works like an admiring disciple. Wagner transcended the philosophy of Kant and exemplified the philosophy of Schopenhauer. Wagner represented the Dionysian spirit and his "music dramas were pictures of the ruling primordial will."[42] Music was the best means for expressing the will, for penetrating beyond the human "illusions" of words. And Wagnerian music achieved this breakthrough (think of the "ride of the Valkyrie").

The Untimely Meditations

Nietzsche struggled with his adopted art of writing, and published four essays in his immediate post-Wagner period (1873-76):

David Strauss, The Confessor and Writer,
The Use and Abuse of History for Life,
Schopenhauer as an Educator, and
Richard Wagner in Bayreuth.

These Untimely Meditations, as Nietzsche labelled them, contained statements of his discipleship and of his doubts. He also confronted his era with his hopes.

These long essay length writings were meant to function as polemics for the Wagnerite movement. Wagner evidently encouraged Nietzsche to choose David Strauss as the topic for the first one. Strauss, whom Nietzsche had read with great approval in 1865 in his pre-Wagner days, had recently written a new work following up on his shocking Life of Jesus (1835). Forgetting Strauss's achievement and courage in having attacked the Jesus myth, Nietzsche attacked Strauss for his endorsement of current German Protestant culture and its love for science. Nietzsche went on to criticize contemporary culture in general in comparison to ancient Greek culture as the Wagnerites idealized it. Finally, Nietzsche expressed his goal: "to assist the coming generation . . . to a truly German culture."[43]

Nietzsche had not publicly responded to the philological community's attack on the Birth. A friend of his had written a rejoinder, but it was not effective outside of sympathetic listeners. In his second Untimely Meditation, The Use and Abuse of History for Life, Nietzsche launched a counter-attack through an attack on academic trends in history and philology. He contrasted a concept of history which enhances life with one which was merely a look into the past:

Man is encased in the stench of must and mold; through the antiquarian approach he succeeds in reducing even a more creative disposition, a nobler desire, to an insatiable thirst for novelty.[44]

17

Scientific scholarship is accused as the murderer of worthwhile historical writing. Nietzsche saw the claimed objective method producing merely meaningless tracts. The philologists, in particular, were singled out as men who had mastered a set of techniques and a small body of knowledge and yet claimed to be producing "wisdom."

Praise of the Greeks was offered as an antidote to modern worship of the factual. Nietzsche saw the classical Greeks as an "essentially unhistorical culture."[45] He called for a new rejection of oppressive historicism, to rise "against that blind power of the factual and the tyranny of the actual."[46] Nietzsche reminded his contemporaries that it had always been the "thus it shall be" that drove men forward. Morality was always an opposition to "thus it is" with its "it ought to be thus." And worship of the factual, and science as its handmaiden, would not yield an "it ought to be thus," a new ideal. Only individuals, creators, artists could produce an ideal for the foundation of a new harmonious culture: "a unison of living, thinking, appearing and willing."[47] Nietzsche saw a goal outside of the mass movements of the late nineteenth century:

> To what end the "world" exists, to what end "mankind" exists, ought not to concern us. . . . No the goal of humanity cannot lie in its end but only in its highest exemplars.[48]

Schopenhauerian geniuses were sought. Men who were individuals who could place science's world of becoming and mechanism behind their need to know themselves. Nietzsche concluded Use by asking for 100 men to come forward to begin the effort at this new cultural reformation. None came forward as the essay went unnoticed.

Nietzsche began to recognize his loneliness, now that he was separated from the Wagners and his writings were not receiving any acclaim outside of the Wagnerites. He already sensed his individual stature: "Here and there the judgment and taste of individuals may be higher and finer than the rest."[49] As he realized his isolation was caused partly by his new philosophical vocation, he pictured the result of his care for truth as one who "ends his days as a lonely philosopher, with the wisdom of disillusion."[50] Following his ideal models he had no desire to be an academic philosopher, but rather, he wanted to live his philosophy and prove his own remark false: "No one dares fulfill the law of philosophy in himself."[51]

In Schopenhauer as an Educator, Nietzsche was looking for his own, true self and he stated a method for such discovery:

let the youthful soul look back on life with the question, "what has thou up to now truly loved, what has drawn thy soul upward, mastered it and blessed it too?" Set up these things . . . and maybe they will show thee, in their being and their order, a law which is the fundamental law of thine own self.[52]

Still a romantic, Nietzsche went on to say that "Intuition is still the first requisite" and "Only what compels the response of love is true."[53] Desperately, he sought a goal, a mission:

Not to drag their generation to the grave, but to found a new one--that is the motive that ever drives them onward . . . and future generations will know them only as the first comers.[54]

His search for a new integrating world view which could mold a generation was a religious quest. Something beyond Christianity was needed in his view.

In these Untimely Meditations, Nietzsche achieved separate insights on his own future course. He played with his vision of "first comers"--of a new transformation, of a course beyond Christianity and its philosophical allies. He cryptically stated the new path: "The way to redemption lies only through joyousness."[55] This was not explained, but a crass hedonism was not implied. The individual was definitely the focus: "the time will come . . . when we shall no more look at the masses but at individuals who form a sort of bridge over the wan stream of becoming."[56] This (probably self-reflective) comment led to the now infamous conclusion: " the goal of humanity cannot lie in its end but only in its exemplars."[57] Nietzsche, of course, saw himself, Wagner and Schopenhauer as among these highest exemplars. He called for others to reach for high status:

Ask thyself to what end thou art here, as an individual; and if no one can tell thee, try then to justify the meaning of thy existence *a posteriori*, by putting before thyself a high and noble end. Perish on the rock! I know no better aim for life than to be broken on something great and impossible.[58]

Once again the passionate soul of a romantic youth was openly portrayed.

Nietzsche had decided for himself that he would pursue the high and noble purpose of Truth. He specifically stated that "great and impossible" something that would be the aim of his life: "to shake to their foundations the present conceptions of 'health' and 'culture'".[59] Nietzsche, who would later characterize

19

his thoughts as "philosophizing with a hammer", appears in this light as having a goal well established before his major philosophical works were even begun.

This third <u>Meditation</u> represented Nietzsche's public homage to Schopenhauer. His example of how a non-Christian could thrive amid the nihilism of modern thought was proclaimed. Schopenhauer's tragic life led from "heights of sceptical gloom to the heights of tragic contemplation."[60] Nietzsche saw Schopenhauer's philosophy as a statement of an individual which gave "insight into his own want and misery, into his own limitations."[61] His philosophy revealed the "antidotes and consolations" which were necessary: "sacrifice of the ego, submission to the noblest ends, above all to those of justice and compassion."[62] Nietzsche then revealed his own history of nihilism as mirrored in Schopenhauer:

> neither riches nor honors nor erudition can lift the individual out of the profound depression he feels at the valuelessness of his existence, and how striving . . . acquires meaning only through an exalted and transfiguring overall goal: to acquire power so as to aid the evolution of the *physis* (Nature) . . . in the end for everyone . . . a striving which by its nature leads toward resignation.[63]

Nietzsche had contrasted three modern types of man, Rousseau, Goethe and Schopenhauer, and endorsed his mentor:

> <u>Schopenhauerian man voluntarily takes upon himself the suffering involved in being truthful</u>, and this suffering serves to destroy his own wilfulness and to prepare that complete over-turning and conversion of his being, which it is the real meaning of life to lead up to.[64]

The final liberation of the Schopenhauerian conversion was compared with the East Indian release from desires: "over into the domain of peace and denial of the will, across to the other coast of which the Indians speak."[65]

A meaningful life to Nietzsche demanded a metaphysical answer. Modern, secular men faced the truth of Nature as constant change, or becoming: "In becoming everything is hollow, deceptive, shallow and worthy of our contempt; the enigma which man is to resolve he can resolve only in . . . the imperishable."[66] Therefore, "That is why the truthful man feels that the meaning of his activity is metaphysical, explicable through the laws of another and higher life."[67] The religious quest has been refocused in metaphysical philosophizing, with the addition of Schopenhauer's goal of individual geniuses: "and who are they who lift us? They are those true <u>men, those who are no longer animal, the</u>

philosophers, artists and saints."[68] And finally, Nietzsche returned to his theme of the need for a new culture:

> a mighty community held together . . . by a fundamental idea . . . of culture. . . . but one task: to promote the production of the philosopher, the artists and the saint within us and without us and thereby to work at the perfecting of nature. . . . Only by your living for the good of the rarest and most valuable exemplars . . . so that at last the man may appear who feels himself perfect and boundless in knowledge and love, perception and power, and who in his completeness is at one with nature.[69]

Nietzsche's own quest was thus embedded in a philosophy of culture. His own soul's "desire to look beyond itself and to seek, with all its might for a higher self as yet still concealed from it"[70] had been satisfied in Schopenhauerian Wagnerism. Culture was given a metaphysical value. Nietzsche had tried to live his philosophical perspective. He sought to become a philosopher and warrior for the new culture. He realized that "A scholar can never become a philosopher",[71] and that true philosophers of genius are disturbing and must demonstrate by "their deeds that love of truth is something fearsome and mighty."[72]

Nietzsche's final Untimely Meditation, though he planned more at several points, followed his praise of Schopenhauer with an equal offering to his other god, Wagner. It was Wagner's life again that captivated Nietzsche:

> how he started darkly and restlessly, how he stormily sought relief, strove for power and intoxication, often flew back in disgust, how he wanted to throw off his burden, longed to forget, to deny, to renounce.[73]

Finally, Wagner's music was his gift: "one who unites what he has brought together into a living structure, a simplifier of the world."[74] Wagner brought together Greek tragedy, Schopenhauerian philosophy and modern nihilism and rebellion and had created musical art which sought harmony, which made life appear simple. Such great art, such tragedy, was the best man could do:

> The struggles it depicts are simplifications of the real struggles of life; its problems are abbreviations of the endlessly complex calculus of human action and desire. But the greatness and indispensability of art lie precisely in its being able to produce the appearance of a simple world, a shorter solution of the riddle of life. . . . art exists so that the bow shall not break.[75]

21

The tragic perspective has an individual moral directive:

> The individual must be consecrated to something higher than himself--that
> is the meaning of tragedy; he must be free of the terrible anxiety which
> death and time evoke in the individual . . . [so that] he may encounter
> something holy that endlessly outweighs all his struggle and all his
> distress--this is what it means to have a sense for the tragic.[76]

Nietzsche foresaw that this "sense of the tragic" was crucial to secular man:

> There is but one hope and guarantee for the future of man, and that is that
> his sense of the tragic may not die out. If he ever completely lost it, an
> agonized cry, the like of which has never been heard, would have to be
> raised all over the world.[77]

Wagner, through his music dramas, was able to communicate the mythic
message of the tragedy of life while other modern media had failed. His triumph
of artistic power reflected his personal will and self-overcoming. The harmony
produced in the audience recreated the achievements of Heraclitus in classical
Greek culture:

> Wagner's music as a whole is an image of the world as it was understood
> by the great Ephesian philosopher: a harmony produced by conflict, the
> unity of justice and enmity.[78]

These Untimely Meditations were the public production of Nietzsche, and
they showed a committed Wagnerite. But they were a veneer over a period of
intellectual and personal change. Personal relations with the Wagners deteriorated.
His intellectual commitments were placed in doubt as he wrote quite differently
in his unpublished notes.

NOTES

1. Quoted in O'Brien, Son of the Morning, p. 103.
2. The Birth, Golffing, p. 21. (Nietzsche's writings are referred to by the title of
   the book as listed in the bibliography, with translators, or dates, listed to
   indicate specific sources.)
3. The Birth, Golffing, p. 5.
4. The Birth, Golffing, p. 41.

5. The Birth, Golffing, p. 66.
6. The Birth, Golffing, p. 142.
7. The Birth, Golffing, p. 53.
8. The Birth, Golffing, p. 101.
9. The Birth, Golffing, pp. 102-3.
10. The Birth, Golffing, p. 103.
11. The Birth, Golffing, p. 50.
12. The Birth, Golffing, p. 35.
13. The Birth, Golffing, p. 108.
14. The Birth, Golffing, p. 31.
15. The Birth, Golffing, pp. 29-30.
16. The Birth, Golffing, p. 93.
17. The Birth, Golffing, p. 92.
18. The Birth, Golffing, p. 95.
19. The Birth, Golffing, p. 95.
20. The Birth, Golffing, p. 90.
21. The Birth, Golffing, p. 132.
22. The Birth, Golffing, p. 133.
23. The Birth, Kaufmann, p. 112.
24. Quoted in Steiner, Friedrich Nietzsche, p. 143.
25. Quoted in Jaspers, Nietzsche, p. 56.
26. Quoted in Lea, The Tragic Philosopher, p. 18.
27. Thoughts Out of Season, vol. 5, p. 114.
28. Thoughts Out of Season, vol. 5, p. 114.
29. Schopenhauer, World as Will and Representation, vol. I, p. 310.
30. The Essential Schopenhauer, p. 81.
31. Lea, The Tragic, p. 24.
32. Nietzsche-Wagner Correspondence, pp. 4-5.
33. The Birth, Golffing, p. 127.
34. Gutman, Richard Wagner, p. 139.
35. Barzun, Darwin, Marx and Wagner, pp. 236-7.
36. Thoughts Out of Season, vol. 4, p. 165.
37. Nietzsche-Wagner, p. 112.
38. Quoted in Gutman, Richard Wagner, p. 315.
39. Quoted in O'Brien, Son, p. 72.
40. Quoted in Lea, The Tragic, p. 31.
41. Quoted in Lea, The Tragic, p. 32.
42. Steiner, Friedrich Nietzsche, p. 133.
43. Untimely Meditations, p. 34.
44. Untimely, p. 75.

45. Untimely, p. 103.
46. Untimely, p. 106.
47. Lea, The Tragic, p. 80.
48. Untimely, pp. 112 & 111.
49. Thoughts, vol. 4, p. 31.
50. Thoughts, vol. 5, pp. 27-8.
51. Thoughts, vol. 5, p. 27.
52. Quoted in Lea, The Tragic, p. 83.
53. Quoted in Lea, The Tragic, p. 83.
54. Thoughts Out of Season, vol. 5, p. 59.
55. Thoughts Out of Season, vol. 5, p. 59.
56. Thoughts Out of Season, vol. 5, p. 59.
57. Untimely, p. 111.
58. Thoughts, vol. 5, p. 61.
59. Thoughts, vol. 5, p. 71.
60. Untimely, p. 141.
61. Untimely, p. 142.
62. Untimely, p. 142.
63. Untimely, p. 142.
64. Untimely, p. 152.
65. Untimely, p. 143.
66. Untimely, p. 155.
67. Untimely, p. 153.
68. Untimely, p. 159.
69. Untimely, pp. 160 & 162-3.
70. Untimely, p. 163.
71. Untimely, p. 181.
72. Untimely, p. 194.
73. Untimely, pp. 202-3.
74. Untimely, p. 209.
75. Untimely, p. 213.
76. Untimely, p. 213.
77. Thoughts, vol. 4, p. 131.
78. Untimely, p. 242.

CHAPTER 2 THE TRANSITION

False Starts and Philosophy

One of Nietzsche's main research topics during his philological study was the works of Theognis. This post-Homeric Greek writer stressed "man's helpless dependence on an arbitrary power" and established "a new bitter emphasis on the futility of human purposes."[1] The immature Nietzsche who may have associated with this extreme pessimism and fatalism was left behind with philology when he ventured into broader concerns in the years after The Birth. Nietzsche would never shed his philologist past, and he especially retained the model of the scholar that Ritschl had imprinted on him: a man ceaselessly engaged in critical struggle with his own ideas.[2]

In lectures he gave in the year after The Birth was published, Nietzsche openly criticized the educational system in Germany, which had channeled himself into philology. His academic interests moved from tragedy to the Greek pre-Socratic philosophers. The pre-Socratic material existed in fragments and so allowed Nietzsche great freedom in his interpretation of their thoughts. No well worked-over, dusty manuscripts existed. The philologist could relax and the cultural historian and philosopher could empathetically relive the tragic age of Greece.

By examining Nietzsche's unpublished book fragment, Philosophy in the Tragic Age of the Greeks, which was written in 1872-3, we can see the philosopher at work on other philosophers. Nietzsche is no longer a mere philologist, rather he empathizes with those he considers the tragic heroes of philosophy, and of Greek culture. He admitted he was not doing critical history, rather he was pointing to the philosophical style and personality of the pre-Socratics as he found them. The visions of these thinkers were styled philosophy, but on the whole their likeness to myths is clear. Nietzsche's comments in this study threw light on his own self image: "The philosopher seeks to hear within himself the echoes of the world symphony and to re-project them in the form of concepts."[3] This view of a creative essence in philosophy, similar to great symphonic music, sums up Nietzsche's life-work concept better than any commentator has ever done. He described the philosopher by analogy with the traits of others:

1. contemplative and perceptive as an artist,
2. compassionate as the religious,
3. a seeker of causes and purposes like the scientist,
4. mirrors the world like a poet.

These traits also seem to indicate what he would hope to achieve in his future philosophic writing.

Nietzsche described clearly what was the essence of Greek culture that he could never praise enough:

> Man for them was the truth and the core of all things; everything else was but semblance and the play of illusion. For this very reason they found it unbelievably difficult to comprehend concepts as such. Herein they were the exact opposite of modern man. For us, even the most personal is sublimated back into an abstraction: for them, the greatest abstraction kept running back into a person.[4]

Any delving into early Greek philosophy does give one the impression that abstract conceptions did give them great difficulty. Nietzsche read this as a virtue, that they still felt the anti-humanity of such abstract levels.

Heraclitus is Nietzsche's favorite pre-Socratic philosopher, and Nietzsche's own later proclamations sound many themes straight from Heraclitus' thoughts. Nietzsche draws a portrait of Heraclitus as a Kantian critic. While discussing Heraclitus, Schopenhauer is cited to clarify the anti-Kantian meaning of Heraclitus' metaphysics. The Kantian philosophical perspective and its criticism is crucial to understanding Nietzsche's own thought because this approach would remain Nietzsche's basis for a criticism of all Western metaphysics.

For Kant, the foundation of all man's knowledge was centered in three things: the things of the world, the knower, and the mediation between things and knower. This image was usually referred to in traditional philosophical terms:

1. The world is "the-thing-in-itself" (*ding-an-sich*),
2. The knower is the human self (soul), and
3. The mediation consists of the elements of mind, namely, perceptions.

26

The Transition

It was clear to Kant, and the empiricist philosophical tradition, that all knowledge came from man's sense perceptions and his reflections upon these. All the contents of awareness, objects of perceptions and thoughts were mental contents of the individual soul. How did the self, mind, receive these notions? The common sense answer was that the world causes our perceptions, and that the perceptions correspond to the real world. But, that world was also in some sense constructed by our minds. We never directly grasped the world as something beyond our mind. Our empiricism and sensationalism has forced us to the predicament of Bishop Berkeley: we have a mind with many representations of the world, but we have no direct knowledge of other minds or even our own body! Kant did not want this skeptical position. He wanted to justify the knowledge of science--as being of the world and not just of the representations in our mind. Kant developed a complex philosophy which attempted to justify empirical knowledge while preserving a skeptical perspective on the "thing-in-itself." For Kant, this unknown was originally described as the cause of all sensation, but because it, in itself, was without the form given to all sensation by the human mind, it must necessarily be outside of human knowledge. Many interpreted Kant as really leaving only a faith that the outside world was there. This became a stumbling block for many philosophers who followed Kant. They hoped, and longed for knowledge on a more certain foundation. They wanted direct access to reality.

Nietzsche was securely anchored in this Kantian metaphysical problem. In a 1866 letter to a friend, Nietzsche had already shown this Kantian perspective:

1. The sensual world is the product of our organization.
2. Our visible (physical) organs are, for all other parts of the external world, merely images of an unknown object.
3. Hence, our real organization remains as unknown to us as real external things. All we ever face is the product of both of them . . .
not only is the true essence of things, the thing itself, unknown to us, its very concept is nothing more or less than the final product of an antithesis that is stipulated by our organization, and of which we do not know whether it has any significance beyond our range of experience.[5]

The really real as a static substance is not available in the Kantian world view. What then was the real? This was a question dear to the pre-Socratics. Heraclitus said that "becoming" was the real, that change or activity was the essence of reality. Nietzsche approved of this way around the "ding-an-sich", despite the fact that this was a chilling thought: "The everlasting and exclusive coming-to-be, the impermanence of everything actual . . . is a terrible, paralyzing thought."[6]

Heraclitus went on to see all as a game of Zeus. Zeus, the chief of the Homeric gods, played and in so doing created the world. However, as in play, he also destroyed and recreated out of the desire to play again. Nietzsche saw the Heraclitean world as innocent and amoral. But it was a tragic world: "it views man as a completely unfree necessity."[7] Again the fatalistic pessimism of Theognis was accepted. Man could merely view the world as artistic creation.

Thus, the Nietzsche of The Birth was still present. The artist was the cultural hero: not only for his work itself, the needed "illusion", but because his life re-enacted the primordial creation of the world out of play. But the primordial creation was a myth, an "illusion." Nietzsche had no criticism of this, and instead criticized the developments in early Greek philosophy after Heraclitus.

Where Heraclitus had accepted all of the world as real, Parmenides began the division of the all into the real and the only apparent. Their logic was as follows:

> The Eleatics were persuaded that reason informs us of certain truths which are altogether contrary to what sense experience shows. But it is self-contradictory to deny a rational truth. Sense, opposed then to rational truth, must be inconsistent. But no rational person would affirm an inconsistent proposition. Hence no rational person can accept propositions based on the senses.[8]

Consequently, sense perception was swept aside. The mind would be the medium to truth and the real. The avenues would be the abstractions of thought. And the fuel would be the logical drive in man. The unique philosopher's claim was first made: "we have an organ of knowledge which reaches into the essence of things independent of experience."[9] The mind had access to the realm of the really real. The realm turned out to have nothing in it like the things found in ordinary experience. Parmenides' real was motionless and unitary. There was no space or time. He had a real of which little could be said. A real reached by mental conception, practically meditation. Logical exercises replaced prayer or other rites, but the result was the same: a world other than the everyday world was praised as the true world--and as worth knowing at the expense of everything in the everyday world. Plato would strengthen this tradition and pass it on into Western philosophy for all time. Nietzsche saw that Indian philosophy showed a similar development. Both displeased him, actually sickened him when he thought of their result in Western and Eastern civilizations: "I hate that overleaping of this world which occurs when one condemns this world wholesale."[10] He summed up his distaste for the overly rational development of

Greek philosophy in an 1875 note: "Ancient philosophy in its entirety is a strange labyrinthian aberration reason."[11]

Platonic and Eastern philosophies resulted in a disvaluing of our experienced reality. They turned things upsidedown. Lange, who Nietzsche had read in 1866, said this about Plato: "The further he was from the facts, the nearer he thought himself to the truth."[12] Nietzsche agreed and opposed the Platonic view with what he took to be Heraclitus' view: "the whole of reality lies simply in its acts."[13] Nietzsche quoted Schopenhauer to clarify his position: "'the whole nature of materiality: its being as its activity . . . its whole being and nature consists only in orderly change which one of its parts produces in another.'"[14] Lange was embraced, the Kantian "thing-in-itself" rejected: "Through words and concepts we shall never reach beyond the wall of relations to some sort of fabulous primal ground of things."[15] All knowledge was the result of the relation of the self, a mere object, and the objects of perception and thought. There was no knowledge of anything outside of such a perspective, such relativity. In 1868, Nietzsche had said:

> At all events you do not write a criticism of a world view. Rather, one understands it or does not understand it; a third standpoint is unfathomable to my way of thinking.[16]

However, as we have seen, some five years later, he was criticizing a major world view, that of Platonism, and Christianity and all other-worldly metaphysics. His attempt to compose his attack on the evils of the traditional world view of the West was his next task.

His writings and lectures on the Pre-Socratic philosophers did not develop into the book he was planning (Nietzsche constantly noted down book plans throughout his career--most of which remained just that). Breazeale has called this project the "Philosophers' Book." It was to be made up of "Philosophy in the Tragic Age of the Greeks," plus elements from several unpublished fragments which Nietzsche completed during the time he was publishing his Untimely Meditations, 1872-1875. These notes indicate he was still working out his efforts at a synthesis which he described in 1875 thusly:

> I wish to combine Schopenhauer, Wagner, and early Hellenism . . . to show how life, philosophy, and art can have a more profound and congenial relationship to each other.[17]

Breazeale offered an explanation for Nietzsche's change of direction into more strictly philosophical themes in the unpublished work of the mid-1870's:

Nietzsche's general interest in culture led him to an investigation of the problems of a culture "based upon knowledge," and in order to investigate this possibility he was forced to delve rather deeply into narrower questions concerning the nature, origin, and value of knowing.[18]

This concentration on knowledge led him directly into a confrontation with the dominant Kantian position which he had acquired from his Schopenhauerian tutelage. Nietzsche came at the problem with a "deep and abiding commitment to the correspondence ideal,"[19] that is, that truth must somehow represent the really real world, but he seemed to change to a view "of the metaphysically real world as a primal, unformed chaos."[20] Nietzsche noted his advance beyond the conceptual position of a Kantian thing-in-itself:

> We far too readily confuse <u>Kant's</u> "thing in itself" with the <u>Buddhist's</u> "true essence of things." On the one hand actuality exhibits nothing but <u>illusion</u>; on the other, it exhibits an <u>appearance which is totally adequate to the truth</u>.[21]

This dual perspective was announced by Nietzsche and he never really gave it up in all his later published works. Reality as we "know it" in Kantian terms was "illusion," that is, it was something created by the knowers. What appears to us as the objects of perception, "appearance," was what we measure truth against, was the basis of true judgments. There was no way to jump over the objects of appearance to "know" a non-illusive metaphysical reality. Schopenhauer was rejected along with the Kantian thing-in-itself: "We can say nothing about the thing in itself, for we have eliminated the standpoint of knowing.[22]

Nietzsche never finished the "Philosophers' Book" and Breazeale wondered why. During this intellectually turbulent time after the Wagners had moved to Bayreuth, Nietzsche had plenty of time to do philosophy--without the shadow of Schopenhauer, as played by Wagner, bearing down on the young former philologist. The result was a philosophic development which eclipsed the pessimistic genius and ushered in a new scepticism, a more philosophically mature scepticism. The fragments of 1872-1876 document a philosopher struggling with his Schopenhauerian positions and moving towards a new position. His published works of this time remained Schopenhauerian and Wagnerian (his sister reports that he purposely refrained from criticisms of Wagner, even though he made notes of such from 1874 onward.[23]). The Pre-Socratics would remain an important source for Nietzsche, but they were also being relegated to his past. The "Philosophers' Book" would have been a monument to Nietzsche the Classicist and Schopenhauerian Wagnerite. He had grown beyond this perspective by 1875 and just let the project drop. He went on to deal with his new, mature scepticism in Human, All Too Human.

But all did not work out as smoothly as might be believed from this retrospective. Nietzsche's health was deteriorating, it had never been good. His discipleship to Wagner had broken up. Nietzsche was left with himself and a few friends. He had revealed in Schopenhauer how great of a stress his own experience of a Schopenhauerean loneliness was to him (he admitted these were autobiographical comments in 1888):

> The threatening danger that this great deed would be undone simply through indifference created in him a terrible, barely controllable agitation . . . hunting for the slightest sign that he was not utterly unknown. . . . he was a total solitary; he had not a single companion truly of his own kind to console him. . . . Because of this a cloud of melancholy gathers . . . more hateful than death itself . . . [this causes] perpetual bitter, resentment . . . [which issues in revenge of] words and deeds and then explosions.[24]

Nietzsche here had prophetically laid out his future stormy life. But greater loneliness lay beyond 1875.

A Third Force: Burckhardt

Nietzsche had come to Basel in 1869, having received an university appointment before he completely finished his Leipzig University schooling due to the recommendation of Ritschl. He had been considering leaving philology when this opportunity put off second thoughts. He spent most of his next ten years in Basel, a period in which he made the transition from philologist, Schopenhauerian and Wagnerite to his own philosophy. Other than the two gods who dominated the early part of this period, a third figure now entered his life.

Jacob Burckhardt was a senior faculty member of the University of Basel. He had been there for 24 years when the 25 year old Nietzsche joined him as a colleague. Nietzsche and Burckhardt probably would have eventually met based on similar interests, however fate effected an early meeting. All university appointments at Basel, being a rather small school, included teaching duties at the preparatory academy. It was here that Nietzsche and Burckhardt had the same period off and struck up a friendship that Nietzsche would remain true to until his final days. As Wagner receded from Nietzsche's life, Burckhardt remained. Even after having left Basel, Nietzsche corresponded with him on a regular basis, and sent him every new work he published.

"The Philosopher" meant the same thing to Burckhardt and Nietzsche in 1869, namely, Arnold Schopenhauer. When this common love was added to Burckhardt's expertise in Greek cultural studies--the very field in which Nietzsche was trying to draft his first book--a strong ground for meaningful conversation was available. Burckhardt also had no love for modern mass movements as he saw them. Here he reflected Basel itself: a very conservative city-state attempting to remain outside of 19th century political and social change. Basel also reflected Nietzsche's sheltered past in Naumberg and Pforta. Burckhardt openly feared the cultural consequences of the loss of the classical traditions in European life. Prussian imperialism, economic commercialism and mass democracy were seen as destroying the best of old Europe without offering any hope of better times. Modern man was forgetting the value of societal restraints on the individual. Instead a new "ethic" of "Let everyone get what he can, and devil take the hindmost" was coming to dominate the young.[25]

Nietzsche would, in his later works, have much to say about modern decadence, but initially his concerns were with changing modern culture through Wagnerism. This was the primary difference between Burckhardt and Nietzsche in 1869. Heated discussions were bound to ensue between the young disciple of Wagner and the defender of the noble European tradition. Burckhardt posed as the realist. He accepted the Greek tragic view of man in opposition to modern Rousseauism or Wagnerism. While Rousseau had led to faith in man's rational ability to build a society to release man's essential goodness, Burckhardt steadfastly saw man as basically beset by evil in every historic civilization. Moral regeneration could not be achieved through the state, or a social/cultural movement, but only through the individual. He saw "The Philosopher" as offering only such individual hope. Only a contemplative life could release one from the powers of evil inherent in the striving, doing and suffering of the desire-filled life. Burckhardt saw his life of contemplation through the study of the history of culture as fulfilling the Schopenhauerian imperative.

When Wagner left the Basel environment in 1872, Nietzsche offered his services full-time to the "movement." Clearly then, Burckhardt's influence had not yet swung Nietzsche away from the dreams of Romantic social activism. However, the influence of Burckhardt was surely present in Nietzsche's The Birth. Nietzsche may have used this book for Wagnerite ends, but the form of the work reflects Burckhardt's views on philology and cultural history. Burckhardt held that a history of culture approach was necessary if one wanted to gain an understanding of ancient civilizations. The narrow confines of philology were not able to reveal the context of ancient texts, and so could not reveal the true perspective on the culture. Nietzsche followed this image in his presentation in

The Transition

<u>The Birth</u>. Nietzsche was attacked by the philologist wing which was anti-Burckhardtian.

Part of the reason why Nietzsche had offered his services to Wagner in 1872 probably stemmed from the disaster of <u>The Birth</u>'s reception in the philologist's community. Nietzsche had been professionally discredited. Students stayed away from his philology lectures. One can imagine Burckhardt's difficult position. He had probably agreed with the historical form of exposition for <u>The Birth</u>, but decried the Wagnerite overlay. Now Nietzsche had received only public praise from the Wagnerites. His philological career appeared ruined. Evidently, Burckhardt was able to help Nietzsche through this period, as he helped him through the Franco-Prussian War experience, and he would have applauded Nietzsche's decision to pursue a philosophy career. Burckhardt ranked the role of the philosopher at a high level. This Schopenhauerian belief had been shared by Nietzsche. Nietzsche himself had thought about a philosophical career just before the Ritschl offer came through. Wagner rejected Nietzsche's full-time services and left for Bayreuth. Nietzsche penned these thoughts about philosophers in 1872:

> There are times of great danger in which philosophers appear-- ... when philosophers and artists assume the place of the dwindling mythos. They are far ahead of their time. . . . A people which becomes aware of its dangers produces the genius.[26]

Nietzsche grasped Schopenhauer again as his refuge. He could become the philosopher genius and stir mankind from the dangers of modern decadence.

The transition would be difficult. Wagner had been loved. The ensuing years after 1872 would manifest a love-hate relationship between Wagner and Nietzsche more like that between ex-spouses. Nietzsche was periodically attracted, but always repelled on close contact. At the end of the summer in 1872, it was Nietzsche who refused Wagner when invited to Bayreuth. He also refused an invitation by the Wagners for Christmas that year, the first time in three years. Nietzsche also put aside his work on the Greek Pre-Socratic philosophers. Philosophy itself moved into first place ahead of philology.

Unpublished Thoughts

While Nietzsche published polemics for the Wagnerite and Schopenhauerian causes, he wrote philosophy and about philosophy for himself. Between 1872 and 1876 several essay length works and lesser fragments were penned by Nietzsche. These writings revealed Nietzsche's doubts and hopes for his philosophic beginnings. Included were a series of notes critical of Wagner. Schopenhauer was still the dominant philosophic influence. Ideas from The Birth were still being reworked. The objective was now not Greek culture and philosophy, but philosophizing for now.

The role of "Great Men", a topic dear to Burckhardt's lectures on the history of culture, took on a focus in relation to Nietzsche's concern with ethics, culture and art. Nietzsche saw ethics as the rule of custom in a culture. And that the individual great man provided the custom. This provision occurred through the artistic creation of a powerful individual personality. It was not the real facts that captivated, Nietzsche asserted, but rather the "illusion" created which set the example for ethical emulation. Ethical thought itself was seen to be the creation of man based on the "illusion" that the individual was of infinite importance. Nature had not provided this valuation of the individual.

Nietzsche thus continued his thinking about "illusions" from The Birth:

> a beautiful illusion has exactly the same value as an item of knowledge-- provided only that it is an illusion in which one believes--, then one realizes life requires illusions.[27]

And it was powerful individuals who brought the people to believe in cultural "illusions." "Illusion," enshrined as custom, became the truth of a culture. Nietzsche drew the conclusion of pragmaticism: "the true and the effective are taken to be identical."[28] Finally, the striving for truth, that he knew so well, was revealed to him as a "struggle for a holy conviction."[29]

Philosophy, the search for truth, was not an end in itself: "The will to existence employs philosophy for the purposes of a higher form of existence."[30] The Schopenhauerian world as "Will" was implied. Philosophy was not a unique avenue of escape as the Platonic tradition indicated, rather it was "a form of artistic invention," a "continuation of the mythic drive."[31] Philosophy was a religion of concepts. All myth, religion and philosophy were the creation of artistic forces, of the forces in life. Nietzsche then drew the final conclusion in an 1872 piece: "Art is more powerful than knowledge, because it desires life."[32]

Skepticism and pessimism had been common products of the development of modern philosophy (and also in ancient philosophy). Nietzsche saw this danger in the philosophical perspective: "no one can live in this skepticism. We must get beyond this skepticism; we must forget it! Our salvation lies not in knowing, but in creating!"[33] This led Nietzsche to question the role of the philosopher, and his own choice of a future: "He is able to create no culture. He acts as solvent and destroyer."[34] But this last aspect is not bad. Further in "The

Philosopher as Cultural Physician" he went on to list viable functions of this "cleanser" of a culture:

Eliminates the theory of the soul
[provides] Proof of what is absolutely anthropormorphic
Opposes the fixed value of ethical concepts
Opposes hatred of the body[35]

What was bad was that this "cultural physician" tended to dissolve instincts, cultures and customary moralities. Here a quandary arose. Part of philosophy, that critical function similar to scientific analysis, was welcomed by Nietzsche, while other aspects of "positive" philosophizing were feared as avenues to religious or mystical positions. These in turn were usually hostile to science and divorced from actual ethical concerns. Yet "positive" philosophizing was part of "that drive by which we incessantly deal with nature by the means of anthropomorphic illusions."[36] "Illusions" were necessary to life. Nietzsche saw a need for the philosopher:

Philosophers strive to understand that which their fellow men only live through. By interpreting their own existence and coming to understand its dangers, the philosophers at the same time interpret their existence for their people.[37]

This 1875 comment shows that Nietzsche concluded in favor of the philosopher and philosophy. But not any philosophy was acceptable. He wished to "replace the popular picture of the world with a new one."[38]

This new world picture was to be scientific, non-Christian, and non-metaphysical and it was to provide ethical guidance for the current generation. Schopenhauer was the prophet for this new world picture, at least in the beginning. In this perspective, metaphysics, as "positive" claims about real worlds beyond the world of science, was forbidden as non-sense. This critical Kantianism, more pure than Kant himself as claimed by Schopenhauer, forbade discussion of the "thing-in-itself." The relation between such an unknowable and our perceptions was beyond science. One might as well think of it as an "aesthetic relation",[39] that is, as art is to reality, as a creation of man in the world, life's reaction is to living experience. Our world picture was "illusion," the primary "illusion." Nietzsche put it this way in an 1872 note:

There actually exists nothing but an illusion, an image. Matter is in its entirety, nothing but the outside: what truly lives and operates is

35

something entirely different. But our senses are the product of matter and things, as is our mind. I mean to say, to arrive at a thing-in-it-self, one must start from the natural sciences.[40]

This seems to indicate movement from a strict Schopenhauerian position. Schopenhauer was not anti-science, but he did not see natural science as a way to the "thing-in-itself." For the "thing-in-itself" was "Will" for him. Of course, Nietzsche's desire to create a new ethics for a new cultural era was not part of Schopenhauer's teaching.

Nietzsche's disagreements with Schopenhauer had begun the latter's interpretation of Greek tragedy. Where Schopenhauer had seen only resignation at man's tragic fate, Nietzsche saw overcoming of suffering through art. Nietzsche came to see too much pessimism in Schopenhauer: "Here each line cried out renunciation, denial, resignation; here I saw a mirror in which the world, life, my own mind were reflected in fearful grandeur."[41] Burckhardt, too, was too pessimistic for Nietzsche. Burckhardt echoed the Greek maxim in his tragic view: "I would be prepared to exchange my life for a never-having-been."[42] Art was not in service of pessimism nor merely there to be contemplated as a means to resignation. As Nietzsche said later, "Art is essentially affirmation, blessing, deification of existence."[43] "Illusion" as the essence was not a sad revelation, but rather proof of the creative force in life itself. So Nietzsche began his quest for a synthesis of the best in early Hellenism, Wagner and Schopenhauer which was congruent with modern science. He resigned from the university to have time to test his commitment to the truth, and to convalesce. As many great thinkers have been, he was driven to work out his thoughts. The product would be his first work in his distinctive aphoristic style. Its telling title, Human, All Too Human, marked the beginning of Nietzsche's very productive ten year period from 1878 to 1888.

Finding One's Self

Nietzsche was 34 years old when Human, All Too Human: A Book for Free Spirits was published. It was a testament to his new freedom. Not only freedom to try a new style of writing, but also a declaration of intellectual freedom. In a series of related short sections, Nietzsche stated his critique of present culture and thought he pointed a way to a new being. No salvation was promised or painted. But a way for "free spirits" was hinted at, a way to something beyond the common man of current European culture. In his own preface to the work, written 8 years later (1886), he called the work a piece of youthful discovery. In a zest of freedom he posed the ultimate question for "free spirits": "cannot all values be overturned?"[44] Nietzsche did not really answer this question in this one work. In some sense, the remainder of his written output dealt with answering this question, always circling about a clear answer.

An answer had been eluding Nietzsche in his personal quest for a meaningful life. He had originally put aside <u>Philosophy in the Tragic Age of the Greeks</u> to help the Wagnerites with their Bayreuth project in the spring of 1873. During that summer he met Paul Ree and struck up a friendship with this "psychologist" which would last for about 10 years. The "movement" rejected Nietzsche's written proclamation to aid Bayreuth and, as usual, he was crushed and depressed. In this mood he wrote the fragmentary works which probed his role and the philosopher's role in culture. It wasn't until the spring of 1874 that Nietzsche was able to distract himself from depression. Happiness returned through a rereading of "the Philosopher." This led to the third <u>Untimely Meditation</u>. And it may also have sparked more critical thoughts about Schopenhauerian philosophy.

January of 1875 brought more depression to this sensitive soul. Wagner's Parsifal idea struck Nietzsche as the abandonment of his hero to quasi-Christian beliefs. Then a friend, who lived practically with Nietzsche in this period, decided to enter the Church. Depression led to illness and thoughts of his father's early death. He came to the decision that he must thoroughly reanalyze his positions. That summer, spent at a spa, spawned the first jottings destined to become <u>Human</u>. On returning to Basel in the fall of 1875, his illness resumed and he requested a leave of absence from the University. While recuperating, he noted down a title for an <u>Untimely Meditation</u>, "The Free Spirits." This was never to be, but rather a totally new effort was in gestation.

In his state of partial recovery, Nietzsche attended the opening of Wagner's music festival at Bayreuth in the summer of 1876. He had drafted his fourth <u>Untimely Meditation</u> on Wagner, working mainly from earlier notes, for the festival. In spite of this outward faith, the whole festival sickened Nietzsche. He became convinced the Wagnerite movement was a failure. <u>A new</u>, not merely a neo-Christian, ideal was still lacking. The whole summer caused him to make a resolution to give up music. In deep depression, he returned to Basel in the fall.

Nietzsche sought a new climate. Paul Ree and Nietzsche settled in Sorrento for the fall of 1876. It was probably no coincidence that the Wagners were also staying in Sorrento. Nietzsche attempted to reconcile himself to Wagner in the fall, but after Wagner moved on, Nietzsche turned to his own thoughts. Parsifal was on Wagner's mind, and Nietzsche saw this as an unbridgeable chasm between them. An unusual period of happiness and contentment descended on Nietzsche's life in Sorrento, even after the failed Wagner affair and after Ree was forced to depart. Nietzsche was free of university demands. He read, in widely diversified fields. He wrote almost daily. He discussed, explained with a few friends. To one of these, he disclosed that he had finally abandoned Schopenhauer's metaphysics: "I think I <u>know</u> that his metaphysics are wrong."[45] Finally he showed his new production to an older female companion. These notes for <u>Human</u> were shocking to even his friends. For Nietzsche, years of transition were entering a new phase. He resolved to continue his new life and resign from the University.

Basel was the scene of the final drafting of <u>Human</u>. After the glorious 1876-77 period of leisure, Nietzsche rejoined academic life, at least outwardly, in the fall of 1877. Burckhardt was there for daily intercourse. Nietzsche concluded that the format of <u>Human</u> should be short notes, or aphorisms. This manifested a complete break with his romantic style of the <u>Meditations</u>. By the beginning of 1878, <u>Human</u> was complete. Nietzsche received a copy of Wagner's latest effort, <u>Parsifal</u>, at this time. Nietzsche paused before responding, then sent <u>Human</u> to Wagner. And thus independence was proclaimed, ten years after their first meeting.

<u>Human</u> contained a great deal of auto-biographical material. Some of it was transparently so, other parts were probably not meant so by Nietzsche, but are apparent when looking back. In one respect, the entire work is a mirroring of his valuation of his own intellectual achievement. Counting himself among the "free spirits" he referred to, Nietzsche praised the enlightenment of true scientific knowledge which produced "free spirits." These newly emancipated saw the errors of the past. The biggest errors were:

1. belief in free will and the concept of responsibility and,
2. faith in justice.

He proclaimed the nonexistence of free will and justice and equated morality with egoistical actions. And he hinted that the "free spirits", possessed of a similar enlightenment, would reach a new morality. Although Nietzsche did not use the term *Übermensch* (variously translated as "superman", "overman" or "higherman"), its meaning was foreshadowed throughout <u>Human</u>.

After demolishing the basic concepts of morality in <u>Human</u>, Nietzsche went on to indict religion as the opponent of science and truth. Religion was castigated for changing man's perceptions of reality without allowing one to analyze the facts scientifically. The Christian religion was painted as the religion of the weak. This religion had constantly made man see himself as sinful, and had taught man to devalue nature, in himself and in the whole cosmos. Lastly, Nietzsche branded the ascetic phase of religious being as wrong-headed egoism. Asceticism was still ego driven, but driven from a perspective where all natural, physical desires were evil. Religious phenomena were only to be praised when they led to the self-perception of sinlessness: he claimed this was the achievement of Christ and some Hindu sages.

Once most of the religious and the ethical valuations were demolished, Nietzsche attacked art, previously his own favorite way to judge life as worthwhile following Schopenhauer. Nietzsche thus proclaimed his progress beyond The Birth. Art is "illusion", but now, an "illusion" harmful to social activity. Although art can tame misery, as it did with the Greeks, the "fearless ones" had to do more than use art to say life is good. Art was to be replaced by science for "free spirits." However, these new science prophets had to learn the methods of the artists: "so the relief-like, incomplete representation of a thought, or a whole philosophy, is sometimes more effective than its exhaustive realization."[46] Nietzsche expressed his own method when he called for us to "take pleasure in the uncertainty of his horizon, as if the road to various other thoughts were still open."[47]

Nietzsche painted an image of scientific causality which indicated a quasi-religious perspective of science:

man's every action, not only his books, in some way becomes the occasion for other actions, decisions, and thoughts; that everything which is happening is inextricably tied to everything which will happen; then one understands the real immortality, that of movement: what has once moved others is . . . enclosed and immortalized in the general intertwining of all that exists.[48]

One is also reminded of Heraclitus' perspective, and Nietzsche's fondness for his philosophy. This was not a cold scientific attitude, but a sample of science beyond art--helping affirm that life is good.

After a short critique of the values of the masses, Nietzsche went on to preach for a new science, one not estranged from art. He acknowledged that such an achievement will involve a necessary tension because science as the objective seeks to destroy myth while art builds "illusion" to proclaim its messages. He wanted his contemporaries to transcend the Greek philosophers who never produced the highest possibility of the philosophic life. He urged the "free spirits" on:

to become a necessary chain of culture-links yourself, and from this necessity to draw a conclusion as to the necessity in the progress of general culture.[49]

39

Nietzsche, like the ancient philosophers, equated knowledge and wisdom: "life which has its zenith in age has also its zenith in wisdom, in that mild sunshine of constant mental joyfulness."[50] Note the "free spirit" was not promised an overwhelming experience, on a model with the Platonic myth, but a gentle sunshine, comforting as a spring day.

After indulging his poetic playfulness, Nietzsche turned to a biting attack of political realities as exemplified in his time. Nietzsche announced an elitist perspective. Democracy was painted as dominance by the mediocre majority, and "free spirits" should step aside from political events as long as the majority did not oppress. He also believed the ease of governing the masses was about to end:

> The subordination which is so highly valued in military and official ranks will soon become <u>incredible</u> to us. . . . its foundation is disappearing, the belief in unconditional authority, in ultimate truth.[51]

The democratic state would then have no obligation of superhuman sanction:

> No longer does anyone feel any obligation toward a law other than to bow instantaneously to the power that introduced it; at once however, people begin to undermine it with a new power, a new majority yet to be formed.[52]

The solution to this problem was pointed to by Nietzsche: "The masses must have the impression that there is a powerful, nay indomitable strength of will operating."[53] This would be when the state and leader were made religious in the eyes of the people. A superhuman obligation was thus reestablished. Socialist revolutionaries would fit a similar mold, as they placed the revolutionary values beyond the mere majority will. Nietzsche, however, saw socialism as a great evil: "it aims at the complete annihilation of the individual."[54] (He did not foresee the possibilities of annihilation which a Nazi leader could produce.)

Nietzsche's political answer was to end nation-states and forget utopian, revolutionary heaven-on-earth plans. "The destiny of men is designed for <u>happy moments</u>",[55] not ideal ages of bliss unending. This wisdom was derived by Nietzsche from analysis of the primitive man: "after powerfully exerting himself in hunting or war, man surrenders to rest, stretches his limbs, and hears the wings of slumber rustle around him."[56] Thus Nietzsche was anti-political and mostly unconcerned with positive political programs.

The final part of <u>Human</u> was labeled "Man Alone by Himself." In it, Nietzsche hints at two themes which were to appear in his later works:

    1. that Truth is not necessarily related to what is good for man, and

The Transition

2. that man should regain a perspective of himself as an animal. He also called for the achievement of a mental state for "free spirits":

> a third state, which is related to play as gliding is to dancing, as dancing is to walking, a blessed, tranquil movement; it is the artists' and philosophers' vision of happiness.[57]

Thus the "free spirits" were not to be "true believers" who were convinced of their mission in life and worked to achieve it at all costs. Nietzsche understood that the activities of men with solid convictions had made possible the civilizations and cultures of man, yet "free spirits" were to look objectively, scientifically, and see these convictions as errors. A history of convictions men have held revealed the strengths of the human will over the uncertain. However, Nietzsche demanded more of his "free spirits":

> He who has attained intellectual emancipation to any extent cannot, for a long time, regard himself otherwise than as a wanderer on the face of the earth--and not even as a traveler towards a final goal, for there is no such thing.[58]

And he closed the book describing the time ahead for "free spirits": "alternately merry and thoughtful, are wanderers and philosophers . . . they seek the ante-meridiem philosophy."[59]

Finding a Method

Nietzsche had called his method of analysis in Human "historical philosophy." Traditional philosophers had ignored the truth that man was historical:

> A lack of historical sense is the congenital defect of all philosophers. They will not understand that man has evolved, that the faculty of knowledge has also evolved . . . everything has evolved; there are no eternal facts, nor are there any absolute truths.[60]

Darwin's insight was applicable to even philosophy: "life and experience--has gradually evolved, indeed is still evolving."[61] Even the essence of traditional philosophy, metaphysics, had to be understood as having an historical origin which was crucial in understanding it: "to overcome metaphysics, . . . [we] must

41

first understand both the historical and the psychological justification [for it]."[62] Nietzsche's dream was of "a truly liberating philosophical science."[63] A new discipline was envisioned. Science was to be intimately joined with philosophical analysis. An important step in the study of anything was to be the analysis of historical causes, psychological causes. Nietzsche would employ his new critical analysis in most of his writings from here on.

This new critical philosophizing was devastating when applied against Schopenhauer, and even so against some of Kant. Yet Nietzsche could not sever his whole education in neo-Kantian thought. His critical scalpel was applied to metaphysics, that is, to thought about extra-historical reality. Such a "possible" something was to be ignored:

> It is true, there might be a metaphysical world; one can hardly dispute the absolute possibility of it. . . . [but] there is nothing at all we could state about the metaphysical world except its difference, a differentness inaccessible and incomprehensible to us. . . . the most inconsequential of all knowledge.[64]

Thus, the "thing-in-itself" and all of Schopenhauer's assertions about it as "will" were unallowable, and even if some knowledge could be had, it would be inconsequential to historical human existence.

"Religion, art, and morality do not enable us to touch 'the essence of the world in itself.'"[65] They were merely parts of human history. No conclusions about human life were valid based on the metaphysical pretensions of religion and morality: "it is self-evident that the world is not good and not evil . . . we must in every case dispense with both the reviling and glorifying view of the world."[66] And Schopenhauer's valuation of the world as primarily suffering must also go. All such resignation and pessimism was founded on errors of metaphysical judgment. Individuals naturally affirm life. The moral view point, especially the Christian version of "guilty man", was an error. At the base of this error was the concept of "free will." Moral responsibility was dependent on "free choice." Now all this was reduced to causal understandings. Moral actions were not supra-historical, or metaphysical. They were human actions like all other actions. Neither did music somehow communicate the metaphysical. Music was a human invention, a cultural, historical product.

Nietzsche had documented his rejection of the essence of Schopenhauerian thought. He was clearly rejecting his past in philology and ancient Greek philosophy as well. Of philology he said, "everything essential has been found and all that is left for the researcher is a scanty autumn gleaning."[67] Of the formerly beloved pre-Socratics he said, "it seems to me extraordinarily difficult to see any philosopher from Thales to Democritus clearly."[68]

Only Wagner remained undisposed of in Human. No real direct attacks were mounted against his former idol. Schopenhauer, art, music, and the Greeks all were devalued, and thus indirectly, Wagnerism was repudiated. But Nietzsche clung to the ideal of new cultural ideal--now it would be Nietzsche's creation, not Wagner's.

NOTES

1. Dodds, The Greeks and the Irrational, p. 30.
2. Jaspers, Nietzsche, p. 30.
3. Philosophy in the Tragic Age of the Greeks, p. 44.
4. Tragic Age, p. 41.
5. Quoted in Frenzel, Nietzsche, pp. 32-3.
6. Tragic Age, p. 54.
7. Danhauser, Nietzsche's View of Socrates, p. 135.
8. Danto, "Nietzsche's Perspectivism," Nietzsche: A Collection, p. 41.
9. Tragic Age, p. 82.
10. Philosophy and Truth, p. 112.
11. Philosophy and Truth, p. 130.
12. Lange, History of Materialism, p. 73.
13. Tragic Age, p. 53.
14. Tragic Age, p. 54.
15. Tragic Age, p. 83.
16. Unpublished Letters, p. 47.
17. Philosophy and Truth, pp. 133-4.
18. Philosophy and Truth, p. xxxi.
19. Philosophy and Truth, p. xxxi ftn.
20. Philosophy and Truth, p. xxxii ftn.
21. Philosophy and Truth, p. 41.
22. Philosophy and Truth, p. 37.
23. Nietzsche-Wagner, pp. 199-204.
24. Untimely, pp. 139-40.
25. Force and Freedom, p. 30.
26. Quoted in Heidegger, Nietzsche, vol. 1, p. 3.
27. Philosophy and Truth, p. 16.
28. Philosophy and Truth, p. 17.
29. Philosophy and Truth, p. 17.

30. Philosophy and Truth, p. 17.
31. Philosophy and Truth, p. 19.
32. Philosophy and Truth, p. 66.
33. Philosophy and Truth, p. 32.
34. Philosophy and Truth, p. 71.
35. Philosophy and Truth, p. 73.
36. Early Greek Philosophy, p. 154.
37. Philosophy and Truth, p. 141.
38. Philosophy and Truth, p. 141.
39. Philosophy and Truth, p. 86.
40. Philosophy and Truth, p. 151.
41. Quoted in Brinton, Nietzsche, p. 19.
42. Quoted in Heller, The Importance of Nietzsche, p. 53.
43. Will to Power, #821, p. 434.
44. Human, Faber, p. 8.
45. Selected Letters, p. 162.
46. Human, Faber, #178, p. 118.
47. Human, Faber, #207, p. 125.
48. Human, Faber, #208, pp. 125-6.
49. Human, Zimmern, #292, p. 265.
50. Human, Zimmern, #292, p. 265.
51. Human, Zimmern, #441, p. 320.
52. Human, Faber, #472, p. 222.
53. Human, Zimmern, #472, p. 332.
54. Human, Zimmern, #473, pp. 343-4.
55. Human, Faber, #471, p. 222.
56. Human, Faber, #471, p. 222.
57. Human, Zimmern, #611, p. 386.
58. Human, Zimmern, #638, p. 405.
59. Human, Zimmern, #638, p. 405.
60. Human, Faber, #2, p. 14.
61. Human, Faber, #16, p. 23.
62. Human, Faber, #20, p. 27.
63. Human, Faber, #27, p. 32.
64. Human, Faber, #9, p. 18.
65. Human, Faber, #10, p. 18.
66. Human, Faber, #28, p. 33.
67. Human, Faber, #257, p. 156.
68. Human, Faber, #261, p. 160.

CHAPTER 3 PHILOSOPHER IN DEVELOPMENT

To Surpass His Background

In <u>Human</u>, Nietzsche had set the table for most of his writing in the ensuing 10 years of his productive life. Themes established were embellished, perfected or revised in later efforts. His major themes can be described as these:
  a) a quasi-religious perspective on scientific reality,
  b) an emphasis on the dominance of the animal will in man,
  c) a destructive critique of Christian values, especially the ascetic ideal, and
  d) a denial of absolute values or a final goal for man.
Slowly, his thinking matured and his "faith" in science was shaken, until it too was almost merely another perspective on reality. Additionally, Nietzsche came to value "illusion" again, and, in his 1886 preface to <u>Human</u>, stated that "life, in spite of ourselves, is not devised by morality; it <u>demands</u> illusion, it <u>lives</u> by illusion."[1] Lastly, in this preface, he continued: "My philosophy advises me to be silent and not to question further."[2] This statement indicates an obscure element of Nietzsche's method which was to grow after <u>Human</u>.

Nietzsche had definitely abandoned the model of Schopenhauer's genius with the completion of <u>Human</u>. His replacement was the "free spirit":

> the thinker who is not bound by custom, convention, even by 'truth', who follows his ideal as a Don Juan, who regards custom as a shackle, who admits no allegiance except to his own honesty and his own intellectual freedom.[3]

Williams continued his description pointing out the nihilistic point Nietzsche had reached:

> no absolute truths or values, everything is in a flux of change. . . . All belief is a reflection of our state of pain or pleasure . . . such criticism undermines the whole basis of any metaphysical thinking.[4]

Wagner received Human as the announcement that Nietzsche had rejected the movement. Wagner's placed his polemical comments in the movement's newspaper. Only implying Nietzsche was his target, he labelled philologists as being overly critical in areas far beyond their narrow specialty. He also indicated his displeasure at his perceived abandonment by Nietzsche. Nietzsche's attack on metaphysics was just ignored by Wagner. O'Brien summarized the polemical response: "Wagner concluded by sneering at these Goliaths of knowledge who acknowledge no reality that was not visible from their University chairs."[5] It was clear that Nietzsche had grown apart from Wagnerism in his philosophical development.

Nietzsche explained how he pushed on in his 1886 preface to Miscellaneous Maxims and Opinions and The Wanderer and His Shadow (two works originally published independently in 1879 and 1880, but later issued as volume II of Human): "we investigate ourselves the terrible and problematical elements characteristic of all existence."[6] He commented retrospectively that his results in these works testified to the strength of the will, or intellect to pursue the truth. He had called for such a relentless pursuit in his Untimely Meditations. Even his own artist hero of The Birth was a victim of this will to truth.

Now Nietzsche took on the philosophers, including his former mentor Schopenhauer. Metaphysical aspects of philosophy were indicted because they tore man away from reality, the reality of ordinary life. The metaphysical philosopher distorted ordinary reality "into the uncertain, the illusory, the spurious, the impure, the sinful, sorrowful, and deceitful."[7] He quoted Schopenhauer as glimpsing the proper limits to philosophical creativity: "Insight into the stern necessity of human actions is the boundary line that divides philosophic from other brains."[8] Nietzsche concluded that the necessity involved in human action leads to viewing freedom of the will as unreal. And most traditional, metaphysical philosophers stressed freedom of the will as essential to a self so that a choice of the "right way" could be made, this was especially so in the Christian tradition. (Even Schopenhauer saw man as able to choose the life of artistic contemplation and resignation.) Lea summarized Nietzsche's position thusly:

what the metaphysicians have persistently done, he concludes, is to treat certain habits of mind implanted by the religions of the past as though they were an irreducible datum, and to erect their systems upon them.[9]

Nietzsche had already established that everything has evolved: "there are no eternal facts, nor are there any absolute truths."[10]   He had gone on to say that: "the needs which have been met by religion and are now to be met by philosophy are not unchangeable: these themselves can be weakened and rooted out."[11] His "free spirits" were to embark on this new areligious conditioning. Morality, religion and art existed, but their existence was not evidence of the truths the metaphysicians were after. Rather, these cultural forms revealed truths about man's history, development.

The errors of the philosophers, as well as of scientists, artists, politicians or economists, were identified with simplification. The grasping onto one perspective and then trying to persuade others to it has led mankind "to pay a heavy price".[12] This price came from ignoring the extensive and wide ranging needs of humanity. Instead of such simplification, he called for a "cult of culture," an acceptance of "all this is necessary" as the correct perspective.[13] The Greeks were praised for achieving this:

> They continually found new motives for feeling happy, for celebrating festivals, being inventive with all their wealth of shrewdness and reflection . . . With regard to suffering existence, the ancients sought to forget or in some way to convert the sensation into a pleasant one.[14]

Nietzsche complained that Christianity never understood the wisdom of pagan culture: the acceptance of the "all-too-human as unavoidable."[15] They did not deny expression to human urges, but defined and limited them to definite cults and celebrations (the actual historic church also accepted the cultic from the pagans, although Nietzsche did not point this out). The pagan culture as a result was a delight in reality, a reality enhanced through art and celebration.

Christianity's philosophers, Nietzsche held, had turned man away from what was important, namely, the close at hand realities. The result, as he pointed out in The Wanderer and His Shadow, was that no one thinks about every-day matters and, therefore, habit and custom rule. This makes for a dissatisfying and painful existence for many. The individual's health and satisfaction were transcended by "the salvation of the soul, the service of the State, the advancement of science, or even . . . social position and property."[16] Nietzsche then applauded the solution of Epicurus for adapting to life's events. Epicurus saw the solution of theoretical problems as unnecessary. Epicurus' two methods were judged as still valid:

> 1. remain indifferent to such philosophical problems, for they do not concern you; and
> 2. be indifferent to philosophical claims because they are not definitely established.

Nietzsche then continued:

> We have no need of these certainties about the farthermost horizons in order to live a full and efficient human life, any more than the ant needs them in order to be a good ant. Rather we must ascertain the origin of that troublesome significance that we have attached to these things for so long. For this we require the history of ethical and religious sentiments, since it is only under the influence of such sentiments that these most acute problems of knowledge have become so weighty and terrifying.[17]

Ordinary realities, Nietzsche ascertained, had not been involved in these quests of the philosophers:

> For ages men have let their imaginations run riot where they could establish nothing, and have induced posterity to accept these fantasies as something serious and true.[18]

Incredibly, faith in these fantasies was raised above knowledge of things near to man. Nietzsche wished to turn this on its head (as his contemporary Marx did also): "Everything must lie nearer to us than has hitherto been preached to us as the most important thing."[19]

Nietzsche was continuing in his pursuit of a new mental toughness, a will to truth unlimited by traditional morality, religion and metaphysics. As he glimpsed the results of his efforts, he saw traditional perspectives were destroyed. He saw clearly that "the drop of life on the earth is without significance for the total character of the mighty ocean of birth and decay."[20] Within his attempt to revisualize human life, he stumbled onto an explanation of conscience (anticipating Freud) as an internalization of societal authority: "our conscience is all that has regularly been demanded of us, without reason, in the days of our childhood, by people whom we respected and feared."[21] He concluded that the conscience was "the voice of some men in man."[22] Some spirit or other daemon was not needed, was not possible since Nietzsche had eliminated metaphysical realms in general.

The effects of conscience were real, but so also were the effects of man's predilection toward competition and victory. And Nietzsche declared that societal thinking must recognize egoism as real, must analyze utopian schemes for the failure to be cognizant of this truth. Too often moralists, preachers and philosophers have forgotten man's reality, founded on his actions. The result of 2,000 years of "significant errors of moral, religious, and metaphysical ideas"[23] was portrayed by Nietzsche at the end of the Wanderer:

Man has been bound with many chains, in order that he may forget to comport himself like an animal. And indeed he has become more gentle, more intellectual, more joyous, more meditative than any animal. But now he still suffers from having carried his chains so long, from having been so long without pure air and free movement.[24]

Nietzsche carefully explained his role, and the limits of its application:

At present we stand in the midst of our work of removing the chains, and in so doing we need the strictest precautions. Only the ennobled man may be granted freedom of the spirit . . . [to others it] . . . would be dangerous.[25]

As Nietzsche ends the Wanderer, he has definitely distanced himself from even Kant and Schopenhauer, "both of whom, though in differing ways, conceived of morality as bringing man into connection with a supersensible, metaphysical world."[26] Nietzsche was struggling with a new philosophy which could not appeal to any metaphysical realm, yet he wished to found a position on reality. Salter summarized Nietzsche's position on moral matters into four conclusions:
1. "the whole circle of ethical conceptions can be explained without going out of the realm of human relations."
2. Morality is not the supreme element in life, but is a means which has been made an end; and it is a means only to one type of life (social), not the highest type of life.
3. "Conscience is a social product, and may vary as social standards vary."
4. There are no moral acts (free and unegoistic), or moral phenomena, but only a moral interpretation.[27]

For Nietzsche, what was real was the way we act, not as free agents, but as determined beings:

49

Everything is necessity: this is the new knowledge, and this knowledge itself is necessity. Everything is innocence: and knowledge is the way to insight into this innocence.[28]

But Nietzsche realized it would take time to change man, maybe thousands of years before humanity could:

produce wise, innocent (conscious of their innocence) men as regularly as it now produces unwise, unfair men, conscious of their guilt,--these men are the necessary first stage, but not the opposite of those to come.[29]

How were these innocent "free spirits" to be created? Nietzsche did not yet have the path completed in the Wanderer. He evidently felt he was close to the answers he was after.

The Convalescent

Nietzsche's own path into the philosophy of Human had not brought the public acclaim for which he was desperate. Within Human even, Nietzsche had seen merely writing as no way: "To think of writing as one's life's profession should by rights be considered a kind of madness."[30] He was still hoping to influence others, to ignite a movement toward a new culture. He didn't give up in the summer of 1878, but rather had tried to perfect his message and his style in gleanings from the same notes which he had used in composing Human. The result, Miscellaneous Maxims, was composed into a book during the 1878-79 academic year.

Nietzsche was very ill again by winter. His sister joined him in Basel to aid him. He finally resigned from the University in the spring of 1879 and moved away from Burckhardt, one of his only supporters, and Basel for good. Nietzsche discovered Sils Maria in the Italian Alps in March of 1879. This became his favorite summer place for the rest of his life. Here his illness and depression passed (they usually appeared and disappeared together). He drafted The Wanderer and His Shadow during this first Sils experience. This happy period passed when he returned to Naumberg in the fall of 1879. Soon extreme illness overtook him again. The winter of 1879-80 in Naumberg was one of his worst. Even a visit from Ree didn't snap him out of it.

When Nietzsche began to write again, it was through using his illness as a topic for comment. At first, he fought against his pain, as we all do naturally. Nietzsche then recognized that the pain had become a new stimulus to life--that his life arrogantly struggled to overcome even severe pain. His convalescence physically also brought philosophic redemption:

> Redeemed from scepticism.-- . . . out of a general moral scepticism . . . braver and healthier than ever, again in possession of my instincts . . . I have again learned to affirm.[31]

As his personal crisis was overcome through affirmation, so the philosopher was to affirm life. The Christian and Schopenhauerian labeling of life as bad was a form of cultural illness. There was no cure for life. Neither metaphysics, morality, art or religion could cure man of life. Life was greater than all this.

The renewed clarity spread reflectively over Nietzsche's past. His concentration on the Greeks now seemed incomprehensible:

> Nothing grows clearer to me year by year than that the nature of the Greeks and antiquity . . . is very hard to understand, indeed is hardly accessible at all.[32]

A mere twelve years since he had struggled with writing of The Birth had wrought a complete change of focus. Art too was not the way, but rather an imitation of happiness. Metaphysics, whether as in Plato or in Schopenhauer, was firmly repudiated: "For that to which they want to show us the way does not exist."[33] All cults of feelings and mysteries were overthrown through a new appreciation for science with the hope of a new enlightenment. Science was to be the new foundation for the ideals of the new culture Nietzsche still hoped for.

In his next book, The Dawn (published in 1881), he set out to definitively defeat traditional understandings of morality--a defeat which had to be achieved before the path to the new culture and "free spirits" could be made clear. Traditional morality was clearly defined in The Dawn:

> morality is nothing else . . . than obedience to customs, of whatsoever nature they may be. But customs are simply the traditional way of acting and valuing. Where there is no tradition there is no morality.[34]

Nietzsche's "free spirits" would be immoral: "The free man is immoral, because it is his will to depend upon himself and not upon tradition."[35] Tradition, and morality, were relative to history and without other value: "What is tradition? A higher authority, which is obeyed, not because it commands what is useful to us, but merely because it commands."[36] Utility was not the basis of moral commands, this view was a development and rationalization: "All things that live

51

long are gradually so saturated with reason that their origin in unreason thereby becomes improbable." [37] Rational morality was the creation of the philosophers. Kant's entire philosophical construction, Nietzsche contended in the preface to The Dawn, was to provide a solid foundation for his rationalist moral beliefs.

The essence of traditional morality was the sacrifice of the individual to societal dominance. In ancient times this reality was clothed in religion and unquestioning acceptance. To acquire a clear knowledge of this fact, Nietzsche said, was to gain knowledge of yourself. Book I of The Dawn ends with a call to all atheists to come together (echoing the call in Use)--to bring a new era into being. He styled this new movement "European Buddhism," and referred to himself as the "teacher of the religion of self-redemption."[38]

In Book II of The Dawn, Nietzsche discussed the human condition from the perspective of the new amoralists. The primary conclusion reached was that "our moral judgments and evaluations too are only images and fantasies based on physiological processes unknown to us."[39] He asserted that physiological causes truly determine all human actions. Given this fact and the nonreality of any moral realm, he called for a revaluation of the egoistic/unegoistic dichotomy which had dominated Western moral philosophy since Christianity's ascendence. He concluded Book II with a promise to liberate "selfish" actions from their evil image.

In Book III, Nietzsche examined the morality dominating his own time. He found a people who knew how to obey and who valued labor. He insightfully analyzed the work ethic:

> severe toil from morning til night--we have the feeling that it is the best police . . . For work uses up an extraordinary proportion of nervous force, withdrawing it from reflection, meditation, dreams, cares, love and hatred; it dangles unimportant aims before the eyes of the worker and affords easy and regular gratification.[40]

Hence, the work ethic was useful to societies (he paints work as the opiate of the social masses), but the real key stress was "the easy and regular gratifications." He glimpsed what drove men forward:

> the strongest tide which carries them forward is the need for the feeling of power. . . . when man experiences the sensation of power he feels and calls himself good.[41]

He also saw that, in the era of capitalism, "money now stands for power,"[42] and that "What was once done 'for the love of God' is now done for the love of money."[43]

While there was no worry of seeing money as an ultimate good, at least in philosophical circles, why had philosophers persisted in ignoring actual motives in their pursuit of the truly good? Nietzsche again took up the battle against this mind set:

> There is nothing good, nothing beautiful, nothing sublime, or nothing evil in itself, but that there are states of soul in which we impose such words upon things external to and within us.[44]

We have our valuations. They are relative to our societal reality: "there are no means of exit or escape to the real world!"[45] Philosophers can ponder and introspect all they wish Nietzsche implied, but no key to the "really real" will be found:

> When we try to examine the mirror in itself we discover in the end nothing but the things upon it. If we want to grasp the things we finally get hold of nothing but the mirror.--This . . . is the history of knowledge.[46]

Merely substitute self or consciousness for "the mirror" and everyday objects for "the things reflected" and we have Nietzsche's repudiation of the Kantian road to metaphysical realities.

The days of the philosophers of old were gone Nietzsche proclaimed--the era of the scientists was emerging. The old metaphysical workers were described as follows:

> To solve everything at a single stroke, with one word --this was the secret desire; . . . no one doubted that it was possible to reach the goal of knowledge . . . and to settle all questions with one answer.[47]

Nietzsche contrasted this magical conception of the knowledge of reality (which obviously had Schopenhauer's "will" in view) with science and its piecemeal process which gradually produced results. He saw science as exhibiting the laws of behavior--laws which need not show man as rational. These scientific seekers would liberate man from the need for salvation. Men would be free to experiment. Hence, the dawn of a new era in human action was at hand.

The negative approach to philosophy had dominated in Nietzsche's productions from <u>Human</u> through <u>The Dawn</u>. His "historical philosophy" lent itself to a debunking of earlier philosophies, religions and moralities. Yet even he recognized that mere antiquarian critiques would not deal with things near at hand and important to man of his day. For this reason, Darwinian concerns were ignored, whether looking backward to the ape or looking forward to new evolutionary change for man. Science was lauded for its concentration on the here and now of analysis. Causal analysis led to practical knowledge of human action.

Moral thinking as currently undertaken needed analysis. The level of analysis was to be restricted to psychological factors, with metaphysical perspectives eliminated. What then was the moralist saying at bottom:

> How many there are who still conclude: "Life could not be endured if there were no God!" (or, as it is put among the idealists: "Life could not be endured if its foundation lacked ethical significance!")--therefore there <u>must</u> be a God (or existence <u>must</u> have an ethical significance)! The truth, however, is merely that he who is accustomed to these notions does not desire life without them.[48]

Religious belief in God was equated with metaphysical belief in an ethical reality. Both were reduced to acquired beliefs which historically created the strong psychological need for them. Nietzsche wished to strip this ideological approach from moral thinking. Although he didn't have this worked out in <u>The Dawn</u>, he stated that he wanted a morality without any attachment to reality claims which psychologically gave the feeling of identification with a powerful force. He wanted moral commitment of the individual which was real self-sacrifice--without mysterious participation, intoxication through ritual or Wagnerian music, or other metaphysical excesses.

Such a pure morality was a new orientation for Western man. Nietzsche recognized the newness of his approach:

> To <u>recommend</u> a goal to mankind is something quite different: the goal is then thought of as something which <u>lies in our own discretion</u> . . . it could in pursuit of it also <u>impose</u> upon itself a moral law, likewise at its own discretion.[49]

Unlike discovering the will of God or Nature, man himself was to be the director of his moral actions. Man alone was to rise up and set a goal and an appropriate morality. This was what Nietzsche wanted his "free spirits" to accomplish.

However, Nietzsche's remaining Schopenhauerian thought about the individual was not really congruent with this praise of self-direction. Throughout The Dawn, the self, our conscious self, is debunked as an unreality. This position destroyed the possibility of a self directing his own actions:

> The unknown world of the "subject" . . . The primeval delusion still lives on that one knows . . . how human action is brought about. . . . no amount of knowledge about an act ever suffices to ensure its performance.[50]

Nietzsche continued from this to debunk the basic dynamics of moral decision based on a weighing of consequences and motives. His assertion was that real causal events were below consciousness, and hence, moral consideration and judgment were not truly effective in producing actions. So-called "will" and intentions were a mere facade in human consciousness: "perhaps there exists neither will nor purposes, and we have only imagined them. . . . our most intentional actions do no more than play the game of necessity."[51] How the self is driven was not known to Nietzsche. Consciousness was only the appearance of hidden causes: "Consciousness is a more or less fantastic commentary on an unknown, perhaps unknowable, but felt text?"[52]

How was this tension between self-direction and a merely surface-self resolved by Nietzsche? It wasn't resolved in The Dawn, and in fact, it was never adequately resolved in the later Nietzsche either. Nietzsche grasped both sides of the dilemma openly and proclaimed this perspective of a truly determined self as a liberating vision. With the realm of human will and purposes eliminated, the self fell into the realm of causes (Kant undone)--a realm where determinism was the rule. But at the same time man was thus liberated from the traditional Western dogmas of moral existence:

1. Human actions were not performed by "free will".
2. Human actions were the determined result of causes.
3. Human actions were not deserving of blame for evil.
4. Human actions were innocent.

This freedom from guilt was joined to the freedom from the religious burden placed on the individual:

> mankind's most useful achievement is perhaps the abandonment of its belief in an immortal soul . . . For in the past the salvation of the "eternal soul" depended on knowledge acquired during a brief life time, men had to come to a decision over night-- "knowledge" possessed a frightful importance.[53]

Man for Nietzsche thus had no religious or moral commandments based on a dogma of human and metaphysical reality. "Free spirits" were free to experiment.

Finding Philosophy in Psychology

In The Dawn, Nietzsche scattered comments on what drove men. The unknown causes of human action were not ignored. Knowledge was still very meaningful to Nietzsche, and with the benefit of hindsight, concerns with "power" can be drawn together. Nietzsche had always recognized the effectiveness of pain and happiness (pleasure) on human motivation. He sought deeper however, and said that there were "two species of happiness (the feeling of power and the feeling of surrender)."[54] He also saw that the valuing of self-control by noble individuals was in part caused by the pleasure of the feeling of power in self-mastery. Much of social dynamics was viewed as a striving for dominance, as "lust for power."[55] Nietzsche even called this "the need for the feeling of power" in a political perspective.[56] This led to the realization that a remedy for depression lay in "a new excitation of the feeling of power."[57] Nietzsche's repeated emphasis on the feeling of power carried over into his discussion of a new moral goal:

> to pursue more distant goals even at the cost of the suffering of others--
> . . . [We can] through sacrifice . . . strengthen and raise higher the general feeling of human power, even though we might not attain to more. But even this would be a positive enhancement of happiness.[58]

The beginnings of a positive philosophy were in The Dawn. Nietzsche still retained doubts however. He worried over his "free spirits," of whether their courage and innocence might not lead to "the supreme form of arrogance" and feel themselves "above man and things."[59] He also worried that his own philosophy was really, merely, a reflection of his life:

> Does it do more than translate as it were into reason a strong and constant drive, a drive for gentle sunlight, bright and buoyant air, southerly vegetation, the breath of the sea, fleeting meals of flesh, fruit and eggs, hot water to drink, daylong silent wanderings, little talking, infrequent and cautious reading, dwelling alone, clean, simple almost soldierly habits, in short for all those things which taste best and are most endurable precisely to me?[60]

Philosopher in Development

His positive moral beginnings were similarly austere. They were also open, as the sunny sea coast of Sorrento. Nietzsche hoped they were refreshing as the sea breeze--light and free of heavy metaphysical trappings. It was a morality he was after despite the new orientation:

> I do not deny. . . . that many actions called immoral ought to be avoided and resisted, or that many actions called moral ought to be done and encouraged--but I think one should be encouraged and the other avoided for other reasons than hitherto. We have to learn to think differently . . . to feel differently.[61]

Nietzsche was still driven by a lust for knowledge like that he described in The Dawn:

> a greedy longing for knowledge as a law ruling over you . . . a duty to desire to be present as a witness whenever knowledge is present and to let nothing escape again.[62]

This Faustian striving conflicted with his desire to be part of a movement, a community no matter how small, because his pursuit of knowledge had driven him into isolation. Yet Nietzsche recognized his communal drive as potentially dangerous to one's thought production. He described the philosopher's danger thusly:

> he can no longer endure at all the dreadful isolation in which every spirit lives who flies on out ahead; he henceforth surrounds himself with objects of veneration, communality, emotion and love; he wants at long last to enjoy what all the religious enjoy and celebrate within the community . . . indeed, in order to possess this community he will invent a religion.[63]

Nietzsche held himself back from this pathetic picture. He did not seek a new religion. Although disillusioned by the results of his quest after knowledge and disappointed in the lack of appreciation from the outside world, he stuck to his quest. He kept writing, creating. He saw the artist in man as driven, but yet content with his drivenness:

> when he is feeling his best, when he is creating, he does so because he forgets that he is at precisely this time doing--and is bound to be doing--something fantastic and irrational (which is what all art is) but with the highest degree of purposiveness.[64]

57

The complex marriage of determinism, creativity and self-direction was not well developed at the time The Dawn was completed. Nietzsche obviously felt he was on the verge of something--a new dawn for man, and for himself.

NOTES

1. Human, Zimmern, p. 3.
2. Human, Zimmern, p. 12.
3. Williams, Nietzsche and the French, p. 30.
4. Williams, Nietzsche and the French, p. 39.
5. O'Brien, Son of the Morning, p. 179.
6. The Philosophy of Nietzsche, 1965, p. 110.
7. The Philosophy of Nietzsche, 1965, p. 554.
8. Human, part II, p. 28.
9. Lea, The Tragic, p. 116.
10. Human, Faber, #2, p. 15.
11. Human, Faber, #27, p. 32.
12. Human, part II, p. 100.
13. Human, part II, p. 100.
14. Human, part II, p. 101.
15. Human, part II, p. 113.
16. Human, part II, p. 187.
17. The Philosophy of Nietzsche, 1965, p. 555.
18. The Philosophy of NIetzsche, 1965, p. 555.
19. The Philosophy of Nietzsche, 1965, p. 555.
20. Human, part II, p. 194.
21. Human, part II, p. 224.
22. Human, part II, p. 224.
23. Human, part II, p. 363.
24. Human, part II, pp. 362-3.
25. Human, part II, p. 363.
26. Salter, Nietzsche the Thinker, p. 323.
27. Salter, Nietzsche the Thinker, pp. 324-6.
28. Human, Faber, #107, pp. 75-6.
29. Human, Faber, #107, p. 76.
30. Human, Faber, #194, p. 121.
31. Daybreak, #477, p. 197.
32. Daybreak, #195, p. 116.
33. Daybreak, #474, pp. 196-7.

34. The Dawn, #9, p. 14.
35. The Dawn, #9, p. 14.
36. The Dawn, #9, p. 15.
37. Daybreak, #1, p. 9.
38. Daybreak, #96, p. 55.
39. Daybreak, #119, p. 76.
40. The Dawn, #173, pp. 176-7.
41. Daybreak, #189, pp. 110-1.
42. The Dawn, #203, p. 209.
43. The Dawn, #204, p. 210.
44. Daybreak, #210, p. 133.
45. The Dawn, #117, p. 123.
46. Daybreak, #243, p. 141.
47. The Dawn, #547, p. 378.
48. Daybreak, #90, p. 52.
49. Daybreak, #108, p. 63.
50. Daybreak, #116, p. 72.
51. Daybreak, #130, pp. 81-2.
52. Daybreak, #119, p. 76.
53. Daybreak, #501, p. 204.
54. Daybreak, #60, p. 36.
55. Daybreak, #113, p. 69.
56. Daybreak, #189, p. 110.
57. Daybreak, #140, p. 88.
58. Daybreak, #146, p. 92.
59. Daybreak, #551, p. 222.
60. Daybreak, #553, pp. 223-4.
61. Daybreak, #103, p. 60.
62. Daybreak, #270, p. 148.
63. Daybreak, #542, p. 216.
64. Daybreak, #263, p. 146.

CHAPTER FOUR   JOY AND LOVE

Work to Be Done

Nietzsche produced the following works after 1881:

    The Joyful Wisdom (1882 & 1886)
    Thus Spoke Zarathustra (1883-84)
    Beyond Good and Evil (1886)
    Genealogy of Morals (1887)
    The Wagner Case (1888)
    Twilight of the Idols (1881)
    The Antichrist (1888)
    Ecce Homo (1888)

An impressive production by a man who was chronically ill, and struggling with his sight. He suffered a breakdown in 1889 and wrote and talked no more as a philosopher. His body lived on for another 11 years.

There was no progressive system, or comprehensive elaboration laid out in the eight works. Thus Spoke Zarathustra was regarded by Nietzsche as his masterpiece. It reads like a mythic tale. It was an attempt at poetry, myth, literature and philosophy: one might say, a Wagnerian effort at synthesis, although Nietzsche would never have agreed to such a characterization. The Joyful Wisdom contained most of the ideas in Zarathustra, but in the style of Human. The style of Beyond Good and Evil and Genealogy of Morals was the furthest from that of Human. Ecce Homo reads like the autobiographical notes of a feisty old man; they seem only partly serious. The Twilight of the Idols and The Antichrist were in an extreme aphoristic or short paragraph form. Most of Nietzsche's unpublished notes were in this same form. Some of these notes were published after his death under the title of The Will to Power (This publication is not discussed as a unity here because it was not a product which he had prepared for publication). There is some indication that The Antichrist was to be part of a grand trilogy, but such a summing up never was produced.

With The Dawn completed early in 1881, Nietzsche turned to a heavy reading program until fall. From what he requested to be sent to him, we know he read a lot of current natural science. This program continued after he left Genoa for Sils Maria in the summer. There his natural science immersion was joined to a secure solitude and his usual long mountain walks. He also had time to discover Spinoza from among the great predecessors in philosophy. In a letter to a friend, he stated the similarities of his views with Spinoza: "closest to me in these points precisely: he denies free will, purposes, the moral world order, the nonegoistical, [and] evil."[1] During this blissful period, a pivotal idea came to him. He subsequently referred to this as the idea of eternal recurrence. His description of these times in a letter of August 14, 1881, revealed Nietzsche experienced more than a new idea:

> The intensity of my sentiments made me shudder and laugh--twice already I have had to stay in my room, and for a ridiculous reason; my eyes were inflamed, Why? Because while I walked I had cried too much, but tears of joy; and I sang and said idiotic things.[2]

Nietzsche was grasping for a way to found an ethical perspective which was not metaphysical, i.e., not based on the ultimate nature of reality. Individualism, as egoism, had to be transcended. How to justify such, or to found a new non-egoistic vision was problematic. Nietzsche checked what natural science had to offer. But he never found a goal for man in science. In a note from this period he stated his goal for this new ethical foundation: something "Beyond 'me' and 'you'! To feel cosmically."[3] This quest reflected what Schopenhauer had offered his disciples. But such an offering had a metaphysical price which Nietzsche would not pay. From a scientific perspective without metaphysics, Nietzsche could not offer any similar support.

The Kantian model would also have been available to Nietzsche, but he had rejected it because its foundation was also metaphysical at base. So instead of escaping the determinism of natural science through metaphysics, Nietzsche grasped this horn of the dilemma. Determinism was affirmed as the good instead of the evil. Science's view of all as inextricably linked in a causal nexus could be seen as giving value to every action as a part of the whole determined world. The individual could view his every action as a part of the whole, as vitally important to the resultant actions to follow from his actions. Finally, Nietzsche relied on current scientific/mathematical understandings of infinite time to see each life, and each action, as bound to recur again and again. How to present what seemed to him this grand solution to the major modern problems of ethics was an issue he would grapple with throughout his next three works. He was aware that it was problematic.

Before he could draft his new ideas into a workable product, illness and depression beset Nietzsche again in the fall of 1881. The catalytic event was the absence of any response to the publication of The Dawn (in the summer of that year). Genoa was not a happy place this time. But he gradually worked himself out of it as he began what was to become The Joyful Wisdom. As he wrote, he held back on his insight of "eternal recurrence." This idea did not appear until the fourth book, the final book of the original version. His fourth book followed from a joyous new year for 1882. He recorded his resolution to achieve the fruits of eternal recurrence in his life in the beginning of this book:

> I want to learn more and more to see as beautiful what is necessary in things . . . *Amour fati*: let that be my love henceforth! . . . some day I wish to be only a Yes-sayer.[4]

The title for this work described Nietzsche's elevated mood going into the new year. The mood was also reflected in his return to music after his self-imposed five year abstinence.

Wisdom, which spans the Zarathustra period, when considered in its 1886 version, seems to reveal the meaning of Zarathustra.[5] The spirit of Nietzsche was incarnate in the works of 1882-1885. While Wisdom seems to reveal all, his jewel, Zarathustra was a well-polished presentation that hides as much as it discloses. Nietzsche's creativity, heightened by his love for Lou Salome, spun out a production for a wider audience. Zarathustra, taken by itself, (which teachers of Nietzsche wrongly do), is obscure in its total effect. The background of Wisdom is necessary to penetrate to the meaning of this epic poem. For Zarathustra is not even a hint at an argument, and the arguments which support it must be exposed if one is to grasp Nietzsche's intent.

The Joy of Wisdom

Wisdom was written in two distinct periods: the first four books were completed just prior to Zarathustra and the fifth book was not written until after his next work, Beyond Good and Evil. Book IV has elements which foreshadow Zarathustra, and Book V assumes knowledge of the Zarathustra themes. The first four books should be seen as a unit, as the final preparation for Zarathustra. The title page of the original edition labels <u>Wisdom</u> the completion of Nietzsche's six year effort starting with <u>Human</u>.[6]

The major development in <u>Wisdom</u> was the dethroning of the science/knowledge quest from a preeminent place. Nietzsche also presented a clear rejection of much of Schopenhauer's thought for the first time. Wagnerian romanticism was also surpassed, but the individual and the passions were still highly valued. Lastly, a full affirmation of life in all its aspects was proclaimed. And with science dethroned, a mythic production like <u>Zarathustra</u> could be accepted.

In Book I, Nietzsche began with a reanalysis of the dominance of the animal will in man. The individual was portrayed as of less value than the species in overall events of man and nature. Despite this Darwinian and Schopenhauerian perspective, the great tragedy of man was that he searches for a meaning for existence. Man had hoped to find that X is the meaning of existence. He had believed that he could be certain about X and its function. "Higher man" had especially been driven by this quest after certainty in knowledge about existence. These comments were probably reflective of Nietzsche's own life, as well as the Western intellectual tradition (and this author's).

Nietzsche went on to set up an opposition between the "higher men" (formerly "free spirits") and "lower men." The "lower men" were styled after the traditional moral zealot of the Christian tradition. The Christian model of the conscious individual driven by ethical obligations was the ideal "lower man." "Higher man" had broken out of this mold and was searching beyond these values, beyond the acknowledged goods, therefore toward evil. Nietzsche equated the morality of the "lower men" with anti-individualism, as a belief in the individual's subservience to society which created and inculcated moral value in men. Such a morality was directed at achieving the greatest good for society without regard to individuals, while "higher men" rebelled against this self-sacrifice. In the Christian moral tradition, science/knowledge was perceived as a handmaiden to discovering the good society (once science was accepted). Nietzsche asserted that science succeeded because of three false assumptions:

1. that science was the best way to understand God's goodness and wisdom;

2. that scientific knowledge would facilitate morally appropriate actions; and

3. that scientific endeavors would be harmless.[7]

Nietzsche implied that science, as it developed, proved these assumptions false, and left a major question: could science furnish a goal for human action after it had destroyed the validity of all previous goals (which had existed in the Western

Christian tradition)? Nietzsche, as was his style, did not answer this question directly. Instead he turned to critique science and the quest for Truth itself.

Testability was determined to be the new criterion for scientific truths according to Nietzsche. Thus, he anticipated the thrust of philosophy's main stream in the next century. But he went further, anticipating Wittgenstein of the mid-Twentieth Century, and questioned the concept of truth. Nietzsche implied that there was no X which when observed, or tested, by all would be judged as true. Instead of this model, he proposed the following:

> And man's greatest labor so far has been to reach agreement about very many things and to submit to a law of agreement--regardless of whether these things are true or false.[8]

Nietzsche could have said that science had to do with the current forms of agreement. He was not this clear, and continued to use the word "true" to refer to the belief in a vision of reality which did not acknowledge the role of human convention or agreement. He was attacking the Kantian position also. For the Kantians had a faith in an X which was more than the fruits of human agreement. The fruits of human agreement, or experience, were characterized as mere appearance by the Kantians and as not of the really Real. However, science pertained to appearances for them. Nietzsche sought to cut-off the really Real and save appearance: "What is "appearance for me now? Certainly not the opposite of some essence . . . . Appearance is for me that which lives and is effective."[9] But as the fruits of agreement, appearance would not be granted the absolute character of the really Real. That possibility was banished. The "free spirits" were allowed, encouraged, to question the given truths of appearance, of society. The "higher men" challenged the reign of agreement. This has always been the role of creative individuals: poets, artists, and philosophers.

Nietzsche called out for the individual as the proper focus of value. The free individual, not subject to a faith or another's will, was the ideal. A passionate individual who directed his own activity was praised. A creative individual who dominated appearance through his use of it was the pinnacle of man. Yet, in Book II, it was not an irrational, arbitrary life that he wanted to recommend:

> The greatest danger-- . . . the eruption of madness--which means the eruption of arbitrariness . . . the enjoyment of the mind's lack of discipline, the joy in human unreason.[10]

Neither irrationalism nor the Romantic facade of heightened passions were approved of by Nietzsche. He called all such attempts to provide intoxication of the senses "aping the high tide of the soul."[11] Art needed to be more than "a little intoxication and madness."[12]

Not only did Nietzsche clearly separate himself from Romaticism in Wisdom, he finally made clear what he wished to reject in Schopenhauer's philosophy. Nietzsche mentioned these specific positions which he rejected:

1. "the denial of the individual"
2. "his ecstatic reveries about genius"
3. "'the pure, will-less, pain-less subject of knowledge'"
4. that pity allows one to escape individuality
5. that pity is the source of all morality
6. "'dying is really the purpose of existence'"
7. his concept of "will".[13]

Overall, Nietzsche presented Schopenhauer as "seduced and corrupted by the vain urge to be the unriddler of the world."[14]

All of Schopenhauer was not rejected. Nietzsche admitted he retained:

1. "the intellectuality of intuition"
2. "the a priori nature of the causal law"
3. "the instrumental character of the intellect"
4. "the unfreedom of the will".[15]

Nietzsche did not elaborate on these acknowledged borrowings, but their acceptance clearly indicates indicates some affinities with the neo-Kantianism then in fashion. One of the difficulties with interpreting Nietzsche's thought stems from the problem of determining how much of Schopenhauer's metaphysics he retained. Only hints are offered in the remainder of his works. This entry in Wisdom was a rare direct comment on his philosophical development.

Nietzsche was no longer a disciple of anybody, and this is what he wanted of his "free spirits": "'Be a man and do not follow me--but yourself! But yourself!'"[16] The secret to your own path had to come from within: "We, too, shall grow and blossom out of ourselves, free and fearless, in innocent selfishness."[17] To point out his message, Nietzsche then repeated what he had said years earlier in his fourth Untimely Meditation:

> That passion is better than Stoicism and hypocrisy, that being honest in evil is still better than losing oneself to the morality of tradition . . . the unfree human being is a blemish upon nature . . . that everyone who wishes to become free must become free through his own endeavor, and that freedom does not fall into any man's lap as a miraculous gift.[18]

Joy and Love

Looking back to his first book, he concluded Book II with a message recalling the theme of The Birth:

> As an aesthetic phenomenon existence is still bearable for us . . . At times we need a rest from ourselves . . . an artistic distance, laughing over ourselves or weeping over ourselves . . . we must occasionally find pleasure in our wisdom . . . we need exuberant, floating, dancing, mocking, childish blissful art . . . we should be able to stand above morality-- . . . to float above it and play.[19]

This also foreshadowed Zarathustra: a dancing, mocking, childish art, which was a free floating creative act of Nietzsche.

But Book III was deadly serious in tone. Nietzsche began with a way of describing the effects of modernity which carried forward to today:

> God is dead; but given the way of men, there may still be caves for thousands of years in which his shadow will be shown.--And we--we will still need to vanquish his shadow too.[20]

Nietzsche meant much more than that theological beliefs about God were irrelevant. The whole archetypical method of world characterization was now inoperative for the "free spirits." The world should not have been characterized as an organism, a machine, or a divine unity. Characterizing appearance as a world, a nature, may even have been too much. It is indifferent to man and his conscious appraisal. Returning to his earlier theme, even material reality, the things of common sense, are only the result of the human conditions of life. They are only from our perspective. The conceptions interwoven in our common reality are the result of human needs, human utility. Even these very fundamental truths are not evidence for Truth: "Thus the strength of knowledge does not depend on its degree of truth but on its age, on the degree to which it has been incorporated, on its character as a condition of life."[21] The traditional wisdom of man has also, thusly, been a development out of fundamental beliefs which had utility--but there is no guarantee their development continued to serve utility.

Nietzsche set out what he saw as the four basic erroneous beliefs which man had developed:

1. that man was imperfect;
2. that man was rational and had free will;
3. that man was qualitatively above all animals; and
4. that value systems were eternally and unconditionally valid.[22]

67

These beliefs were foundational to the development of Christian individual morality. Nietzsche's "free spirits," of course, would believe the contrary to the above:

> 1. that man is as he is, and is not an imperfect copy of something other;
> 2. that man is not rational and does not have free will;
> 3. that man is an animal; and
> 4. that every belief is valid only from a perspective.

Nietzsche had asked: "When will we complete our de-deification of nature? When may we begin to "naturalize" humanity in terms of a pure, newly discovered, newly redeemed nature?"[23] Parts of a new naturalized man and redeemed natural world were hinted at by Nietzsche in Wisdom. Man had evolved: "Gradually, the human brain became full of such judgments and convictions, and a ferment, struggle, and lust for power developed in this tangle."[24] Science endeavored to describe the natural world, not to explain by reference to metaphysical forces: "we do not explain any more than our predecessors . . . we have merely perfected the image of becoming without reaching beyond the image or behind it."[25]

Instead of positing "will" behind all as Schopenhauer had, Nietzsche tried to analyze human willing. First, he clearly stated that "willing" applied only to intellectual beings, humans. He held that "willing" was a mechanism, and not a simple one. It was involved in the execution of action after interpretations had been made by the intellectual functions. "Willing" was not a quasi-magical force or some manifestation of a metaphysical reality. "Willing" was part of the natural man, a resultant of organic processes.[26]

The intellect had a role in the guidance of the organism:

> Even the determination of what is healthy for your body depends on your goal, your horizon, your energies, your impulses, your errors, and above all on the ideals and phantasms of your soul.[27]

The individual, each individual, thus would set values for himself. Everything must be evaluated from the perspective of what is good for the individual--nothing is eternally set: "man alone among all the animals has no eternal horizons and perspectives."[28] Rather, man must continue his experiments in living.

Nietzsche concluded Book III protesting that he did not seek followers, or disciples, but rather free individuals who would develop on their own:

For an individual to posit his own ideal and to derive from it his own laws, joys, and rights--that may well have been considered hitherto as the most outrageous human aberration and as idolatry itself.[29]

But it is this "evil" that Nietzsche preached.

Book IV (the end of the original work) was the proclamation of the joyful wisdom, a new gospel. An age of innocence was proclaimed. An egoism without Christian guilt was offered. A salvation equal to Christianity's was not offered. Nietzsche proclaimed himself as the prophet of contemporary self-knowledge. The ideal proclaimed was the opposite of the ascetic ideal: total, joyous affirmation of life, including the necessity of death, of all necessities. As tips to achieve this, Nietzsche offered his discussion of the actions of "higher men" and "free spirits." There was no one way for all. One should de-emphasize the contemplative and re-emphasize action. For action remained mysterious, susceptible of neither rational reduction nor moral guidance. The active life represented a life better than the ideal of contemplative thought which was the result of a rational reduction of life to certain principles. The "higher men" must acknowledge accept and then joyously affirm life in its manifold diversity.

Nietzsche created a rule for judging one's life in light of the joyful wisdom: live so that one could be supremely happy with the possibility of living the exact life over forever and ever.[30] This moral maxim was later dramatized into the myth of eternal recurrence in Zarathustra. In Wisdom its meaning was clear: it is a tough standard for appraising one's actions, an ideal, not a true rule which could be followed. Nietzsche also posed an important reminder: "Only we have created the world that concerns man! . . . we fail to recognize our best power . . . we are neither as proud nor as happy as we might be."[31]

Hope for Love

Nietzsche seemed not to heed his own advice and ended his happiness in the spring of 1882 with a trip to Sicily. He became ill on the journey and returned in poor spirits. Wagner was in Sicily, and this apparently indicated that Nietzsche had hoped for some sort reconciliation--although there was no basis for such. Nietzsche thus refused to accept his own history, i.e., his break with Wagner and the popular romanticism of his followers.

In May of 1882, Frau von Meysenbug, an old friend, invited Nietzsche to Rome. He had spent time with her and Ree when he was drafting notes for Human. Nietzsche accepted, probably hoping for a renewal of happy times. Frau von Meysenbug evidently had been seeking a marriage match for him--a subject he off-handedly considered from time to time. She had a young, intelligent candidate in Lou Salome. Lou had already struck up an acquaintance with Paul Ree. Nietzsche looked forward to a reunion of the 1876-7 times when he first tasted freedom, now with the addition of a lively female to increase interests.

Both Ree and Nietzsche professed no marriage interests. Lou's mother seemed to prefer Ree to the recluse philosopher. Nietzsche, however, was quickly smitten. He had never had a first love (there is some question about his relationship to Cosima Wagner), nor any serious relationship with a young lady. He was naive, very Victorian, and not a free thinker in this area. He did seem happy enough in the summer of 1882 to let events happen. Lou was at least intrigued and led him on as to her interests in him.

Lou received Nietzsche's outpouring after years of solitude. They traveled to Triebschen together. Here at the scene of Nietzsche's greatest happiness with the Wagners, he recounted his sadness at joys now denied. He admitted to Lou that Schopenhauer and Wagner had inspired him, had replaced the awe which had been missing since abandoning his Christian upbringing. This sharing bound Nietzsche to Lou.

But Lou was more free in these matters than Nietzsche. She was of the coming generation--a liberated woman. So when Nietzsche asked Ree to present his love to Lou, in line with formal tradition, Lou refused and indicated she wasn't interested in marriage. Nietzsche had withdrawn to Basel and he poured out his love-sick heart to the Overbecks in June of 1882. He asked Lou again, and she refused again. Then Nietzsche moved off to Berlin, and then positioned himself near Bayreuth for the scheduled opening performance of Parsifal. He received a poem from Lou and was overjoyed.

While Nietzsche pined away hoping for a summons from Wagner, Lou attended the festival with Ree. After the festival Lou and Nietzsche were together again. He set about transforming her into a disciple. He was still confident of a long-term relationship. Lou however had no such plans. While Nietzsche was in Leipzig in September of 1882, Lou visited him, but she came with Ree. Nietzsche became possessive and denounced Ree to Lou. This backfired and precipitated the end of this Platonic threesome. Lou went off with Ree and Nietzsche concluded he had been betrayed by all. He left for Rapallo in October to be alone and to work.

Ways of living endorsed in Wisdom were probably on Nietzsche's mind: "The Epicurean selects the situation, the persons, and even the events that suit his extremely irritable, intellectual constitution."[32] He followed his own advice: "Live in seclusion so that you can live for yourself."[33] His flurry of activity with people was over. Later he saw the Lou episode as comic: "Love is the danger for the most solitary man, . . . Indeed, my foolishness and modesty in love is laughable!"[34] He returned to an image of life presented in <u>Wisdom</u>: "the idea that life could be an experiment of the seeker for knowledge . . . . 'Life as a means to knowledge'."[35]

NOTES

1. <u>Selected Letters</u>, p. 177.
2. Quoted in Halvey, <u>The Life of Friedrich Nietzsche</u>,   p. 232.
3. Quoted in Shapiro, <u>Nietzschean Narratives</u>, p. 92.
4. <u>Gay Science</u>, #276, p. 223.
5. This author found <u>Wisdom</u> to be the pivotal book in understanding Nietzsche.
6. <u>Gay Science</u>, p. 30.
7. <u>Joyful Wisdom</u>, #37, pp. 75-6.
8. <u>Gay Science</u>, #76, p. 130.
9. <u>Gay Science</u>, #54, p. 116.
10. <u>Gay Science</u>, #76, p. 130.
11. <u>Gay Science</u>, #86, p. 142.
12. <u>Gay Science</u>, #89, p. 144.
13. <u>Gay Science</u>, #99, p. 153.
14. <u>Gay Science</u>, #99, p. 153.
15. <u>Gay Science</u>, #99, p. 153.
16. <u>Gay Science</u>, #99, p. 155.
17. <u>Gay Science</u>, #99, p. 156.
18. <u>Gay Science</u>, #99, p. 156.
19. <u>Gay Science</u>, #107, p. 164.
20. <u>Gay Science</u>, #108, p. 167.
21. <u>Gay Science</u>, #110, p. 169.
22. <u>Joyful Wisdom</u>, #115, p. 160.
23. <u>Gay Science</u>, #109, p. 169.
24. <u>Gay Science</u>, #110, p. 170.
25. <u>Gay Science</u>, #112, p. 172.
26. <u>Gay Science</u>, #127, pp. 183-4.
27. <u>Gay Science</u>, #120, p. 177.
28. <u>Gay Science</u>, #143, p. 192.
29. <u>Gay Science</u>, #143, p. 191.
30. <u>Joyful Wisdom</u>, #341, pp. 270-1.
31. <u>Gay Science</u>, #301, p. 242.
32. <u>Gay Science</u>, #306, p. 245.
33. <u>Gay Science</u>, #338, p. 271.

34. <u>Zarathustra</u>, Hollingdale, p. 175.
35. <u>Gay Science</u>, #324, p. 255.

CHAPTER 5 THE CREATION OF A FREE SPIRIT

Poetic Philosophy

The experimenter returned to long walks in the cold and wet winter of 1882-83 around Rapallo. His mind must have been a ferment of activity. He still had the "eternal recurrence" idea to work out. He now could add in the love experience and the final acceptance that Wagner was behind him (Wagner died in February of 1883). He had spoken to Lou about "the impossibility of founding his hypothesis in reason."[1] He had also talked of creating a fictional progeny. These thoughts came to a head in ten weeks that winter.

The idea Nietzsche grasped was that of creating a fictional character, Zarathustra, to present his ideas. This creation seemed to free his ability to work out his feelings and his thoughts. As he had said in Wisdom, he "had not discovered any other way of getting rid of" his thoughts.[2] Later, Nietzsche claimed his Zarathustra effort was produced as if inspired. But the effort itself was well honed, cogent from part to part, though it spanned a couple of years, and unified. And we know Nietzsche was a perfectionist in presentation, ever looking for the correct style. This lyric, epic, poetic effort probably was not the work of mere days as claimed. Nietzsche's comments otherwise were self-serving. They were meant to add to the fictional setting of a religious prophet's handing down of the gospel. Nietzsche was too crafty for his interpreters in this effort. As he said with Also Spoke Zarathustra: "I will fence my thoughts round, and my words too: so that swine and hot fanatics shall not break into my garden!"[3] And an even more telling entry was made in Human:

The artist knows that his work has its full effect only when it arouses belief in an improvisation, in a wondrous instantaneousness of origins; and

73

so he encourages this illusion and introduces into art elements of inspired unrest . . . deceptions that dispose the soul of the viewer or listener to believe in the sudden emergence of perfection.(emphasis added)[4]

Zarathustra was Nietzsche's primary creative effort and he never repudiated it. He wrote the first part in the winter of 1882-83. It was published in June of 1883.

In this self-proclaimed masterpiece, a new creativity was unleashed. Many of his old themes were woven into this mythic story. Nietzsche was free to craft symbols, that is, presentations not molded on rigorous argument, rather than to draft clear philosophic conceptions. In this respect, Zarathustra was the zenith of his art. He may have thought he had realized his goal as proclaimed in The Birth: "Dionysus speaks the language of Apollo, but Apollo, finally, the language of Dionysus . . . the highest goal of tragedy and art."[5] Zarathustra, as a character created by Nietzsche, was a symbol who used symbolic presentations. No wonder many contemporary philosophers have labeled him a literary artist rather than a philosopher.

Many students of Nietzsche have found Zarathustra enigmatic (including this author). Contemporaries were also not sure what to make of this poetic creation. Nietzsche remained convinced it was his finest creation. He claimed it was the product of an enraptured state. He completed the first two parts in spurts. Part III required more time and Part IV was executed much later, and originally it was only circulated privately. (There were plans for additional parts, but none were written.) The central ideas of Zarathustra were developments from his earlier thoughts. From Wisdom (the first 4 parts), "eternal return" was developed into the central concept. "Will to power" and the "*Übermensch*", however, were new terms with unique treatment in the symbolic Zarathustra.

By spring of 1883, Thus Spoke Zarathustra (Part I) was written. Nietzsche's intention was to use this effort as a way to make his eternal recurrence concept more available; at least, this was what he said in 1884 when looking back at the work. Actually, his whole philosophy was set forth, although not in a discursive fashion.

Part I did not directly illuminate eternal recurrence. Nietzsche created a new term, *Übermensch* (which I shall not translate because connotations of translations usually given outweigh the advantages) and Zarathustra's role was that of the herald of the *Übermensch*. Zarathustra was a prophet, or holy man, or sage, who was returning to civilization seeking disciples. Zarathustra's message was Nietzsche's position of the last seven years. Instead of "free spirits" or "higher men", it was now the *Übermensch* as the ideal man and central focus.

Before Nietzsche could stress the *Übermensch* as an ideal, he developed a naturalistic position on man. Zarathustra espoused his first commandment: "Be loyal to the earth!" Man was a natural creature, a product of the earth like all else on its surface. Even the individual, the human self, was fundamentally body, that is, an animal organism. But Nietzsche and Zarathustra did not stop at this foundational level of human reality. The healthy man was seen as one who creates, and he creates out of his own ego. Egoism, thus understood, was rehabilitated:

> I teach mankind a new will: to desire this path that men have followed blindly, and to call it good and no more to creep aside from it, like the sick and the dying.[6]

A very realistic affirmation of natural living was given prominence as opposed to a view of the natural as sinful. Zarathustra wanted a return to innocence. Such innocence could not be achieved if natural desires were evil. Hölderlin's feeling for nature had finally borne fruit in the mature Nietzsche.

Within this naturalistic perspective, Nietzsche brought forward his new concept of "will to power". It first appeared in a discussion of values created by a people. It ran thusly: "A table of values . . . the table of its overcomings . . . the voice of its will to power."[7] The idea projected was that of a primal force guiding change, or even causing change or resistance to change. (The word "overcomings" was meant to tie in with "*Übermensch*" which literally could be translated as "over-man".) Nietzsche did not further elaborate at this point.

With extra-earthly values eliminated in a naturalistic perspective, the source of all values was man himself: "men have given themselves all their good and evil . . . created the meaning of things, a human meaning!"[8] And one thing man had created, and thus valued, was the modern concept of the individual: "the individual himself is still the latest creation."[9] All our creations have been the product of our driving emotions, of love and anger, of our will to power. Zarathustra did not seek to undo any of man's creations, especially not the creation of the individual. Rather, modern man needed a goal, a new value. This new value was to be the *Übermensch*, and Zarathustra was the bringer of this new goal. As Zarathustra said, "The world revolves about the inventor of new values."[10] And now Nietzsche hoped it would revolve about Zarathustra. The *Übermensch* was the meaning of the earth, the new goal for earthly man. The *Übermensch* was to be achieved through healthy overcoming, through creating and valuing out of man himself.

Part I alone was very cryptic. Without looking back at Nietzsche's earlier works, there was no way one could read his intentions. Nietzsche met his personal test of the affirmation of life and his history in the winter of 1882-83. On Christmas day of 1882, he was crushed and poured his soul out to his friend Overbeck in Basel: "to prove that for me 'all experiences are useful, all days holy, and all human beings divine!!!!'"[11] This was quite a challenge in the winter depression following the Lou and Ree affair. By February, he was already looking back, distancing himself from his personal abyss: "This winter was the worst of my life."[12]

He felt like he had shed a great burden. Zarathustra, his fictional progeny, had been born. Nietzsche had also come to terms with his Lou infatuation, and Wagner no longer menaced him. Nietzsche moved on to Rome after completing Part I and was in Sils Maria when it was published in June of 1883. When Zarathustra provoked no response, Nietzsche was very disappointed. He harnessed his anger and frustration into energy to write Part II--which was completed in days.

Zarathustra, like Nietzsche, had given up on his audience. Part II displayed the conclusion that Zarathustra alone must bear the burden of the *Übermensch*. His disciples were not capable of what was required. God was dead but most were not ready for this message. Zarathustra also openly rejected ways of life other than his own. His listing was fairly exhaustive of current types:

      a) The pious life
      b) The realist who can only tear down
      c) The contemplative life
      d) The scholarly life
      e) The poets
      f) Schopenhauer and all philosophical pessimists.

In addition to these types, Zarathustra heaped scorn on all the "preachers of equality." This group's message was directly contrary to Zarathustra's naturalism: "Men are not equal. And they should not become so either!"[13] Zarathustra, and Nietzsche, saw the "preachers of equality" as insidious in their revengefulness, in their acting against the natural divisions among men, against a natural order of rank. This order had the *Übermensch* at the top. The creative thinker was the highest man, the highest of the highest creature in a world without God. Such a man was the creation of the earth, the goal, the value for all.

Not only without God, Zarathustra's reality was also without any metaphysical world. Schopenhauer, as part of the long tradition from Plato, had resurrected the metaphysical world, a changeless, ideal realm. Zarathustra disposed of such: "I call it evil and misanthropic, all this teaching about the one and the perfect and the unmoved and the sufficient and intransitory."[14] And Schopenhauer's position that the will could cease willing was repudiated:

will might redeem itself at last and become non-will--but you all know this fairytale song of insanity, my brothers! I led you away from such fairytale songs when I taught you "will is creative."[15]

A very positive acceptance of life was at the core of Zarathustra's gospel. "Willing" remained a central focus, but not as something to be eliminated:

Willing liberates: that is the true doctrine of will and freedom--thus Zarathustra teaches you. . . . In knowing and understanding, too, I feel only my will's delight in begetting and becoming[16]

An image Nietzsche penned summed up his deep affirmation of living: "like the sun do I love life."[17]

Zarathustra was poetically modeled as a redeemer, as similar to Jesus Christ, in the role he was to fulfil. This task of redemption had fallen on Zarathustra's shoulders, as his disciples were not worthy of the challenge. But it should not be forgotten that Zarathustra was the instrument of "will to power" or life itself. Life's "way" was striving: "Life must overcome itself again and again!"[18] Even Zarathustra's wisdom was an effect of "will to power." "Will to power" did not eliminate suffering, as Schopenhauer preached, it requested it in the dynamics of overcoming. Redemption was achieved in this process of creation:

Creation--that is the great redemption from suffering, and life's easement. But that the creator may exist, that itself requires suffering and much transformation.[19]

Eternal recurrence was brought back into focus at this point. Belief in eternal recurrence was the task required of Zarathustra, of the *Übermensch*: "To redeem the past and to transform every 'It was' into a 'I wanted it thus!'--that alone do I call redemption!"[20] What was being done in this redemption was the removal of all conditional acceptance of life as it was and had been. The harboring of contempt for past actions, of *ressentiment* against what had happened had to be eliminated if total affirmation of life was to be achieved. Belief in eternal recurrence fit with what Zarathustra had asked for earlier in Part II, in contrast to metaphysical images: "the best images and parables should speak of time and becoming: they should be a eulogy and a justification of all transitoriness."[21] All of Zarathustra was Nietzsche's effort to craft a parable to justify the transitory reality he saw. And eternal recurrence was an image, in connection with "will to power", crafted to allow the best of men to free themselves from *ressentiment*, free themselves for creativity and joyous affirmation of life whole and dynamic. And even the creation of eternal recurrence was the fruit of "will to power."

Creating an image, working with an idea, was not willing the reality of it. Willing it was the burden for Zarathustra and the *Übermensch*. Part II ended with this test ahead. Nietzsche ended it calling Zarathustra "A seer, a willer, a creator, a future itself and a bridge to the future."[22]

By September 1883, Nietzsche had put Part II behind him. He traveled to his home in Naumberg and was beset by family squabbles with his mother and sister. This atmosphere drove him back to Genoa, and from there he moved to Nice in November. The winter of 1883-84 was the incubation period for Part III. It did not flow out as the first two parts had. Nietzsche struggled over the form and made many changes. But all was finished by spring and Part III was published in April of 1884.

The subject of Part III of Zarathustra was Zarathustra's redemption through the willing of eternal recurrence. Nietzsche's problem was how to present this innately personal experience of an individual. This presentation was more difficult because what Zarathustra had to do, as each man would have to do if he took up the quest, was "to seek one's own." Willing eternal recurrence was "to learn to love oneself,"[23] only more thoroughly and fully than one had ever thought possible. Zarathustra, speaking for Nietzsche, had to accept and love himself as he was. This goal meant "experiencing solitude as bliss"[24] --something Nietzsche was near achieving. One's own evils and *ressentiments* were the focus of struggle in the battle for total affirmation. One had to overcome such contempt, fear, and anger. It was an internal, individual struggle which Nietzsche did not attempt to portray. He merely indicated the difficulty of individual overcoming and the resultant state of accomplishment.

Zarathustra was portrayed as completely drained by the experience, by willing eternal recurrence. Nietzsche had Zarathustra's animals prattle on about eternal recurrence as if it was another creed--but it was not to be some formula like the Christian creed "believers" could mouth but then do nothing different in their lives. This was a creative change in one's life, the result of supreme effort, self-overcoming. The result was transformation, revaluing.

Nietzsche reset his basic revaluations in this context. He was continuing from Part I and from earlier works when he painted these three items as virtues: Sensual Pleasure, Lust for Power, and Selfishness. Lust for Power was merely the manifestation of "will to power" in the individual. The other two were part of natural innocence. Sensual Pleasure was no longer evil, but the "earth's garden-joy" and the "great restorative" of man.[25] Selfishness was merely a natural result "that issues from a mighty soul."[26]

The Creation of a Free Spirit

This man who had overcome even history was described in an image by Nietzsche: "the dancer . . . the self-rejoicing soul."[27] Why rejoicing? Because Zarathustra had liberated himself and all men who achieve the same willing of eternal recurrence. Zarathustra explained it thusly:

> Truly, it is a blessing . . . when I teach: "Above all things stands the heaven of chance, the heaven of innocence, the heaven of accident, the heaven of wantonness." . . . I have released them [all things] from servitude under purpose. I set this freedom . . . when I taught no "eternal will" acts over them and through them. . . . with all things one thing is impossible--rationality![28]

Things merely recur eternally. If one can free oneself from taking any other attitude toward becoming or its affects, then one is free to will, to create, to overcome everything. As Zarathustra said: "Willing liberates: for willing is creating . . . you should learn only for creating!"[29] Nietzsche had Zarathustra use eternal recurrence against the "haters of life", against the Schopenhauerian pessimists. Echoing back to a theme of his Untimely Meditations' days, Nietzsche had Zarathustra seek the creators of a new era: "Oh my brothers, I direct and consecrate you to a new nobility: you shall become begetters and cultivators and sowers of the future."[30] Zarathustra's gospel was complete. He had given man a goal. He had given a meaning to the earth. He had created a new future. Zarathustra was "the advocate of life, the advocate of suffering, the advocate of the circle."[31] In other words, "will to power", overcoming of the übermensch, and eternal recurrence were the heart of the message, the teaching, the gospel.

How did Nietzsche deal with the truth of eternal recurrence? He veiled his position, commenting through the thoughts of Zarathustra right after he had recovered from the redemptive experience:

> How sweet it is, that words and sounds of music exist: are words and music not rainbows and seeming bridges between things eternally separated? Every soul is a world of its own; for every soul every other soul is an afterworld . . . For me--how could there be an outside-of-me? There is no outside! But we forget that, when we hear music; how sweet it is, that we forget! . . . Speech is a beautiful foolery: with it man dances over all things.[32]

This difficult section in Part III was followed by Zarathustra's animals' song about eternal recurrence. Zarathustra said no more--he did go on to rejoice in song, with the refrain "For I love you, O Eternity!" What Nietzsche let us see was how easy it was to move off into metaphysical traps ("no outside of me") which must be avoided if total affirmation was to be obtained. Words and music were wonderful, joyous and innocent, but they could be used to achieve other ends, namely, life hating metaphysics. Words and music were tools of "will to power", but only mere tools that must be overcome in achieving the total affirmation which was Zarathustra's and Nietzsche's ideal.

Afterthoughts

Nietzsche had completed three parts of <u>Zarathustra</u> which appeared complete as a work of art. But he had contemplated more parts. After a pleasant spring in 1884 in Venice, the continued failure of <u>Zarathustra</u> to produce public response depressed Nietzsche again. He admitted during this period that he himself had not achieved what his fictional sage had:

> I do not wish to live <u>again</u> . . . How have I borne life? by creating. What has made me endure? The vision of the *Übermensch* who affirms life. I have tried to affirm life <u>myself</u>--but ah![33]

Nietzsche's life of solitude and suffering was now without even a disciple. Lou had been a goal, a meaning, a spur. She was gone. No one had discovered his <u>Zarathustra</u>. In a letter to his sister at this time, he dwelled on his loneliness:

> I do not . . . consider myself in the least a secret or furtive or mistrustful person; quite the reverse! <u>If I was that, I would not suffer so much!</u> But one cannot just simply communicate, however much one wants to; one has to find the person to whom communication can be made.[34]

His mission still burned in his mind. Nietzsche wrote to his Basel friend in May 1884: "Indeed, who can feel with me what it means to feel with every shred of one's being that the weight of all things must be defined anew."[35] He took this burden and quest to Sils Maria, as usual, for the summer of 1884. But this summer proved unusual. Nietzsche received a visitor who had sought him out. The young Wagnerian, named Heinrich von Stein, came as a potential disciple. Nietzsche relished this moment as one could well imagine. It had been eight years of seeking in the wilderness since his mental revolt from Wagnerism and Schopenhauer. Other than correspondents and assistants, Nietzsche had not discovered a mind he could truly communicate with. When von Stein left, it was not as a convert, but Nietzsche didn't care. He had the chance to deliver the message. He hoped discipleship would come.

Nice was once again selected by Nietzsche as his winter quarters for the 1884-85 season. He was still explaining the importance of his concepts to his Basel professor friend: "If it is true, or rather: if it is believed true--then everything changes and revolves and all previous values are devalued."[36] Nietzsche's usually productive period was interrupted by a second arrival at his door: Paul Lanzky. This short interlude was followed by von Stein's letter announcing that he would remain a Wagnerian. Nietzsche's depression bore fruit again in a new part to Zarathustra. This production was a continuation, but it came after distinct second thoughts which he had expressed in a letter of September 1884:

> Zarathustra retains only its entirely personal meaning, being my "book of edification and consolation"--otherwise, for Everyman, it is obscure and riddlesome and ridiculous.[37]

Part IV was more of an afterthought or post-script. Later, when he prepared a version of Zarathustra for a new edition, he included only the first three parts. He even asked for all the copies back of Part IV which he had mailed after having to publish it himself (no publisher wanted it).

Part IV of Thus Spoke Zarathustra was completed by March 1885. No new insights were revealed by Zarathustra. The main purpose was to reemphasize that no one was ready for Zarathustra's gospel of eternal recurrence. Only Zarathustra, or the *Übermensch*, was capable of self-redemption through overcoming the past. Nietzsche had Zarathustra simply state the message: "God has died: now we desire--that the *Übermensch* shall live."[38]

From a positive perspective, affirmation of life in total was still the clear refrain: "Did you every say 'Yes' to one joy? Oh my friends, then you said 'Yes' to all pain. All things are entwined, enmeshed, enamoured--"[39] The affirmation was to be joyous: "But joy . . . accepts itself, accepts everlasting flow, accepts itself returning."[40] Zarathustra still bettered Nietzsche's own resolve: "'So that was Life?' I'll say to Death. 'Very good: *da capo!*'"[41] Thus, willing eternal recurrence was the final hurdle, the redemptive accomplishment. Only Zarathustra had achieved it.

The nihilism and its consequent pessimism which Nietzsche had shown in its fullest in Human was overcome in the Zarathustra ideal of total affirmation of life. Nihilism and pessimism made sense only in relation to belief in the existence of a real world of which we could have no knowledge despite its ultimate importance to our lives. Zarathustra's new gospel was the liberation from such a true world. Everything was brought back to man. He alone was the focus of value and the creator of the true. Thus, Nietzsche's initial nausea at the vision of the eternal recurrence of all civilization, of even the herd of Christians, was overcome. He described his own reaction, or revelation: "no longer human--one changed, radiant, laughing!"[42] The newly freed man, with joyful wisdom, proclaimed:

> And we should consider every day lost on which we have not danced at least once. And we should call every truth false which was not accompanied by at least one laugh.[43]

Nietzsche was thus reaching out to overcome his own past, that of the over-serious philosopher confined to meditate over his own problems which he saw as the most serious problems of the world. His own personal history was to be overcome, but not resented. As Kaufmann has put it, the *Übermensch* must:

> be able to give up what life takes away, without being unable to enjoy what life gives us in the first place . . . to relish our triumphs and to endure our defeats without resentment.[44]

This was truly what Nietzsche was achieving with regard to his own sickly, sheltered, and apparently unsuccessful life.

NOTES

1. Halvey, The Life of Friedrich Nietzsche, p. 255.
2. Gay Science, #93, p. 146.
3. Zarathustra, Hollingdale, p. 207.
4. Human, Faber, #145, p. 103.
5. The Birth, Golffing, p. 131.
6. Zarathustra, Hollingdale, p. 60.
7. Zarathustra, Hollingdale, p. 84.
8. Zarathustra, Hollingdale, p. 85.
9. Zarathustra, Hollingdale, p. 85.
10. Zarathustra, Hollingdale, p. 78.
11. Quoted in Halvey, The Life of Friedrich Nietzsche,　p. 232.
12. Quoted in Donadio, Nietzsche, Henry James, and the Artistic Will, p. 117.
13. Zarathustra, Hollingdale, p. 124.
14. Zarathustra, Hollingdale, p. 110.

15. Zarathustra, Cowan, p. 165.
16. Zarathustra, Hollingdale, p. 111.
17. Zarathustra, Hollingdale, p. 146.
18. Zarathustra, Hollingdale, p. 125.
19. Zarathustra, Hollingdale, p. 111.
20. Zarathustra, Hollingdale, p. 161.
21. Zarathustra, Hollingdale, p. 111.
22. Zarathustra, Hollingdale, p. 161.
23. Zarathustra, Hollingdale, p. 211.
24. Shapiro, Nietzschean Narratives, p. 73.
25. Zarathustra, Hollingdale, p. 207.
26. Zarathustra, Hollingdale, p. 208.
27. Zarathustra, Hollingdale, p. 208.
28. Zarathustra, Hollingdale, p. 186.
29. Zarathustra, Hollingdale, p. 223.
30. Zarathustra, Hollingdale, p. 220.
31. Zarathustra, Hollingdale, p. 233.
32. Zarathustra, Hollingdale, p. 234.
33. Quoted in Heller, The Importance of Nietzsche, p. 78.
34. Selected Letters, p. 241.
35. Quoted in Heller, The Importance of Nietzsche, p. 113.
36. Quoted in Morgan, What Nietzsche Means, p. 285.
37. Quoted in Heidegger, Nietzsche, vol. 1, p. 13.
38. Zarathustra, Hollingdale, p. 297.
39. Zarathustra, Cowan, p. 388.
40. Zarathustra, Cowan, p. 387.
41. Zarathustra, Cowan, p. 381.
42. Zarathustra, Kaufmann, p. 272.
43. Zarathustra, Kaufmann, p. 264.
44. Kaufmann, From Shakespeare to Existentialism, p. 181.

CHAPTER SIX EXPLAINING HIS GOSPEL

The Master Offers his Wisdom

Nietzsche never repudiated his achievements in <u>Wisdom</u> and <u>Zarathustra</u>. In a letter written in 1883, he clearly indicated the philosophic value of <u>Zarathustra</u>:

> Behind all the plain and strange words stand my <u>most serious intention</u> and <u>my whole philosophy</u>. It is the beginning of a process of revealing myself--nothing more.[1]

Therefore, his succeeding works must be viewed as explications of his positions, or examples of what his converts should do. The poetic presentation of <u>Zarathustra</u> was not reused. The following two works, <u>Beyond Good and Evil</u> and <u>Genealogy of Morals</u>, were written in a style that was closer to normal discursive prose than anything he had written since the <u>Untimely Meditations</u>. His later works returned to the brief, aphoristic style.

Loneliness and depression dogged Nietzsche in the spring of 1885 while at Venice. He freed himself from these reliable companions through writing: notes for a new work were penned. After May, no more sketches for a continuation of <u>Zarathustra</u> were made. As he looked back he couldn't be sure that he had achieved what he had set out as the criteria of good books. Back in 1878, he had said good books were those which: "elicit a feeling of high-spirited freedom, as if man were rising on tiptoe and simply had to dance out of inner pleasure."[2] Surely, at times <u>Zarathustra</u> and <u>Wisdom</u> had achieved this. But on reflection the whole effort seemed incomplete. Nietzsche had also praised this strategy of presentation in <u>Human</u>: "incomplete representation of a thought, or of

85

a whole philosophy, is sometimes more effective than its exhaustive realization."[3] Nietzsche had no idea of the effect that Zarathustra would have. He knew only the silence of no response.

Nietzsche returned to Sils Maria for the Summer of 1885. He remained convinced of his view of reality. Megill has described this vision succinctly:

> an open and indeterminate universe of chance and spontaneity . . . [the] impossibility of a completely rational teleological, or mechanical explanation of things . . . the impossibility is a blessing . . . [men] are not governed by a purpose from beyond them.[4]

In Zarathustra, Nietzsche did not argue for a hypothesis, he spoke from a convictional stance. Once again, Megill has captured this insight:

> a world in which the death of God is a reality dwarfing all others--is presumed to be obvious to all sensitive souls. Those who accept Zarathustra's vision put themselves within the Nietzschean realm of discourse; those who do not are beyond the pale. The Zarathustrian mind is a mind so convinced of the correctness of its vision that it seeks only to work out the implications of that vision, not to establish its grounds.[5]

Nietzsche was human, however, and the lack of response to his gospel caused him to continue his quest for a better way to deliver his message. Zarathustra had apparently failed. After saying good-bye to his sister, who was off to a utopian colony scheme in South America, Nietzsche met another potential disciple in the fall of 1885. Nothing really came from this and Nietzsche returned to Nice and productive activity for the 1885-86 winter. He culled his notes of the past four years and the result was a book entitled Beyond Good and Evil, which was complete by the spring of 1886. This title harked back to Zarathustra and eternal recurrence: "For all things are baptized at the fountain of forever, beyond good and evil."[6] The new gospel was explained in Beyond Good and Evil. This work was broken into nine parts. Nietzsche stressed certain themes in trying to highlight valuations already disclosed in his two preceding works.

The First Article of Beyond was entitled "Of Philosophers' Prejudices." Nietzsche roamed over many key disputes he had with traditional philosophers as he knew them. The target was the Christian metaphysics as understood in Kantian dress and married to a simplified mechanistic science. In a dangerously self defeating game, he attempted to throw doubt on the achievements of such philosophers by asserting that their positions were the result of non-rational forces, i.e., instinctual drives. Nietzsche seemed to overlook the application of this critique to his own philosophy. He wanted to stress that thinking was the result of organismic drives--that as such, thinking was a tool of the organism for its purposes (namely, "will to power"). Philosophy was not exempt from "will to power", but was another manifestation of it:

> It always creates the world in its own image; it cannot do otherwise. Philosophy is this tyrannical drive itself, the most spiritual will to power, to the "creation of the world".[7]

All purposes of organisms were, according to Nietzsche, reducible to "will to power": "A living thing seeks above all to <u>discharge</u> its strength--life itself is <u>will to power</u>."[8] This over-arching purpose encompassed the narrow will to survive (then in the spotlight due to Darwinian and Schopenhauerian ideas). Simple mechanistic dynamics were dumped as Nietzsche labelled cause and effect and determinism as conventional fictions.[9] Neither free will nor determinism applied to reality. Both were interpretations which were created by man, but, Nietzsche said, misunderstandings arose: "when we mix this world of symbols with the world of things as though the symbols existed 'in themselves,' then . . . we are creating myths."[10] The classic example used by Nietzsche was "soulism": "the <u>soul atomism</u> . . . regards the soul as something indestructible, eternal, indivisible, as a monad, as an atomon: this belief ought to be expelled."[11] He requested that such metaphysical approaches be dropped. He had said as much in <u>Zarathustra</u>, but not as clearly: "I shall repeat it a hundred times; we really ought to free ourselves from the seduction of words!"[12] Instead he urged a realistic description of what people do. In this endeavor the new science of psychology was to be welcomed as a way to expose the reality of human action (Nietzsche did not foresee the new dogma of Behaviorists). What he was concerned with was not philosophical determinism, but the actuality of "<u>strong</u> and <u>weak</u> wills".[13]

Nietzsche attempted to clarify his psychological philosophy

> as morphology and <u>the doctrine of the development of the will to power</u> . . . a doctrine of the reciprocal dependence of the "good" and the "wicked" drives . . . a doctrine of the derivation of all good impulses from wicked ones . . . even the effects of hatred, envy, covetousness, and the lust to rule as conditions of life, as factors which, fundamentally and essentially, must be present in the general economy of life (and must therefore, be further enhanced if life is to be further enhanced).[14]

He also posed the question about his own position, of whether "this also is only interpretation--"? And his answer has surprised many: "well, so much the better."[15] Nietzsche's perspective was not to be evaluated against a criteria which allowed for a true perspective. Instead the intention was to evaluate based on the meaning of the perspective for life.

The description of the free thinker or "free spirit" was the subject of the Second Article. Nietzsche identified the philosopher as a "free spirit" and a "higher man." He styled the surpassing of morality as the distinct achievement of the modern era. He laid out a developmental analysis of the valuation of human actions:

1. Pre-Moral Period--actions judged only by their consequences;
2. Moral Period--actions judged by the intent of their agents; and
3. Amoral Period--the intentions of agents revealed as caused by non-moral factors.[16]

The enlightenment contained in the amoral perspective was not a reason to celebrate the falsity of morality, but rather an incentive to a grand perspective which recognized organismic needs in the moral valuations. This grand perspective grew out of the "will to power" thesis:

> Let us assume that nothing is "given" as real except our world of desires and passions, that we cannot step down or up to any kind of "reality" except the reality of our drives.[17]

Nietzsche reduced all to "will to power": "our entire instinctual life as the development and ramification of one basic form of will (of will to power, as I hold)."[18] The free thinker acknowledged "will to power" as the reality behind human actions. He was aware then that the faults of existence didn't lay in the structure of society and that he must not tie himself to social actions aimed at ameliorating the misery of the masses. Instead, the "free spirits" were to experiment with living and with knowing their own selves. The "free spirit" was to be detached as the Buddhist sage (Nietzsche had referred to his message as European Buddhism in earlier works), but he would not be limited to one path-- rather, each would create his own path.

Nietzsche changed course in the Third Article and considered the nature of religion--as one of the impediments to becoming a "free spirit." The totally committed Christian was shown as manifesting solitude, fasting and sexual abstinence. Nietzsche's description of the fanatical Christian has been seen as an early try at a neurosis concept,[19] i.e., a special fixation which drives the religious adept. He styled Christianity as a religion of sacrifice and servitude. The persistence of the religious phenomena forced Nietzsche to conclude that this manifestation must represent the result of a religious instinct. As such, he hoped to replace Christian theism and its dogmas with a faith in "eternal recurrence." This secular "faith" was really in an ideal of human being:

> the ideal of the most high-spirited, alive, and world affirming human being who has not only come to terms and learned to get along with whatever was and is, but who wants to have <u>what was and is</u> repeated into all eternity.[20]

Such a change would undo the Christian valuation--which was a revaluation of the noble values of ancient times. "Eternal recurrence" sanctified every facet of life, but without any religious baggage from pagan times. Faith in "eternal recurrence" allowed an open experimentation with life and reduced religion to a means to life, instead of being the end of life.

The Fourth Article was a collection of mixed subject aphorisms. Within this crazy quilt, Nietzsche stressed that there were no moral phenomena, only moral perspectives on phenomena. He also stated that all truth was reducible to sense contents, i.e., the last resort was always to a perception of man.

"Contribution to the Natural History of Morality" was the title of the Fifth Article (somewhat anticipating his next full work). Nietzsche did <u>not</u> decry morality as a human creation. He did express his concern with how philosophers had dealt with morality. Basically, he accepted the necessity of a value system for man which teaches man obedience through self-restraint of the human desires. The relation of reason and instinctual drives was problematic for Nietzsche. He listed four historic ways which attempted to deal with the passions:

1. Cure of the passions with a no-weep, no-laugh formula (the Stoics and Spinoza),
2. Tone down the passions in promoting harmony (Aristotle),
3. Adulteration of the passions into new drives (love-of-man, love-of-God, love-of-nation),and
4. Undisciplined release of the passions (Goethe).[21]

Zarathustra did not preach any of these ways, because each man had to find his own way.

Nietzsche switched from this theme to commenting on the moral tendencies of the masses. He concluded, very perceptively, that man had learned to obey:

> there have been human herds . . . and very many who obeyed compared with few who were in command; since, therefore, obedience was the trait best and longest exercised and cultivated among men . . . it has become an innate need, a kind of <u>formal conscience</u>.[22]

Nietzsche followed this with a prophecy that the Europeans were ready for a new strong leader (nicely available for Nazi propaganda).

This article concluded with a deprecation of moralities of resignation (Christianity, Epicureanism, Buddhism) and utilitarian principles (socialism). Nietzsche listed four great men: Alcibiades, Julius Caesar, Frederick II and Leonardo da Vinci. In trying to characterize the center of their greatness, he pointed to their war with themselves, i.e., taking life as a great challenge. Only moralities which permitted great men were acceptable to Nietzsche. Only such moralities allowed man's potential to be tapped.

"We Intellectuals" was Nietzsche's next subject. He discussed seven distinct aspects of his fellow "free spirits:"
1. They were scientific.
2. They were anti-positivist in philosophy.
3. They were experimental toward ways of living.
4. They were anti-academic.
5. They were opposed to objectifying man.
6. They would create values.
7. They would have a "great spirit."[23]

The "free spirits" were driven by the "most spiritual will to power and overcoming of the world."[24] They were to be philosophic in an active way. Such a philosopher "demands of himself a judgment, a Yes or No . . . about life and the value of life--. . . . he risks himself constantly.[25] Such a philosopher was not a scholar or scientist, which Nietzsche deprecated clearly:

> He is only an instrument; . . . he is no "end in himself". . . . whatever still remains in him of a "person" strikes him as accidental, often arbitrary, still more often disturbing. . . . he is no goal, no conclusion and sunrise, no complementary man in whom the rest of existence is justified.[26]

The genuine philosophers, "free spirits", were "tough, powerful, self-reliant" and wanted to be "master."[27] These "commanders and legislators" say "'Thus it shall be!'"[28] They were *Übermensch* who were to "create values" which would become dominant and be seen as "truths":

> they reach for the future, and all that is and has been becomes a means for them, an instrument, a hammer. Their "knowing" is creating, their creating is a legislation, their will to truth is--will to power.[29]

The knowledge of these "free spirits" was for action: "to know of a new greatness of man, of a new untrodden way to his enhancement."[30] The term

"*Übermensch*" was not used by Nietzsche, but it was implied, when he explicated a "great spirit" as follows:

> who wants to be himself, who can be different, who can stand alone, and who must live by his own resources . . . the one most capable of solitude, the most hidden, the most deviant, the man beyond good and evil, the master of his virtues, the one whose will can overflow.[31]

Of course, many of these descriptions fit only Nietzsche and Zarathustra.

The final three articles dealt with diverse topics. Nietzsche covered current subjects including political ideas. He again stressed his new egoism, individualism and naturalism. He turned his naturalism into a rationalization for evils that existed in human society:

> Life itself is essential assimilation, injury, violation of foreign and the weaker, suppression, hardness, the forcing of one's own forms upon something else, ingestion and . . . exploitation.[32]

But it wasn't as a rationalization that Nietzsche endorsed "evil", but rather "evil" was necessary:

> The discipline of suffering, of great suffering . . . has created all enhancements of man so far. . . . there are higher problems than all problems of pleasure, pain, and pity; and every philosophy that stops with them is a naivete.[33]

Nietzsche explained that "Almost everything we call 'higher culture' was based on the spiritualization of cruelty."[34] Uncontrolled human passions have developed into virtues, have been controlled (in Freudian terms, sublimated). Hollingdale concluded that Nietzsche "does not deny that the will to power is dangerous, but it must be controlled, 'sublimated', not weakened and destroyed."[35] Hollingdale continued describing Nietzsche's point:

> All creatures desire power but only man is able to desire power over himself, only man has the requisite amount of power to achieve self-mastery. The distinction between man and animal, obliterated by Darwin, is restored--and without recourse to the supernatural.[36]

Morality itself was a victory of self-mastery. Now a further victory was required of "free spirits," and the *Übermensch*.

The base of Nietzsche's "will to power" idea was in his experience and reflection on the dynamics of human action. He referred to this focus of human being as the "basic will of the spirit." He described it thusly:

> that commanding something which the people call "the spirit" wants to be master in and around its own house and wants to feel that it is master; it has the will from multiplicity to simplicity, a will that ties up, tames, and is domineering and truly masterful. Its needs and capacities are so far the same as those which physiologists posit for everything that lives, grows, and multiplies. The spirit's power to appropriate the foreign stands revealed in its inclination to assimilate the new to the old, to simplify the manifold, and to overlook or repulse whatever is totally contra-dictory. . . . Its intent in all this . . . growth, in a word--or, more precisely, the <u>feeling</u> of growth, the feeling of increased power.[37]

Therefore, "will to power" was the "<u>primordial fact</u> of all history."[38]

A personal core, however, remained untouched in this analysis:

> But at the bottom of us, really "deep down," there is, of course, something unteachable, some granite of spiritual fatum, of predetermined decision and answer to predetermined selected questions . . . [the] unchangeable "this is I".[39]

Nietzsche stressed that we only come to know this "deep self" when certain problems, or solutions to problems "inspire strong faith in us."[40] These convictions however didn't remove the problem for they were only "steps to self-knowledge, signposts to the problem we are."[41]

Nietzsche concluded <u>Beyond</u> with a description of the type of philosopher he admired (which he thought he embodied):

> a human being who constantly experiences, sees, hears, suspects, hopes, and dreams the extraordinary; who is struck by his own thoughts as though they were external to him.[42]

This description reads like a portrait of a philosopher and a recipient of divine revelation combined. Clearly, Nietzsche's ideal philosopher was deeply immersed in his activity. Nietzsche's final point in <u>Beyond</u> was the proclamation that he was the last disciple of Dionysus. The preferred model was again cultic, mythic, not the cold contemplative scientist, or religious ascetic.

Explaining His Gospel

Renewed Hope of Making a Difference

Spring of 1886 found Nietzsche in Venice commiserating with his able assistant Peter Gast. He moved on to Leipzig and visited his former student colleague Rohde, now a professor. Summer brought the usual retreat to Sils Maria. Nietzsche was feeling deserted by his friends. He did send Beyond to Taine and Brandes, two new correspondents. Then, suddenly, interest in his works grew. The publisher decided to bring out a new edition of all his works.

Nietzsche plunged into new activity in connection with these reissuance plans. He wrote a new book for Wisdom, Book V as we know the work today. He also wrote prefaces for all of his works which gave new perspectives on his production over the years. He excluded the Untimely Meditations and Part IV of Zarathustra from this edition. He moved to Rapallo in the fall of 1886 and recaptured the spirit of the birth place of Zarathustra as he prepared his new overtures to his main message.

Book V of Wisdom was a prose recapitulation of the main themes which were dramatically portrayed in Zarathustra. Nietzsche's addition was intended to help his readers enter into Zarathustra. Between Book V and Beyond, the mythic gospel was to be made clear. The primary event of Western Civilization was reannounced (or first announced if his books were read in the order intended by Nietzsche): "God is dead. . . . how much must collapse now that this faith has been undermined . . . the whole European morality."[43] Obviously, Nietzsche wanted his readers to see the downfall of moral rules based on Christian theology. Those who adopted this perspective were described:

> We have become cold, hard, and tough in the realization that the way of this world is anything but divine; even by human standards it is not rational, merciful, or just.[44]

Later he was even more direct in describing the atheists' world: "a de-deified world that had become stupid, blind, mad, and questionable."[45]

Nietzsche's unique twist was to take all of this not as grounds for extreme pessimism, but as basic facts for a new liberation: "They are not all sad and gloomy, but rather like a new and scarcely describable kind of light, happiness, relief, exhilaration, encouragement, dawn."[46] Suddenly, everything was open again: "all the daring of the lover of knowledge is permitted again."[47] Nietzsche was merely restating his insight of Human where he had posited scientific determinism as the cause of his new liberation perspective: "Everything is necessity . . . Everything is innocence: and knowledge is the way to insight into this innocence."[48] Science had achieved the same goal that Nietzsche admired in the Jesus myth:

> through a fantasy . . . he reached the same goal: the feeling of sinlessness, utter freedom from responsibility--a feeling that every one can now attain through science.[49]

But not all men were the same. Some men needed a faith, were weak in Nietzsche's view. Christianity was seen as needed by most men in his time. Some, like Nietzsche himself when young, had replaced this need with a metaphysical need:

> one has become accustomed to the notion of "another world (behind, below, above)"--and when religious ideas are destroyed one is troubled by an uncomfortable emptiness and deprivation.[50]

Even scientists had adopted a version of this need:

> that impetuous <u>demand for certainty</u> that today discharges itself among large numbers of people in a scientific-positivistic form. The demand that one <u>wants</u> by all means that something should be firm . . . --this, too, is still the demand for a support, a prop, in short, that <u>instinct of weakness</u>.[51]

Religion, traditional philosophy and science were retreats for the weak-willed. The "free spirits" had to overcome these props.

With a divine base for morality destroyed, Nietzsche then questioned the value of morality as a form of life, or way of life. How shall we judge the value of morality if divine standards are not provided? We must become naturalists. Man <u>is</u> the valuer, his choices and their effects must be examined. His "free spirits" would drive forward to choices in life out of themselves--without faiths given to them. All men, however, are driven by a human desire for power: "the really fundamental instinct of life which aims at <u>the expansion of power</u>."[52] Nietzsche turned the tables on the naturalistic philosophers who, since Hobbes, asserted that the essence of man's being was the drive to self-preservation. Any such struggle for existence was a mere means to the true end of man: "will to power which is the will of life."[53] But if "will to power" is the essence of being human, what of consciousness (and its proclaimed achievements)? Nietzsche asserted that consciousness was a historical achievement of evolution. It was a response to a <u>need</u> of man in society: the need for better communication.

Explaining His Gospel

However, once it was created, social reality continued to develop this aspect of man and developed self-consciousness. Consciousness and self-consciousness developed in parallel paths with language and society. These assertions led Nietzsche to a tragic view:

> consciousness does not belong to man's individual existence but rather to his social or herd nature. . . . Our thoughts themselves are continually governed by the character of consciousness--by the genius of the species' that commands it.[54]

For Nietzsche, the world of consciousness was not congruent with the reality of the individual. And worse: the individual must use the tools of conscious social life, language, to attempt expression of its self. Therefore, one has knowledge of this self, as we all have knowledge, only in linguistic terms. Nietzsche had beaten Kant at his own game: beyond not knowing the thing-in-itself, one could not know the self-in-itself (a metaphysical self) or make any claim for freedom for this self. A philosophy which begins with facts of consciousness was not starting at the base, that would be to start with the self-before-consciousness. Nietzsche then posed the question, posed originally by Schopenhauer, "Has existence then any significance at all?"[55]

Nietzsche did not really provide a straightforward answer to this question (as was his style). He recognized one could not get to this new self through philosophy. We were all trapped in our human, social, conscious perspective. He went on to summarize his own major perspectives. He rejected his Wagnerian pessimistic romanticism and called for a Dionysian pessimism. To make this clear he drew a distinction between romantic suffering, or suffering of the weak, and Dionysian suffering. The romantic suffered from an "impoverishment of life." The romantic needed rest, redemption, intoxication, that is, ways of escape from the self. The romantic used religion, philosophy and science to banish fear and bring peace and security to his way in the world. The Dionysian suffered from an "overfullness of life." The Dionysian was in constant activity, whether destructive or constructive, creating and overcoming. The Dionysian used art, poetry, music and drama to express overflowing energy and delight with existence despite its necessary suffering.

Replacing the mechanistic world view of 18th century science, Nietzsche proclaimed the rich ambiguity of life. He wanted his joyful wisdom to be liberating, however, any achievements would have to be sobered by the realization that we were imprisoned in "our own human, all too human folly, which we know."[56] Human perspectives could not be transcended:

How far the perspective character of existence extends or indeed whether existence has any other character than this; whether existence without interpretation, without "sense", does not become "nonsense" . . . cannot be decided . . . the human intellect cannot avoid seeing itself in its own perspectives, and <u>only</u> in these. We cannot look around our own corner. . . . we cannot reject the possibility that <u>it may include infinite interpretations</u>.[57]

The ideal men were described as Nietzsche closed this new addition to <u>Wisdom</u>:

> We "conserve" nothing; neither do we want to return to any past periods; we are not by any means "liberal"; we do not work for "progress" . . . "equal rights", or "a free society", "no more masters and no servants" has no allure for us. . . . we are delighted with all who love, as we do, danger, war, and adventures . . . for every strengthening and enhancement of the human type . . . we do not love humanity. . . . we have also outgrown Christianity.[58]

This was as clear as Nietzsche ever was concerning his program for his current "free spirits." In conclusion he set up <u>Zarathustra</u> by describing the "ideal spirit" as one who plays innocently, who creates out of "overflowing power and abundance."[59] These creators were truly healthy, having attained "a human, superhuman well-being and benevolence that will often appear <u>inhuman</u>."[60] Nietzsche had recognized the special status of such creators way back in <u>The Birth</u>: "the imperative necessity of hubris for the titanic individual."[61]

At the end of the revised <u>Wisdom</u>, Nietzsche had put science in its place, thereby criticizing his own earlier love of science which tended to make it a quasi-religious path to Truth. At the same time, he still valued science as a perspective which did a lot for man. It was this, the benefit for man as he lived, which had become the prime value for measuring all things recommended for man, including Christianity and morality.

The Lonely Wanderer

His work on prefaces to his completed works allowed Nietzsche to reflect on his own life, and in his 1886 preface to <u>Human</u> he described his own intellectual and emotional journey. He referred to a "<u>great separation</u>" as a turning point in his life. Nietzsche was apparently referring to his break with

96

Schopenhauerian thought, which he referred to as his "first victory" and an object of love. But he came to see it as "a disease that can destroy man."[62] He then recounted his very critical reaction:

> he rips apart what attracts him . . . he overturns what he finds concealed.
> . . . Behind his raging activity . . . stands the question mark of an ever more dangerous curiosity. "Cannot all values be overturned? And is God perhaps Evil? And God only an invention. . . . Is everything perhaps ultimately false?"[63]

This nihilism was finally seen as an error:

> Such thoughts lead and mislead him, always further onward, always further away. Loneliness surrounds him, curls around him, ever more threatening, strangling, heart-constricting.[64]

Nietzsche had come to recognize the bad effects of his nihilism on himself, on his life. His change to "health" was described:

> It is still a long way from this morbid isolation . . . to that enormous, overflowing certainty and health . . . to that mature freedom of the spirit . . . self-mastery and discipline . . . which permits paths to many opposing ways of thought.[65]

The "will to truth at any price" was superseded by a "tough will to health". He admitted his identification with his "free spirits" in this period of mature growth:

> the free spirit again approaches life . . . as if his eyes were only now open to what is near . . . they now seem transformed! . . . Only now does he see himself . . . all pessimism . . . is thoroughly cured.[66]

Finally, perspectivalism was achieved:

> You had to learn that all estimations have a perspective. . . . You had to learn to grasp the necessary injustice in every For and Against; to grasp that injustice is inseparable from life, that life is determined by perspective and its injustice.[67]

Tragic as this perspective was, Nietzsche had chosen to not be determined by this. Perspectives were just that, one way of viewing something. Nietzsche had sought to reverse the typical religious quest which sought a right way based on a view of reality. In unpublished notes, he had set down his inverted formula: "What must I do to become blissful? I don't know, but I say unto you: be blissful and then do what you feel like doing."[68]

The winter of 1886-87 was unusual for the mature Nietzsche. After his production of the new prefaces, he did not write any more for publication. Instead he read in various areas. The current authors were: Guyau, Bouget, Baudelaire, Zola, and Dostoevski. He also read Renan's Origins of Christianity. He moved to the Swiss Lakes region in the spring and heard of von Stein's death while there. Nietzsche moved on to Sils in June and brooded about the failure of Zarathustra and Beyond to find an audience. Then in July of 1887, he feverishly set to work and completed On the Genealogy of Morals in days. With his promising disciple gone, he tried again to explain his gospel.

In his preface to Genealogy, he explained that his philosophy had not changed in its main elements since 1877. An analysis of his own path to his position in Genealogy was outlined. He looked back to when he was 13 years old. Already he was bothered by the problem of evil. Eventually, he "ceased to look for the origin of evil behind the world".[69] He credited Ree with stimulating him in 1877 to write out his moral ideas in Human. Finally, he recounted his break with Schopenhauer. Praise of the "unegoistic" changed into seeing it as a "no to life." He saw his own life as redeemed in lightheartedness as "the reward of a long, courageous, painstaking, inward seriousness."[70] He also described the experience which was the basis for his *Übermensch* ideal:

> born as one is to a subterranean life of struggle; one emerges again and again into the light, one experiences again and again one's golden hour of victory--and then one stands forth as one was born, unbreakable, tensed, ready for new, even harder, remoter things.[71]

"Will to Power" Explained

Genealogy was divided into three essays. Nietzsche attempted to explicate three of his prime ideas:

1. that man was not a passive mechanism,
2. that healthy man was a self-directed, passionate animal, and
3. that anti-life ideals really demonstrated the actuality of "will to power" in all life.

The First Essay painted the psychologists' image of man as passive. All motive forces in man were described by passive characteristics:

the inertia of habit, in forgetfulness, in the blind and fortuitous association of ideas: always something that is purely passive, automatic, reflexive, molecular, and moreover, profoundly stupid.[72]

This current, scientific image tended to support a passive moral view. Such an image, whether from science or from Christianity's slave morality, was opposed by Nietzsche with a "noble" image of man. Relying heavily on classical Greek models, Nietzsche asserted that the "noble" image had always supported human greatness. The key was that "All truly noble morality grows out of triumphant self-affirmation."[73] Out of self-affirmation came leadership and its traits: powerfulness, vigorousness, courageousness, joyfulness, and self-assuredness. Happiness was achieved in doing. Man was active, enthusiastic and vibrant.

The passive image of man was buttressed in science's view of man as determined, but moralists had always allowed man freedom. Nietzsche's complicated relation to the freedom and determinism issue was made more coherent in his discussion on morality and freedom. Once again it was an image of man that Nietzsche ridiculed. The moralists' image had man with a neutral self, free to choose a moral life style. Nietzsche saw that this then allowed a self-gratifying claim: "I am meritorious because I chose to be moral" (or "I chose to believe in God"). Nietzsche asserted that the moral individual was not free to choose, that is, that he was not a neutral self at the starting point. Rather, Nietzsche held that those who chose the moral (meek and mild) life were driven to that option by their basic character. They chose it at the insistence of the "will to power"--as only through the slave morality could they achieve the feeling of power. Put simply, the slave as a type is not free to be a master. Such claims of freedom were illusory.

Therefore, man was not a passive mechanism. He was not sinful if he embarked on a life of leadership and nobility. In fact, he was more of the type of man Nietzsche sought: "a man who will justify the existence of mankind, for whose sake one may continue to believe in mankind!"[74] The actuality of such a redeemer of mankind was a goal beyond that of the slave morality:

> The welfare of the many and the welfare of the few are radically opposite ends. To consider the former *a priori* the higher value may be left to the naivete of English biologists.[75]

In the Second Essay, Nietzsche turned to the unveiling of the ideal of the few. Nietzsche's ideal was not built in a fantasy-land of unreal beings. He acknowledged man's animality. But this was an active basis, as life itself was active: "the very essence of life . . . the spontaneous, aggressive, overreaching, reinterpreting and reestablishing forces."[76] And within human life, mind was not a mere epiphenomenon, but rather played a "dominant role" which "appears active and shaping."[77]   Man was not a Darwinian pawn, but rather a Dionysian organism with a host of "active emotions."[78] Man was another form of "will to power."

Man had built culture and he had been changed in this historical process. This transformation to the civilized animal had been, and remained, a painful process. The thwarting of animal instincts and old paths to pleasure produced a need to redirect the active emotions. In this long process man produced the man who could be moral: "the man who has his own independent, protracted will and the right to make promises--a consciousness of his own power and freedom."[79] Only such an individual, through time, could have developed concepts of responsibility, guilt, and sin. With these concepts, natural innocence was lost. Man learned how to "suffer from himself."

This path to the ascetic ideal and Christian morality was necessary to the creation of the new individual, Nietzsche's "free spirit." Siegfried-like innocence was to be regained, the suffering of repression reduced and the sickness of *ressentiment* cured in Nietzsche's new man. He described him again and again:

> This autonomous, more than moral individual . . . has developed his own, independent, long-range will.[80]
> men who can command, who are born rulers.[81]
> [those with] minds strengthened by struggles and victories, for whom conquest, adventure, danger, even pain, have become second nature.[82]

Pain was accepted because it was necessary. Happiness as an absence of pain was decried. Pain was part of achieving the pleasure induced by the exercise of one's powers. Nietzsche's ideal man possessed a "self-assured recklessness which is a sign of strong health. . . . superb health."[83] He ended this Essay by referring the reader to his model of this ideal: Zarathustra. Such a man would "make the will free once more" and be "the true Redeemer."[84]

In the final part, Nietzsche made an extended attack on ascetic ideals. Both philosophers and scientists were excluded from being prophets and shown to be rather the expression of asceticism. Even asceticism, of course, was driven by "will to power":

> Every animal . . . instinctively strives for an optimum of favorable conditions under which it can expend all its strengths and achieve its maximal feeling of power.[85]

Ascetics and philosophers needed peculiar conditions to discharge their strengths. These men were "sick": "'what does it mean when a philosopher pays homage to the ascetic ideal?'. . . he wants to gain release from a torture."[86] Such escape into asceticism was not negation of life: "he does not deny 'existence', he rather affirms his existence and only his existence . . . Let the world perish, but let there be philosophy, the philosopher, me!'"[87]

Nihilism, pessimism and asceticism were all egoism disguised. As Nietzsche expanded upon his view of man as driven by the "will to power," he developed a model of man which was proto-Freudian. Man was an energy reservoir and needed constant outlets for discharge of this driving force. Even the ascetic discharged his energy, but he did so in different activities. Nietzsche's point was that all action was thus ego directed, energy driven by the "will to power." The image of the passive soul, awaiting release from the body was incorrect. On the basis of this myth, the whole ascetic dogma was based. Speculating as to the physiological cause of belief in the ascetic dogma, he looked to climatic or racial changes to account for the belief in the man-is-a-sick-soul world-view.

After accusing the religious leaders with preaching the man-is-a-sick-soul faith, Nietzsche examined solutions extended to the believers. He described five methods of religious cure for the sick:

> 1. To reduce self-consciousness through hypnotic techniques (all mystic cults).
> 2. To redirect consciousness to activity (European Protestant work ethic).
> 3. To prescribe the distraction of constant minor satisfactions from good works (Christian/Communist social action).
> 4. To redirect concerns to the community of fellow believers (all utopian cults).
> 5. To prescribe frequent orgies of feeling to exhaust the consciousness (celebration cults, revivalism, drug-based cults).[88]

Zarathustra, of course, did not endorse any of these methods.

Nietzsche posed the following question: Why hasn't the power of the ascetic priest been opposed?[89] He stressed that the essence of the ascetic priest was his faith in his own power, in his way. He then indicted the potential rival ideal types, the scientist and the philosopher for being just varieties of the ascetic ideal. All of these types had faith in Truth. The "free spirits" that Nietzsche prophesied would not have such a faith in Truth, and, consequently, no such "free spirits" had yet existed. He continued and indicted even himself, a philosophic unbeliever:

it is precisely in their faith in truth that they are more rigid and unconditional than anyone. I know all of this from too close up perhaps: that venerable philosopher's abstinence to which such faith commits one; that intellectual stoicism which ultimately refuses not only to affirm but also to deny; that <u>desire</u> to halt before the factual . . . that general renunciation of all interpretation . . . all this expresses . . . as much ascetic virtue as any denial of sensuality. . . . <u>faith in the ascetic ideal itself</u>, even as an unconscious imperative . . . faith in a <u>metaphysical</u> value, the absolute value of <u>truth</u>.[90]

It was the value of Truth itself which Nietzsche wanted to question--he believed he was the first to broach this perspective. How did he begin to judge Truth? He showed what the will to Truth had created in modern science:

Since Copernicus, man seems to have got himself on an inclined plane-- now he is slipping faster and faster away from the center into--what? into nothingness? into a "<u>penetrating</u> sense of nothingness?" Very well! hasn't this been the straightest route to--the old ideal?[91]

Man as a meaningless animal in the cosmos was an image of sickness:

Apart from the ascetic ideal, man, the human <u>animal</u>, had no meaning so far. His existence on earth contained no goal; "why man at all?" was a question without an answer. . . . <u>This</u> is precisely what the ascetic ideal means: that something was <u>lacking,</u> that man was surrounded by a fearful <u>void</u> . . . he <u>suffered</u> from the problem of his meaning.[92]

Man did not succumb to his plight because man "does <u>not</u> repudiate suffering as such: he <u>desires</u> it . . . provided he is shown a <u>meaning</u> for it, a <u>purpose</u> of suffering."[93] And up to Nietzsche's time, the ascetic ideal was the only meaning offered for suffering so far:

man was <u>saved</u> thereby, he possessed a meaning . . . he could now <u>will</u> something; no matter at first to what end, why, with what he willed: <u>the will itself was saved.</u>[94]

The value of Truth was high, supreme, since it permitted <u>meaning</u> and hence <u>willing</u>.

Nietzsche concluded the <u>Genealogy</u> with the final unveiling of the ascetic ideal. The content of the ideal was "hatred of the human, and even more of the animal."[95] He then grasped this as a proof of the omnipresence of the "will to power" when he styled the ascetic ideal as "a will to nothingness" and then said this proves "man would rather will nothingness than not will."[96] The competing Zarathustra ideal was not presented, but Nietzsche had already made it clear that this was the purpose of his epic work.

Nietzsche had rejected any "transcendental solution to life's riddle."[97] This stance was tragic, but the dismissal of absolute Truth was necessary to bring man's focus back to human realities. He recognized that he himself had been driven by the "will to Truth" and that as a thinker he had taken a quasi-ascetic life style as a way to achieve his own strengths. He knew he would continue to will and change. No refuge was available other than death. Man was a bundle of desires and also a cultured citizen of lofty ideals. Life was a "precarious balance between beast and angel."[98] Like Goethe, Nietzsche endorsed this reality of life as "one more enticement to life."[99]

Zarathustra had been Nietzsche's peak. It was as close as he could get to the Wagnerian ideal: "to create an art combining the greatest spiritual and sensual power."[100] Zarathustra, Nietzsche's alter-ego, reached the artistic zenith Nietzsche described: "when he has learned to see himself and his art beneath him, when he is able to laugh about them."[101] Nietzsche however remained all too human. He was crushed by his obscurity, his loneliness. His bottled-up positive emotions poured out in his violent style of writing:

> To wrench the human soul from its moorings, to immerse it in terrors, ice, flames, and raptures to such an extent that it is liberated from all petty displeasure, gloom, and depression as by a flash of lightning.[102]

Although always close to despair over apparently failing in this goal, Nietzsche returned to normal activities after the summer of 1887. A letter to a friend still indicated his philosophic quest was not completed: "I have still not despaired of finding the way out, the hole that will lead us to 'something.'"[103] He read Lange's new edition of The History of Materialism which came out that year, examining this refutation of positive metaphysics for any new insights. He left Sils Maria in the fall and traveled to Venice. He broke off communication with Rohde, his last friend of his old days, because of Rohde's failure to agree with his ideas. But then Nietzsche's spirits were lifted by news from Brandes: he wanted to get to know his work. This good news from a real professor gave Nietzsche hope. To refresh his mind he read Goethe in the winter of 1887-88.

After an unproductive winter, in the spring of 1888 Nietzsche moved to Turin. While there, news of Brandes' interest in offering a course in Nietzsche's thought was received. This seemed to have a catalytic effect on Nietzsche's output of new material. After an unusually long stay in Sils Maria, Nietzsche set to work in late September of 1888 in Turin. Nietzsche did not know it would be his last productive period.

NOTES

1. Quoted in Jaspers, <u>Nietzsche</u>, p. 48.
2. <u>Human</u>, Faber, #206, pp. 124-5.
3. <u>Human</u>, Faber, #178, p. 118.
4. Megill, <u>The Prophets of Extremity</u>, p. 177.
5. Megill, <u>The Prophets of Extremity</u>, p. 62.
6. <u>Zarathustra</u>, Cowan, p. 193.
7. <u>Beyond</u>, Kaufmann, #9, p. 16.
8. <u>Beyond</u>, Kaufmann, #13, p. 21.
9. <u>Beyond</u>, Cowan, #21, p. 24.
10. <u>Beyond</u>, Cowan, #21, p. 24.
11. <u>Beyond</u>, Kaufmann, #12, p. 20.
12. <u>Beyond</u>, Kaufmann, #16, p. 23.
13. <u>Beyond</u>, Kaufmann, #21, p. 29.
14. <u>Beyond</u>, Kaufmann, #23, p. 31.
15. <u>Beyond</u>, Kaufmann, #22, p. 31.
16. <u>Beyond</u>, Cowan, #32, pp. 37-9.
17. <u>Beyond</u>, Cowan, #36, p. 42.
18. <u>Beyond</u>, Cowan, #36, p. 43.
19. <u>Beyond</u>, Cowan, #47, p. 54.
20. <u>Beyond</u>, Kaufmann, #56, p. 68.
21. <u>Beyond</u>, Cowan, #198, pp. 105-6.
22. <u>Beyond</u>, Cowan, #199, pp. 106-7.
23. <u>Beyond</u>, Cowan, #204-12, pp. 117-37.
24. <u>Beyond</u>, Kaufmann, #227, p. 155.
25. <u>Beyond</u>, Kaufmann, #205, pp. 124-5.
26. <u>Beyond</u>, Kaufmann, #207, pp. 126-8.
27. <u>Beyond</u>, Kaufmann, #207, p. 128.
28. <u>Beyond</u>, Kaufmann, #211, p. 136.
29. <u>Beyond</u>, Kaufmann, #211, p. 136.
30. <u>Beyond</u>, Kaufmann, #212, p. 137.
31. <u>Beyond</u>, Cowan, #212, p. 137.
32. <u>Beyond</u>, Cowan, #259. p. 201.
33. <u>Beyond</u>, Kaufmann, #225, p. 154.

34. <u>Beyond</u>, Kaufmann, #229, p. 158.
35. Hollingdale, <u>Nietzsche: The Man and his Philosophy</u>, p. 195.
36. Hollingdale, <u>NIetzsche: The Man and his Philosophy</u>, p. 196.
37. <u>Beyond</u>, Kaufmann, #230, pp. 159-60.
38. <u>Beyond</u>, Kaufmann, #259, p. 204.
39. <u>Beyond</u>, Kaufmann, #231, p. 162.
40. <u>Beyond</u>, Kaufmann, #231, p. 162.
41. <u>Beyond</u>, Kaufmann, #231, p. 162.
42. <u>Beyond</u>, Cowan, #292, p. 231.
43. <u>Gay Science</u>, #343, p. 279.
44. <u>Gay Science</u>, #346, p. 286.
45. <u>Gay Science</u>, #357, p. 309.
46. <u>Gay Science</u>, #343, p. 280.
47. <u>Gay Science</u>, #343, p. 280.
48. <u>Human</u>, Faber, #107, pp. 75-6.
49. <u>Human</u>, Faber, #144, p. 102.
50. <u>Gay Science</u>, #151, p. 196.
51. <u>Gay Science</u>, #347, p. 288.
52. <u>Gay Science</u>, #349, p. 291.
53. <u>Gay Science</u>, #349, p. 292.
54. <u>Gay Science</u>, #354, p. 299.
55. <u>Gay Science</u>, #357, p. 308.
56. <u>Gay Science</u>, #374, p. 337.
57. <u>Gay Science</u>, #374, p. 336.
58. <u>Gay Science</u>, #377, pp. 338-40.
59. <u>Gay Science</u>, #382, p. 347.
60. <u>Gay Science</u>, #382, p. 347.
61. <u>The Birth</u>, Golffing, p. 65.
62. <u>Human</u>, Faber, p. 6.
63. <u>Human</u>, Faber, p. 7.
64. <u>Human</u>, Faber, p. 7.
65. <u>Human</u>, Faber, p. 7.
66. <u>Human</u>, Faber, pp. 8-9.
67. <u>Human</u>, Faber, p. 9.
68. Quoted in Heidegger, <u>Nietzsche</u>, vol. 3, p. 17.
69. <u>Genealogy</u>, Kaufmann, p. 17.
70. <u>Genealogy</u>, Golffing, p. 156.
71. <u>Genealogy</u>, Kaufmann, p. 44.
72. <u>Genealogy</u>, Golffing, p. 158.
73. <u>Genealogy</u>, Golffing, p. 170.

74. Genealogy, Golffing, p. 177.
75. Genealogy, Golffing, p. 188.
76. Genealogy, Golffing, p. 211.
77. Genealogy, Golffing, p. 211.
78. Genealogy, Golffing, p. 206.
79. Genealogy, Kaufmann, p. 59.
80. Genealogy, Golffing, p. 191.
81. Genealogy, Golffing, p. 219.
82. Genealogy, Golffing, p. 229.
83. Genealogy, Golffing, p. 229.
84. Genealogy, Golffing, pp. 230 & 229.
85. Genealogy, Kaufmann, p. 107.
86. Genealogy, Kaufmann, p. 106.
87. Genealogy, Kaufmann, p. 108.
88. Genealogy, Kaufmann, pp. 129-39.
89. Genealogy, Kaufmann, pp. 146-7.
90. Genealogy, Kaufmann, p. 151.
91. Genealogy, Kaufmann, p. 155.
92. Genealogy, Kaufmann, p. 162.
93. Genealogy, Kaufmann, p. 162.
94. Genealogy, Kaufmann, p. 162.
95. Genealogy, Kaufmann, p. 162.
96. Genealogy, Kaufmann, p. 163.
97. Genealogy, Golffing, p. 291.
98. Genealogy, Golffing, p. 233.
99. Genealogy, Golffing, p. 233.
100. Genealogy, Golffing, p. 234.
101. Genealogy, Golffing, p. 234.
102. Genealogy, Kaufmann, p. 139.
103. Quoted in Hayman, Nietzsche: A Critical Life, p. 313.

CHAPTER SEVEN THE FINAL RUSH

Settling Accounts "with a Hammer"

Nietzsche had completed some thoughts on Wagner while at Sils Maria. The Wagner Case was the first of four works Nietzsche would finish in four months. He wanted to clarify his position on Wagner and Wagnerism. In his last work prepared for publication, Ecce Homo, he would finally admit that he had loved Wagner. He also admitted in this work that his praise of Wagnerism in The Birth had been an error. Finally, in Ecce Homo, he said "I name Wagner as the greatest benefactor of my life."[1] He would later gather together notes showing his opposition to Wagner, published under the title Nietzsche Contra Wagner. Nietzsche's stormy relationship with Wagner was finally put to rest.

Other than these Wagner efforts, Nietzsche wrote Twilight of the Idols and The Anti-Christ before New Year's Day 1889. These works were short in length, but their compressed style covered most everything Nietzsche had said in the prior 5 years. Together with Ecce Homo, a self-consciously auto-biographical piece, they summarized Nietzsche's philosophy and critique of culture. He, of course, did not know he would write no more after these works. In January of 1889, he suffered a stroke, collapsing in the street in Turin. He never recovered his mental abilities. Nietzsche's life truly ended in January 1889 at age 44.

Neither Twilight nor Anti-Christ refuted Zarathustra or his recent works. They were new attempts to cause others to become interested in his position, his thoughts. These incisive works were meant to catch the eye of a larger audience which might have been put off by the poetic treatment in Zarathustra. As he was to complain in the preface to Ecce Homo, "people have neither heard me or seen me."[2] These two works were to catapult Nietzsche into popular acclaim, but not until after he was unable to appreciate it (Anti-Christ was not published until 1895). Part of the reason for this acclaim was the perfection of his style in these two works. He finally achieved what he had set out as his goal 21 years earlier.

He had wanted to write as if playing the piano improvisationally, yet to be "still always logical and beautiful."[3]

In Twilight, Nietzsche announced that he was attacking the perennial "idols" of man in civilization. The subtitle, "How to Philosophize with a Hammer," indicated the swift strokes of criticism that he hoped to unleash. His thoughts were compressed into hammer blows, and their meaning would not have been clear from this work alone. At times, however, a new clarity was attempted.

Twilight consisted of 10 parts, which were somewhat related groups of aphorisms reminiscent of Human. The first part was composed of ideas compressed into one sentence units. The second part reiterated Nietzsche's position on Socrates, and therein, Nietzsche stressed an argument previously mentioned in Wisdom: "The value of life cannot be estimated. Not by living man, because he is a party to the dispute."[4] Nietzsche was saying that the value of life could only be objectively judged from "outside" of life--and man cannot be so positioned. Now some such evaluation of life was at the center of the Socratic/Platonic revolution in philosophy (and in the praise of the ascetic ideal). Therein, a judgment was reached in the negative with regard to everyday life. Nietzsche, therefore, asserted that such a judgment was not valid. He furthermore claimed it was a symptom of decadent life, a form of sickness: "To have to combat one's instincts--that is the formula for decadence: as long as life is ascending, happiness and instinct are one."[5] Nietzsche had hinted at this concern with decadence in Zarathustra: "Everything of today . . . is decaying."[6] This concept was to play a major role in his final critique of contemporary culture.

This embedded error of the philosophical tradition had to be exposed. Philosophers had been anti-life:

> Death, change, age, as well as procreation and growth, are for them objections--refutations even. What is, does not become; what becomes is not . . . Now they all believe . . . in that which is. But since they can not get a hold of it, they look for reasons why it is being withheld from them. "It must be an illusion, a deception which prevents us from perceiving that which is. . . . it is the senses!" . . . Moral: escape from sense-deception. . . . denial of all that believes in the senses . . . And away, above all, with the body.[7]

The Socratic/Platonic philosophy had judged life as illusion, as a dangerous distraction from the "true world."

Nietzsche responded for life and the world of our senses:

> the senses . . . they do not lie at all. It is what we make of their evidence that first induces a lie into it. . . . the senses show becoming, passing away, change . . . [this] world is the only one.[8]

Science had achieved everything it had by ignoring the philosophers' reality:

> We possess scientific knowledge today to precisely the extent that we have decided to <u>accept</u> the evidence of the senses--to the extent that we have learned to sharpen and arm them and to think with them through to their conclusions.[9]

The amazing thing was that mankind, and Nietzsche when young, still believed in the "true world", and "should have taken seriously the brainsick fancies of morbid cobweb spinners!"[10] Nietzsche was very clear on where he stood:

1. "the grounds upon which 'this' world has been designated as apparent establish rather its reality--<u>another</u> kind of reality is absolutely undemonstrable."

2. "The characteristics which have been assigned to the 'real being' of things are characteristics of non-being, of <u>nothingness</u>."

3. "to talk about 'another' world than this is quite pointless."

4. "To divide the world into a 'real' and an 'apparent' world . . . is only a suggestion of decadence--a symptom of <u>declining life</u>."[11]

Having disposed of the philosophers' error of the "true world," Nietzsche turned to the moral perspective. This second error of civilization was examined from a Christian, historical point of view. The moral was opposed to the natural, or the instinctual, in the hands of the Church. A new form of hostility to life was the result:

> The Church combats the passions with excision. . . . It never asks: "How can one spiritualize, beautify, deify a desire?"--it has at all times laid the emphasis of its discipline on extirpation.[12]

For Nietzsche, the natural, the instinctual,[13] was the source of all healthy values. Even morality was a product of life, however, of decadent, sick lives:

> life itself evaluates through us <u>when</u> we establish values . . . even that <u>anti-nature of a morality</u> . . . is only a value judgement on the part of life--of <u>what</u> life? of what kind of life? . . . of declining, debilitated, weary, condemned life.[14]

Instead of condemning life, Nietzsche had liberated man for affirmation of all life. Determinism had been embraced as the refutation of moral exhortations:

the individual is, in his future and in his past, a piece of fate. . . . To say to him "change yourself" means to demand that everything should change, even in the past.[15]

Nietzsche's "immoralists" affirmed all of life, even "all that is questionable and terrible."[16] "Moralists" were in error, were unscientific, were decadent.

Now, Nietzsche stated his new thesis distinctly: "Every error, of whatever kind, is a consequence of degeneration of instinct, disgregation of will."[17] An opposition between naturalism (as the good) and decadence explained all of civilization's pitfalls.

Nietzsche claimed to have restored the innocence of becoming through the destruction of the moralists' image of the responsible, conscious self with free will. By taking away free will he actually freed man from a great burden:

No one is accountable for existing at all, or for being constituted as he is, or for living in the circumstances and surroundings in which he lives. The fatality of his nature cannot be disentangled from the fatality of all that which has been and will be. . . . that no one is any longer made accountable . . . this alone is the great liberation--thus alone is the innocence of becoming restored . . . We deny God; in denying God, we deny account-ability: only by doing that do we redeem the world.[18]

This release of the individual from accountability, and therefore guilt, was completed with the logical destruction of Christianity. The Christian concept of God was the linchpin of this world view: "Christianity is a system. . . . If one breaks out of it a fundamental idea, the belief in God, one thereby breaks the whole thing to pieces."[19] Man is released to his own devices: "Christianity presupposes that man does not know, cannot know what is good for him and what evil: he believes in God who alone knows."[20]

The ideal man of Nietzsche was very far from such a meek and subservient being. Confidence in his own abilities was only a first requirement. This innocent man was free to create and he did so out of his own strength: "The man in this condition transforms things until they mirror his power."[21] Man the artist took "joy in himself, in art" and saw "himself as perfection" instead of as a sinful being.[22] This ideal creator did not need any external justification for his life: "What justifies man is his reality--it will justify him eternally."[23] Thus Nietzsche's naturalism was an empowering of man. His ideal was not mere herd existence, but creative greatness. He described Goethe as befitting this ideal:

a strong, highly cultured human being, skilled in all physical accomplishments, who keeping himself in check and having reverence for himself, dares to allow himself the whole compass and wealth of naturalness.[24]

The ideal was no "blond beast." Rather, a nearer image was that of a Renaissance man. One who created, contributed to culture while not denying any aspect of life.

Nietzsche labeled this character ideal Dionysian:

> A spirit thus <u>emancipated</u> stands in the midst of the universe with a joyful and trusting fatalism ... that in the totality everything is redeemed and affirmed--<u>he no longer denies</u>.[25]

Nietzsche used the associations of "Dionysian" with the archaic cult rituals which included orgiastic violence in re-enacting life's abundance. This symbol stood for "an overflowing of life and energy within which even pain acts as a stimulus."[26] Just as the destruction of the god Dionysus was affirmed as part of life's processes, so Nietzsche's Dionysian man affirmed life with "rejoicing in its own inexhaustibility through sacrifice of its highest types."[27] Nietzsche's task for the Dionysian was "<u>to realize in oneself</u> the eternal joy of becoming."[28]

The Zarathustra ideal had been clarified and resupported in <u>Twilight</u>. The key question was now whether the individual represented an "ascending or descending line of life."[29] The individual on the decline was a decadent. He was physiologically the opposite of the ascending, Dionysian type. Nietzsche's worry was that, since Goethe, European culture had seemed to develop only declining types. "An instinct of weariness"[30] had descended over culture. Romanticism was seen as decadence. Schopenhauer's popularity had been symptomatic of this retreat from a strong faith in life. Wagnerism had degenerated into Schopenhauerian retreat from real life. Thus Nietzsche saw his contemporaries without direction toward future life. That was why he gave them the Zarathustra ideal.

The Greek source of Nietzsche's primary ideas was freely admitted in <u>Twilight</u>. Nietzsche related how his study of the Hellenic spirit had led to his concepts of "will to power" and eternal recurrence. He now called the Hellenic spirit the Dionysian and he meant to point to the "exuberant" and "overflowing" character of this spirit. In trying to characterize this human aspect, he had discovered the "will to power":

> I saw trembling at the intractable force of this drive--I saw their institutions evolve out of protective measures designed for mutual security against this <u>explosive material</u> within them.[31]

111

Even Greek art and sport were "for no other purpose than to feel oneself dominant, to show oneself dominant."[32] This "excess energy" was celebrated in the mystery cults:

> Eternal life, the eternal recurrence of life; . . . the triumphant Yes to life beyond death and change; true life as collective continuation of life through procreation, through the mysteries of sexuality. . . . pain is sanctified: the "pain of childbirth" sanctifies pain in general--all becoming and growing, all that guarantees the future, postulates pain.[33]

The Hellenic affirmation was not a retreat from pain and life's challenges, but acceptance--acceptance of reality as it was for all eternity. Nietzsche (and Zarathustra) was this teacher of eternal return. This was his final message of Twilight.

"The Revaluation"

There are indications that Anti-Christ was originally planned as a part of one long work which was to be a new summation of Nietzsche's thoughts. According to Hollingdale, Nietzsche made 25 sketches for this magnum opus, variously titled "Will to Power" or "The Revaluation."[34] He completed one work only, the short book titled Anti-Christ. In Ecce Homo, Nietzsche referred to Anti-Christ as the "Revaluation":

> Now that the yea-saying part of my life task was achieved, there came the turn of the negative portion, which was to deny both in word and deed: the transvaluation of all previous values.[35]

He equated the transvaluation with Christianity, and hence the opposite of Christianity, the "Anti-Christ," would be a revaluation of all Christian values.

Christian valuations were opposed to the Zarathustra ideal of the higher, noble individual. It was a violent opposition in Nietzsche's perspective: "Christianity: it has waged a war to the death against this higher type of man."[36] The *Übermensch* was rejected by Christian philosophy along with affirmation of life: "Christianity, a form of mortal hostility to reality as yet unsurpassed."[37] There was no longer any room for doubt as to where Nietzsche stood:

> What sets us apart is not that we recognize no God, either in history or in nature or behind nature--but that we find that which has been reverenced as God not "godlike" but pitiable, absurd, harmful, not merely an error but a crime against life.[38]

Christianity was the "dark side" of will to power and Nietzsche opposed it with vehemence:

> I condemn Christianity. . . . To me it is the extremest thinkable form of corruption. . . . I call Christianity the <u>one</u> great curse, the <u>one</u> great intrinsic depravity, the <u>one</u> great instinct for revenge . . . the <u>one</u> immortal blemish of mankind.[39]

Life, as the opposite of decadence, was Nietzsche's prime value. Christianity, of course, was rife with decadence. Christianity rejected "all that represents the <u>ascending</u> movement of life, well-constitutedness, power, beauty, self-affirmation on earth."[40] "Will to power" was an essential part of this "ascending" view of life: "life itself [was] instinct for growth, for continuance, for accumulation of forces, for <u>power</u>."[41]

The Zarathustra ideal, the *Übermensch*, was one who lived life with the maximum of affirmation, and "in relation to collective mankind is a sort of superman."[42] Nietzsche admitted his gospel appealed to the elite who could approach such affirmation: "the predominantly spiritual type. . . . the highest caste--I call it <u>the very few</u>."[43] This elite corps had affirmative strength to such an extent that they were even allowed asceticism of a kind:

> "<u>The world is perfect</u>"--thus speaks the instinct of the most spiritual, the affirmative instinct-- . . . . as the <u>strongest</u> . . . their joy lies in self-constraint: with them asceticism becomes nature, need, instinct. . . . Knowledge--a form of asceticism.[44]

With this veiled self-ascription, Nietzsche finally justified his own life of scholarly asceticism.

The pain which Nietzsche knew from first hand experience as a Christian and a philosophical nihilist was exposed in <u>Anti-Christ</u>. He labeled the Christian moral concepts as "instruments of torture" and "forms of systematic cruelty."[45] And the worst part of Christian doctrine was the promise of personal immortality because it guaranteed a turning from this life, our reality, to a fiction, to an illusory reality. It also caused a philosophy whereby all men were leveled in importance, all souls were equal in value. Nietzsche saw that the weapon of the masses was *ressentiment*. It was used with the blessing of Christian doctrine against the elite which Nietzsche saw as "the pre-condition of every elevation, every increase in culture." [46]

Therefore, Christianity as a cultural force was responsible for overturning the great achievements of the Greek and Roman civilizations: "The whole labor of the ancient world <u>in vain</u>: I have no words to express my feelings at something so dreadful."[47] Nietzsche's ideal reality, his Classical life as a scholar of the ancients, had been the victim of Christian decadence. The Roman "yes" to life had been stolen and hidden: "Christianity robbed us of the harvest of the culture of the ancient world."[48] And once Europe had found the lost gold of the ancients in the Renaissance, Christianity robbed mankind again: "The Germans have robbed Europe of the last great cultural harvest Europe had."[49] Luther and the Germans brought the Reformation and the Counter-Reformation which caused the resurgence of Christian morality, of decadence, of anti-life forces.

At the head of such anti-noble crusades were people Nietzsche labeled as redeemer-types. This type had two basic traits:

1. instinctive hatred of reality, and
2. instinctive aversion to resistance.[50]

Both traits led to extreme reactions to ordinary life. The first resulted in fleeing normal intercourse with other people--such contact was too deeply felt. The second resulted in the need to find ways of accepting everything, everyone--love of all was the only avenue available. The resultant individual was oversensitive and overly compliant at the same time. The solution for such an individual was a life apart from society and shunning all needs. The Christian and Epicurean perspectives represented this redeemer-type in the ancient world (the Buddhist represented this type in the East). Nietzsche's conclusion was that the redeemer-type was a physiological error. He was not a god-man, son-of-god, or sage, but rather a decadent. The redeemer-type was an imperfect man, an atypical man, the opposite of the noble type, the Zarathustra ideal.

Such suffering from existence as the redeemer-type manifested was also part of the metaphysical-philosopher type. All those believers in a "real world" beyond our world, such as Schopenhauer, merely expressed their decadence with respect to life:

> this entire fictional world has its roots in <u>hatred</u> of the natural (--actuality!--) it is the expression of a profound discontent with the actual . . . <u>but that explains everything</u>. Who has reason to <u>lie himself out</u> of actuality? He who <u>suffers</u> from it. But to suffer from actuality means to be an abortive actuality.[51]

The healthy, non-decadent, man accepted life as instinctually given: "An action compelled by the instinct of life has in the joy of performing it the proof it is a <u>right</u> action."[52] The decadent received no joy from his actions as normal men did. To achieve such joy as he could required anti-instinctual asceticism. Only through such avenues could he enhance his feelings of power. Such anti-life manifestations were his "good." But the problem was that he did not rest with this self-triumph. The decadent set out to conquer the world. Christianity was his vehicle.

114

The beliefs of Christianity were not that important to Nietzsche. What was at stake was a way of life. Similarly, Zarathustra had asked for no believers, but he wanted to establish "A new way of living, <u>not</u> a new belief."[53] This new way called for individuals to be strong through freedom, not through any faith. The man of faith, the Christian, was "a dependent man--such as cannot out of himself posit ends at all. . . . he needs some one who will use him."[54] The Zarathustra ideal was the self-reliant man of action.

Even Jesus was redrawn by Nietzsche as non-metaphysical--as revaluated:

> Nothing is more un-Christian than the <u>ecclesiastical crudities</u> of God as a <u>person,</u> of a "kingdom of God" which <u>comes,</u> of a "kingdom of heaven" in the <u>Beyond,</u> of a "Son of God," the <u>second person</u> of the Trinity . . . . (rather) The "kingdom of Heaven" is a condition of the heart.[55]

Nietzsche took this interpretation of Jesus and transformed it into a non-Christian model, Zarathustra. The way of Jesus was reestablished without the false psychology of the soul and the metaphysics of a Platonic realm. The same innocence and self-confidence of Jesus were reestablished--transvaluated.

With this perspective, which has been overlooked for the most part,[56] a continuity to Nietzsche's life-long development can be established. A young man raised in a devout Lutheran household lost his firm faith. A reading of Strauss at 20 excited his interests in the "real" history of Christianity.[57] He pursued philology to seek the answers in the ancient documents. He found "the scriptures" a fraud and Christianity a lie, a deceit of the priests from Paul to the present. He plummeted into a nihilism because he saw Christianity as supporting the whole structure of Western values. This lost "soul" was converted to Schopenhauer's atheistic metaphysics. After a period of rapture as a Wagnerian, he returned to reexamine Schopenhauer critically. He returned to a position close to Lange's Neo-Kantian materialism which defeated "real world" metaphysics. From this new beginning he glimpsed the possibilities of science, of knowledge based on our world of the senses. He searched for a new way to values, for a replacement of transcendent sanctions. He finally clawed out the beginnings of a new naturalism, but he had destroyed the ways of rational ethics and philosophy. He needed a new way to present his gospel. The answer was a new Jesus, Zarathustra. And just like the Jesus story, the context of Zarathustra's tales was not important to Nietzsche. It was "A new way of living, not a new belief"[58] that he wanted to proclaim. Yet he never rested with the proclamation. He tried to support, explicate, critique. He sought a following for his Zarathustra ideal. He lost consciousness, at least rational self-consciousness in 1889 (how ironic given his praise of the "non-conscious"), and never knew his fame which began shortly thereafter.

Nietzsche: A Philosophical Biography

His Own Summation

The day before Nietzsche collapsed, January 2, 1889, he had written to his printer and had requested the return of some poems which he had included with his manuscript entitled Ecce Homo.[59] This self-assessment piece was not published until 1908, but it was basically finished before his collapse.

The title Ecce Homo was a phrase from the Bible which was spoken by Pontias Pilate when he introduced Jesus. This was usually translated as "behold the man." Several meanings could have been intended by Nietzsche's use of this phrase for his self-assessment title:

a) Here is the man, Nietzsche revealed;
b) Here is man, not God;
c) Here is another crucified man; or
d) Here is one of equal stature to Jesus.

Probably all of these possible meanings were intended, especially number four, given his view of Jesus as he had recently stated it in Anti-Christ.

Nietzsche had subtitled Ecce Homo "How one Becomes What One Is." His use of this phrase reached back to thoughts of his youth when he had called for "free spirits" to find themselves. Nietzsche had often stressed this theme which praised individualism. In Wisdom, he had put it this way: "What does your conscience say?--'you shall become the persons you are.'"[60] Later in the same work he clarified this: "We, however, want to become those who we are--human beings who are new, unique, incomparable, who give themselves laws, who create themselves."[61] Those with a classicist background would have seen the connection of this Nietzschean theme to the ancient Greek Pindar, who had written a famous saying along these lines. However, Kaufmann has suggested the not so obvious connection to Hegel's similar statement: "the organic individual produces himself: it makes itself what it is implicitly."[62] Thus Hegel wrote exactly what Nietzsche proclaimed throughout his career. Surely, this was not a self-conscious adoption of Hegel's position, for Nietzsche was anti-Hegel (following his mentor Schopenhauer). Yet, the message was clearly the same. Even the explanation by Hegel confirms this: "what man is, is his deed, is the series of his deeds, is that into which he has made himself."[63] Nietzsche in Ecce Homo revealed himself--he was his deeds and he recounted them all, all his books, therein. But this life had not been a planned path: "at no time did I have any intimation of what was growing within me."[64]

And what had been his dominant task? The transvaluation of all values, that is, the overturning of the Christian moral values which were still controlling European civilization. Instrumental to that task, were his major discoveries:

1. that Socrates, the father of philosophy, was a decadent,
2. that morality in its Christian form was a symptom of decadence, and

116

3. that the philosophical, moral, and Christian ways of life were truly degenerate attacks on ascending life.[65]

These discoveries had been clarified in <u>Genealogy</u> when Christian values had been unmasked:

Psychology of Christianity: born out of resentment; "a great rebellion against domination by noble values."

Psychology of Conscience: not "the voice of God in man"; will to power unleashed against the self.

Psychology of the Ascetic Ideal: not power of divine model; only avenue of power enhancement available to decadents.[66]

Thus, Nietzsche was an "Immoralist" with two primary negations of prior values:

I deny the type of man who formerly passed as the highest--the <u>good</u> . . .

I deny that kind of morality which has become recognized and dominant as morality-in-it-self--the morality of decadence, or to use a cruder term, Christian morality.[67]

The "good man" of modern civilization was a coward in Nietzsche's eyes. This type of man was no trouble, he did what was expected of him. He even believed in what he was supposed to. Nietzsche saw this as "the unwillingness to see how reality is actually constituted."[68] The "good man" could live such a life only within a belief structure which falsified reality. The opposite of the "good man" was the *Übermensch*. He acknowledged reality as "will to power." He did what was <u>good for himself</u>. He refused to bow to tradition, or custom. He set his own course. Pain did not mean one had to stop, or that the cause of pain had to be eliminated:

the terrors of reality (in the passions, in the desires, in the will to power) are incalculably more essential than that form of petty happiness, so called "goodness."[69]

The whole man, free and natural, was the ideal. Nietzsche's quest, from his own case, was to reestablish this strong freedom. His use of the term "free spirit" had been meant to capture this: "a spirit that has become free, that has regained possession of itself."[70]   To achieve this regeneration in himself, Nietzsche adopted the maximum affirmation of all of life as his goal: "a yea-saying to the point of justifying, to the point of redeeming all past things."[71] All of <u>Zarathustra</u>, including eternal recurrence, was merely a path to this new healthy affirmation:

My formula for greatness in man is *amour fati*: that a man should wish to have nothing altered, either in the future, the past, or for all eternity.[72]

The term "Dionysian" was merely used as a symbol of all this: "in the Dionysian symbol, the most extreme limits of affirmation are reached."[73]

All this was a restatement of Nietzsche's basic gospel in <u>Zarathustra</u>: "I have not uttered a single word which I have not already said five years ago through the mouth of Zarathustra."[74] No new breakthroughs had been achieved by Nietzsche in his last five years. He had tried to explain his message several times. He was exasperated because no one seemed to understand the critical nature of his doctrine and its foundational discoveries. He still saw his unmasking of Christian morality as an epochal event which "breaks the history of mankind in two."[75] This crisis mentality, plus some measure of sub-conscious hatred for Christianity because of what it had done to him, infected his last writings with extreme comments against Christianity--painting it as if it had been a self-conscious conspiracy against mankind.

But Nietzsche did manage to turn <u>himself</u> away from the hate of nihilism, the hate of many atheists: "I turned my will to health, to <u>life</u>, into a philosophy."[76] Thus, he realized that each individual had to similarly turn towards his own health. He was not to be a religious leader:

> Now I go alone, my disciples, You, too, go now, alone. Thus I want it . . . Now I bid you lose me and find yourselves; and only <u>when you have denied me</u> I return to you.[77]

This use of Christian phraseology to make his own points remained a favorite aspect of his style while his mission remained that of Dionysus versus the Crucified.

Zarathustra was his prophet and he explained the choice of this Persian religious founder as his prophet: the historical Zarathustra created morality and the new Zarathustra was to undo the damage.[78] And how did Nietzsche explain his poetic presentation of <u>Zarathustra</u>: "<u>good</u> is any style that really communicates an inward state."[79] He stressed that he had offered a new ideal type--one to counteract the ascetic ideal of Christianity (and all other-world religions). The inward state of this new ideal, the Dionysian, was clearly restated: "The will to life rejoicing over its own inexhaustibility."[80]

And he still believed that science was an adequate ground for his affirmative vision:

> This ultimate, most joyous, most wantonly extravagant Yes to life represents not only the highest insight but also the <u>deepest</u>, that which is most strictly confirmed and born out by truth and science.[81]

Such a claim seems to cry out for a nice old-fashioned metaphysical grounding-- but none was offered, and, in fact, Nietzsche still claimed to be an enemy of metaphysics. He referred to his achievement in <u>Human</u> wherein he announced the non-reality of an intelligible world (a Kantian/Schopenhauerian word for a metaphysical realm): "as the ax swung against the 'metaphysical need' of mankind."[82] Then, prophetically, he expressed a fear about his achievement: "but whether that will be more of a blessing or a curse for mankind, who could say?"[83] Such is a fitting expression of the quandary that Nietzsche's life work as a whole leaves one with.

NOTES

1. <u>Ecce Homo</u>, Fadiman, <u>The Philosophy of Nietzsche</u>, 1955, p. 39.
2. <u>Ecce Homo</u>, Fadiman, p. v.
3. <u>Selected Letters</u>, p. 22.
4. <u>Twilight</u>, Hollingdale, p. 30.
5. <u>Twilight</u>, Hollingdale, p. 34.
6. <u>Zarathustra</u>, Hollingdale, p. 226.
7. <u>Twilight</u>, Hollingdale, p. 35.
8. <u>Twilight</u>, Hollingdale, p. 36.
9. <u>Twilight</u>, Hollingdale, p. 36.
10. <u>Twilight</u>, Hollingdale, p. 37.
11. <u>Twilight</u>, Hollingdale, p. 39.
12. <u>Twilight</u>, Hollingdale, p. 42.
13. Nietzsche had defined the "instinctual" in some notes of 1872: he did not mean some biological directive or disposition, but a Schopenhauerian essence of an individual, a part of its character. (<u>Friedrich Nietzsche on Rhetoric</u>, pp. 209-10) Nietzsche never reexamined this concept in light of his dropping of Schopenhauer's metaphysics.
14. <u>Twilight</u>, Hollingdale, p. 45.
15. <u>Twilight</u>, Hollingdale, p. 46.
16. <u>Twilight</u>, Hollingdale, p. 39.
17. <u>Twilight</u>, Hollingdale, p. 48.
18. <u>Twilight</u>, Hollingdale, p. 54.
19. <u>Twilight</u>, Hollingdale, p. 69.
20. <u>Twilight</u>, Hollingdale, p. 70.
21. <u>Twilight</u>, Hollingdale, p. 72.
22. <u>Twilight</u>, Hollingdale, p. 72.
23. <u>Twilight</u>, Hollingdale, p. 85.
24. <u>Twilight</u>, Hollingdale, p. 103.
25. <u>Twilight</u>, Hollingdale, p. 103.

26. <u>Twilight</u>, Hollingdale, p. 110.
27. <u>Twilight</u>, Hollingdale, p. 110.
28. <u>Twilight</u>, Hollingdale, p. 110.
29. <u>Twilight</u>, Hollingdale, p. 85.
30. <u>Twilight</u>, Hollingdale, p. 103.
31. <u>Twilight</u>, Hollingdale, p. 107.
32. <u>Twilight</u>, Hollingdale, p. 108.
33. <u>Twilight</u>, Hollingdale, pp. 109-10.
34. <u>Twilight</u>, Hollingdale, p. 15.
35. <u>Ecce Homo</u>, Fadiman, p. 114.
36. <u>Anti-Christ</u>, Hollingdale, p. 117.
37. <u>Anti-Christ</u>, Hollingdale, p. 139
38. <u>Anti-Christ</u>, Hollingdale, pp. 162-3.
39. <u>Anti-Christ</u>, Hollingdale, pp. 186-7.
40. <u>Anti-Christ</u>, Hollingdale, p. 135.
41. <u>Anti-Christ</u>, Hollingdale, p. 117.
42. <u>Anti-Christ</u>, Hollingdale, p. 116.
43. <u>Anti-Christ</u>, Hollingdale, p. 177.
44. <u>Anti-Christ</u>, Hollingdale, p. 178.
45. <u>Anti-Christ</u>, Hollingdale, p. 150.
46. <u>Anti-Christ</u>, Hollingdale, p. 156.
47. <u>Anti-Christ</u>, Hollingdale, p. 182.
48. <u>Anti-Christ</u>, Hollingdale, p. 183.
49. <u>Anti-Christ</u>, Hollingdale, p. 184.
50. <u>Anti-Christ</u>, Hollingdale, p. 142.
51. <u>Anti-Christ</u>, Hollingdale, p. 125.
52. <u>Anti-Christ</u>, Hollingdale, p. 122.
53. <u>Anti-Christ</u>, Hollingdale, p. 146.
54. <u>Anti-Christ</u>, Hollingdale, p. 172.
55. <u>Anti-Christ</u>, Hollingdale, pp. 146-7.
56. Thomas Altizer, in "Eternal Recurrence and the Kingdom of God," <u>The New Nietzsche</u>, p. 238, made a similar comparison between the <u>Anti-Christ</u>'s portrait of Jesus and Zarathustra. C. G. Jung, in <u>Nietzsche's Zarathustra</u>, p. 1539, equated the *Übermensch* and a secular Jesus.
57. <u>Anti-Christ</u>, Hollingdale, p. 140.
58. <u>Anti-Christ</u>, Hollingdale, p. 146.
59. <u>Ecce Homo</u>, Kaufmann, p. 213.
60. <u>Gay Science</u>, #270, p. 219.
61. <u>Gay Science</u>, #335, p. 266.
62. Quoted in Kaufmann, <u>Hegel</u>, p. 254.
63. Quoted in Kaufmann, <u>Hegel</u>, p. 255.
64. <u>Ecce Homo</u>, Fadiman, p. 45.

65. Ecce Homo, Fadiman, p. 66.
66. Ecce Homo, Fadiman, p. 117.
67. Ecce Homo, Fadiman, p. 136.
68. Ecce Homo, Fadiman, p. 137.
69. Ecce Homo, Fadiman, p. 137.
70. Ecce Homo, Fadiman, p. 79.
71. Ecce Homo, Fadiman, p. 111.
72. Ecce Homo, Fadiman, p. 49.
73. Ecce Homo, Fadiman, p. 66.
74. Ecce Homo, Fadiman, p. 143.
75. Ecce Homo, Fadiman, p. 143.
76. Ecce Homo, Kaufmann, p. 224.
77. Ecce Homo, Kaufmann, p. 220.
78. Ecce Homo, Kaufmann, p. 328.
79. Ecce Homo, Kaufmann, p. 265.
80. Ecce Homo, Kaufmann, p. 273.
81. Ecce Homo, Kaufmann, p. 272.
82. Ecce Homo, Kaufmann, p. 289.
83. Ecce Homo, Kaufmann, p. 289.

CHAPTER 8 CONCLUSIONS

THE DOMINANCE OF WAGNER

When one finally looks back at Nietzsche's mature thought, and considers the primary early influences of ancient Greek culture, Wagner, Schopenhauer and Neo-Kantianism, one is not drawn to the Wagner experience as the dominant one. Without Schopenhauer's metaphysics, one could not truly understand Nietzsche's intellectual journey. His Greek cultural basis never leaves him. And Neo-Kantianism is the best label for the philosophic core of this final intellectual position. But it is Wagner's early ideas that are enshrined in Nietzsche's praise of life which directs his mature thought.

The personal bond between Nietzsche and Wagner was very strong on Nietzsche's part. A love relationship was manifested in the dynamics of attraction and repulsion. After 1876, Nietzsche remained ambivalent despite rejecting Wagner's turn toward Christianity and the worst of Schopenhauer's philosophy, and being sickened by Wagner's pandering to the German middle class. Why did Nietzsche remain ambivalent and not just reject Wagner? Was there more than a quasi-love relationship of the son to the father? The answer is yes.

If we consider that Nietzsche read all Wagner's early works during his formative period, then a new perspective opens up. Nietzsche's contact with Wagner's early work came in the proper emotional situation for establishing discipleship. Nietzsche was looking for something new outside of philology, for new ideas. He had a smattering of Schopenhauer from self-study, but he already had disagreements with Schopenhauer's view of art. Then Wagner overpowered him with a set of ideas written with great force, and these ideas were given a musical reality. Within this engrossing situation, Nietzsche studied Wagner's thoughts and became a true disciple. Nietzsche himself recognized the crucial nature of early influences. Thiele records that in 1868:

> Nietzsche wrote that youth's ideals cast a spell on the man from which he never emerges, even though the "idealizing gaze" has long since died out from his eyes.[1]

And Nietzsche's own youthful pro-Hellenism never died out. He described in a letter to his friend in 1869:

> The Greeks believed . . . that man must create his own virtues and his own gods. Imbued with a tragic sense, a courageous pessimism, they never turned from life. There is an exact parallel between them and ourselves; pessimism and courage, and the will to create new beauty.[2]

Wagner's romantic idealism was imbibed by a receptive Nietzsche. Despite the fact that Wagner had fallen for Schopenhauer as Nietzsche had, in the early works he expressed a non-Schopenhauerian faith in life. Wagner also idealized ancient Greece and clothed his arguments in "historical" analyses. Tragedy was held on high and Christianity was the low point in the history of culture. And most importantly, it was all wrapped in a revolutionary fervor. This was not dry disputation over the translation of Greek texts. It was a call to action. A call for disciples:

> I am Revolution, I am the ever-fashioning Life, I am the only God, to whom each creature testifies, who spans and gives both life and happiness to all that is![3]

Nietzsche was swept up in Wagner's surge of ideas. After jettisoning his Schopenhauerian language, Nietzsche returned, without a self-conscious awareness, to a romantic idealism of life. "Will to power", eternal recurrence, and the *Übermensch* idea were all incipient in the early Wagner. Of course, the early Wagner represented the praise of Greek culture then topical in Germany. The whole of Wagner's intellectual context fit like a glove with Nietzsche's own education. The developments in mid-Nineteenth Century science also seemed to support a new animated view of nature. Finally, Nietzsche's own early cultural heroes had messages consistent with romantic idealism: Hölderlin, Goethe, Byron and Emerson. The early Wagner came not as a shock to the young Nietzsche, but as a revelation of how many of his own intellectual aspects could be put together (and by a fellow Schopenhauerian as well).

124

Conclusions

The personification of nature or life abounds in Nietzsche's The Birth, the first work written by Nietzsche after his Wagner immersion. Wagner had also seen nature as the active force: "Nature is so strong, so inexhaustible in its regenerative resources, that no conceivable violence could weaken its creative force."[4] Nietzsche, in The Birth, had nature describe "her" self:

Amidst the ceaseless flux of phenomenon I am the eternally creative primordial mother, eternally impelling existence, eternally self-sufficient amid the flux of phenomena![5]

It was the praise of nature in the ancient Greek Olympian religion that Nietzsche applauded: "the accents of an exuberant, triumphant life, in which all things, whether good or bad, are deified."[6] Nietzsche's faith was already beyond Schopenhauerian pessimism: "Yes, my friends, have faith with me in Dionysian life and in the rebirth of tragedy."[7] And, right after The Birth, in "Homer's Contest" of 1872, Nietzsche attributed all of man's greatness to nature: "Man, in his highest and noblest capacities, is wholly nature."[8]

The main negative thrust of the early Wagner was taken over by Nietzsche as well. Christianity was the inversion of nature worship to the early Wagner. He painted Christianity as a "dread and loathing of actual life" and a "longing for death."[9] Nietzsche had battled Christianity throughout his works and in his mature period he revealed his anti-death stance:

It makes me happy that men do not want at all to think the thought of death! I should like to do something that would make the thought of life even a hundred times more appealing to them.[10]

Nietzsche was continuing the early Wagner's message which called for the end to the "dominion of death over Life."[11] Dionysus over Christ was Nietzsche's symbol of his version of the early Wagner's message:

The God on the cross is a curse on life, a pointer to seek redemption from it. Dionysus cut to pieces is a promise of life: it is eternally reborn and comes back from destruction.[12]

The master, the early Wagner, had a program which was not confined to romantic contemplation of glorious Greece: "We have thus quite other work to do than tinker at the resuscitation of old Greece."[13] Nietzsche was looking for what he could do, how he could move beyond philological irrelevance. The master gave direction: "we desire to grow to fair strong men, to whom the world

125

belongs as an eternal, inexhaustible source of the highest delights of art."[14] The *Übermensch* or "free spirits" jump to mind! But Wagner waxed even closer to this Nietzschean ideal when he described these "fair strong men": "free in willing, free in doing, free in enjoying, shall ye attest the worth of life."[15] Nietzsche's praise of the liberation of man after the rejection of nihilism covers this exact ground. Man was free to create, thus said Wagner also:

> Man's highest good is his fashioning force, the fount whence springs all happiness . . . not in the created, in the act of creation itself, in the exercise of your powers lies your true highest enjoyment.[16]

All of the heart of the mature Nietzsche is encapsulated in this 1849 item of Wagner's: the constant creating, overcoming, as the path to fulfillment, the feeling of power exercised as the true spur to human motivation, and all as driven by the will to power as a natural force. Nietzsche summed up his similar goal for men in <u>Wisdom</u>: "we want to be the poets of our life."[17]

Wagner provided not only the emphasis on the creator which Schopenhauer never offered, but he also preached the value of the individual. Schopenhauer's philosophy devalued the individual, while the mature Nietzsche was the great prophet of individualism. Wagner's individualism arose out of respect for the Greek achievement which saw personality as gaining:

> its liberty and its consciousness of selfhood . . . as it realizes that it is a separate world opposed to the external law, it discovers its own inner laws.[18]

As was the case in Jaeger's view of the Greek enlightenment, Wagner saw the individual of society at the center: "the prime motor of this [social] nature is the individual."[19] And it was not the alienated rational individual, but a passionate animal: "who only in the satisfaction of his instinctive longing for love, can appease his bent to happiness."[20] Not only sexual love was at issue. Wagner saw love as the passion driving even the "will to Truth": "All understanding comes to us through love alone."[21] Passion was revalidated by the mature Nietzsche when he praised the essence in Wagner:

> what is distinctively Wagnerian in Wagner's heroes: I mean the innocence of utmost selfishness, the faith in great passion as the good itself--in one word, what is Siegfried-like.[22]

126

He also saw love as Wagner had, and also saw its relation to creation: "for it is only in love, only when shaded by the illusion produced by love, that man is creative."[23] The Nietzschean emphasis on art, "illusion", creation and passion all comes together out of this Wagnerian insight:

> the power to transform being is produced by the feeling of power one receives through the illusion of a perfected world. Better said, the struggle for perfection produces power, and the illusory glimpse of perfection allowed us in art and love is the necessary stimulant to struggle.[24]

Thiele also cited Nietzsche's own words of <u>Anti-Christ</u>:

> Love is the state in which man sees things most of all as they are not. The illusion-creating force is there at its height, likewise the sweetening and transforming force.[25]

When turned toward the self concept, the Greek concept of "*arete*" was available for Wagner and Nietzsche:

> the highest kind of self-love which makes man reach out towards the highest *arete* . . . sacrifice to an ideal is a proof of highly developed self-love.[26]

This Aristotelian ideal was reappropriated by Wagner and Nietzsche. In his third <u>Meditation</u>, Nietzsche had clearly described the role of love in self-development: "love also creates the desire to get out of one's present self and search, with all one's might, for a higher and nobler self."[27] Wagner joined self-love to total affirmation as the requirements for the ideal man: "the necessity of recognizing and yielding to the change, the many-sidedness, the multiplicity, the eternal renewing of reality and life."[28] Thus Wagner wrote in 1854, and in the same letter, he anticipated the center of Nietzsche's requirement for affirmation of life, namely "amour fati": "to will what necessity imposes."[29] Nietzsche took this idea to the final stage with eternal recurrence: "Immortal is the moment when I produced the recurrence . . . For the sake of this moment I endure the recurrence."[30] Here his unpublished notes show "*amour fati*" in action. Love of all life transforms reality. Thiele put it this way:

> In the realm of love, the line between illusion and reality is not thin: it simply doesn't exist. One must transgress the borders of reality during the

subtle and intricate gymnastics of realizing ideals and transforming potential into actuality.[31]

Nietzsche's peak "illusion" was the creation of Zarathustra, his prophet. One could imagine Zarathustra preaching these early Wagnerian words:

> Life is a law unto itself . . . the only Holiness is the free man . . . ye yourselves are the law, your own free will the sole and highest law, and I will destroy all dominion of death over Life.[32]

And did not Nietzsche's Zarathustra fulfill this early Wagnerian vision of "the God become Man", and even parallel the action? "Rush down to the valleys and plains, and proclaim to all the world the new Gospel of Happiness."[33] Was not Siegfried the proto-type of Zarathustra? Yes, if a dash of Nietzsche's greater intellectualism is thrown in. The Siegfried who was the hero of the Ring before Wagner altered it to twist toward Schopenhauer exemplified the ideal in the early Wagner that Nietzsche remained loyal to in his mature period. In 1881, Nietzsche proclaimed his loyalty in <u>Wisdom</u>:

> Let us remain faithful to Wagner, in what is true, and authentic in him . . . It does not matter that as a thinker he is so often wrong. . . . Enough that his life is justified before itself and remains justified--this life which shouts at every one of us: "Be a man and do not follow me--but yourself! But yourself!"[34]

Thus Nietzsche remained faithful to his purified Wagnerism, and to Wagner as the model of a justified life. And Nietzsche also justified his own turning away from the Master by espousing Goethe's romantic dictum of individualism.

THE TRANSCENDENCE OF SCHOPENHAUER

If Wagner the romantic rebel, creator, musician and individual was the most dominant influence in the mature Nietzsche, then Schopenhauer was the influence that had to be transcended. Schopenhauer had been praised by Nietzsche as the archetype of the seeker of Truth. He had been "the Philosopher" for Nietzsche in the middle years, 1868-1874. Wagner was a converted disciple to Schopenhauer, as was Burckhardt--his two mentors in this same period. Nietzsche's Schopenhauerian conviction had been so strong that it colored all his thoughts in this formative phase.

Conclusions

The conflict between the romantic naturalism of Wagner which Nietzsche finally embraced and Schopenhauer's ultimate pessimism toward life was clear-- but Nietzsche was not able to grasp this clear problem until his mature period. Nietzsche's youthful amalgamation of Wagner and Schopenhauer was stated in a letter of 1868: "What pleases me in Wagner is that which pleases me in Schopenhauer: the ethical breeze, the whiff of Faust, the Cross, the grave, etc."[35] It was because Schopenhauer was a philosopher, as Nietzsche styled himself in his formative period, that Nietzsche was drawn to him. The burning of the "will to Truth" filled Nietzsche as it did Schopenhauer (and as it does in most young philosophers).

Yet Schopenhauer, unlike the Hegelians of his time, focused a significant portion of his writings on everyday reality (sex, included). This apparent agreement of Schopenhauer with the new naturalism of Feuerbach allowed Wagner, then Nietzsche, to graft Schopenhauer onto a romantic naturalism. Schopenhauer was seen as completing such a naturalism. His metaphysical extension of Kant seemed to give the assurance of having attained an extra-human Truth to justify the naturalistic perspective.

But the goal of this metaphysics was anti-life. This Nietzsche came to see, and it led to his recanting of metaphysics, to his refusal to accept an assuring view based on any Truth that was outside of human life. As such, Nietzsche moved back toward Feuerbach, Wagner's first intellectual mentor. Feuerbach had turned from Hegel to a materialism that was naturalistic, not metaphysical:

> Nature . . . is nothing but corporeality . . . The body is the basis, the subject of personality. Only the body is the real personality distinguished from the imaginary one of the spectre . . . But a body does not exist without flesh and blood. Flesh and blood is life, and life alone is corporeal reality.[36]

No Kantian spectre of a person, i.e., a non-physical unknown, was offered here as the essence of the individual. Instead, it was the natural person with body and mind that was the essence of human reality. This was the same position as that of the mature Nietzsche. Feuerbach also clearly placed the mind in a dependent position as Nietzsche would:

> Matter . . . is the basis of intelligence, the basis of personality . . . spirit without Nature is an unreal abstraction; consciousness develops itself only out of nature.[37]

129

Reality was not in essence a "will" which was non-physical. Reality was in essence human animality. This reality was what was worshiped in Greek pagan cults. Feuerbach commented on this, much as Nietzsche could have:

> The shouts of sensual pleasure mingled itself in the worship of the gods . . . it is a sensual God, a God of life, who is worshiped, as indeed the shouts of joy are only a symbolical definition of the nature of the gods.[38]

Dionysus was Nietzsche's symbol for life, which he praised as if it were a god.

Finally, even the mature Nietzsche's doctrine of affirmation of life was in Feuerbach:

> That which exists has necessarily a pleasure, a joy in itself, and loves itself justly; to blame it because it loves itself is to reproach it because it exists. To exist is to assert oneself, to affirm oneself, to love oneself.[39]

And in contrast to this, Nietzsche found the opposite of his grand symbol of affirmation, eternal recurrence, in Schopenhauer:

> the life of the individual, every life-history is a history of suffering . . . at the end of his life, no man, if be sincere and at the same time in possession of his faculties, will ever wish to go through it again. Rather than this, he will much prefer to choose complete non-existence.[40]

Nietzsche finally saw that Schopenhauer's metaphysical "solution" was just this preference for non-existence over life. In fact, Nietzsche accepted Schopenhauer's challenge and proclaimed the belief in eternal recurrence as the test of the Zarathustra ideal. Nietzsche could have used Schopenhauer's own words on the ideal of affirming all of one's life:

> [a man] who found satisfaction in life and took perfect delight in it; who in spite of calm deliberation, that the course of his life as he had hitherto experience it should be of endless duration or of constant recurrence; and whose courage to face life was so great that, in return for life's pleasures he would willingly and gladly put up with all the hardships and miseries to which it is subject; such a man would stand "with firm, strong bones on the well-grounded, enduring earth," and would have nothing to fear.[41]

Siegfried, Zarathustra and Nietzsche exhibited such courage.

130

Conclusions

Dismissing this aspect of Schopenhauer did not help Nietzsche to justify his philosophic quest--for he truly shared this with Schopenhauer. Nietzsche came to see the "will to Truth", the drive which drove him throughout much of his life, as part of the "will to power." But he did not stop with this fitting of the philosophic quest into his overall explanatory scheme. His ideal of "free spirits" or "overmen" envisioned escaping from the "will to Truth". In the Genealogy of Morals, he dismissed atheists, immoralists, nihilists, sceptics and Anti-Christs: "These men are a long way from being free spirits, because they still believe in truth."[42] Nietzsche's own postures as an atheist, immoralist and Anti-Christ were decried. In unpublished notes from 1888, he drew a distinction between the "will to Truth" and the "will to create":

> "will to truth"--as the impotence of the will to create.
> To know that something is thus and thus . . . To act so that something becomes thus and thus.[43]

But he continued doing philosophy! He had also discussed this a few years earlier in Wisdom:

> One day the wanderer slammed a door behind himself, stopped in his tracks, and wept. Then he said: "This penchant and passion for what is true, real, non-apparent, certain--how it aggravates me! Why does this fellow keep following me? I want to rest, but he will not allow it. How much there is that seduces me to tarry! . . . I must go on, I often look back in wrath at the most beautiful things that could not hold me--because they could not hold me."[44]

An unconscious drive was thus credited by Nietzsche with his persistent philosophizing.

As early as 1872, he had seen the quest as not providing satisfaction: "For by its nature every striving for knowledge seems intrinsically unsatisfied and unsatisfying."[45] But back then, he credited his disillusion to a Kantian perspective:

> He is locked within this consciousness and nature threw away the key. . . . the philosopher . . . longs, just once, to peer out and down through a crack in the chamber of consciousness.[46]

The allure of Truth, knowledge, persisted--overrode the Kantian perspective. In a letter of January 1880, he affirmed his continuing quest:

131

in this condition of suffering and almost complete renunciation--this joy in seeking for knowledge carries me to heights where I overcome all torments and all hopelessness.[47]

Yet the quest was always defeated:

the itch and delight in the chase and intrigue of knowledge . . . Until in the end there is nothing left for him to chase except the knowledge which hurts most . . . Perhaps it too will disappoint, as everything that he knows.[48]

And by 1885, five years after this comment from the Dawn, it hurt a lot:

My life is now comprised in the wish that the truth about all things be different from my way of seeing it: if some one would convince me of the improbability of my truths![49]

This desperate plea came after he had written Zarathustra wherein he had asked philosophers to move from being guardians of the Truth to acknowledging the all-too-human nature of philosophy. As Alderman put it in Nietzsche's Gift, "for Zarathustra there is no end to his quest, no final goal, but his self and that is ever being recreated--by himself."[50]

Alderman thus credited Nietzsche with a major change of perspective concerning the role of philosophy, and the philosopher. It was a change which is consistent with some interpretations of the latter Wittgenstein's philosophy. Alderman pointed out that this re-orientation was a risk for the philosopher as an individual. Nietzsche was ambivalent about truly accepting this change. As he said in unpublished notes from around 1880: "I have at all times thought with my whole body and my whole life. I don't know what purely intellectual problems are."[51] This view would make accepting philosophy as less than a pursuit of Truth difficult.

As Heller said in The Importance of Nietzsche, philosophical creations were "dams built against the on rush of emptiness, of the 'nihil', the spiritual vacuity created by the 'death of God.'"[52] The psychological necessity of philosophizing (or creating) consists in the escape from reality, the escape from oneself. Santayana, in Egotism in German Philosophy, drew the conclusion concerning Nietzsche: "human life as it is, and especially his own life, repelled him."[53] Nietzsche also saw this by 1886, maybe not so clearly about himself:

132

Conclusions

what, in the last analysis, did inquiry come to when judged as a symptom of the life process? . . . the "inquiring mind" was simply the human mind terrified by pessimism and trying to escape from it, a clever bulwark erected against the truth?[54]

Even in The Birth of Tragedy, he had seen that the knowledge quest fought basic fears: "mortal man freed by knowledge and argument from the fear of death . . . his mission is to make existence appear intelligible and thereby justified."[55] Much of his life was spent looking for a justification of man. He eventually sided with Goethe's view, as stated by Santayana in Three Philosophical Poets: "The worth of life lies in pursuit, not attainment."[56] But the pursuit in a philosophical perspective does not offer fulfillment. Scharfstein has explained it this way:

We think as much as we do in order to control our lives as well as we can; but the same knowledge that lessens ignorance exposes how much ignorance remains and uncovers threats of which we have not been aware.[57]

The risk of continued philosophy is that the anxiety which led one to philosophy is actually furthered in the pursuit of philosophy. Anxiety is not quelled and fulfillment is not yielded.

Wittgenstein, in the Philosophical Investigations, tried to get a grip on this psychosis and its cure:

The real discovery is the one that makes me capable of stopping doing philosophy when I want to.--The one that gives philosophy peace, so that it is no longer tormented by questions which bring itself in question.[58]

Pitkin, in Wittgenstein and Justice, has described the philosophic disease:

the impulse to philosophy is the impulse to become self-conscious about our concepts and assumptions . . . And what Wittgenstein says about that impulse is not that its aim is impossible, but that where the aim fails the continuing impulse becomes like a disease.[59]

A short-hand way of describing Wittgenstein's cure for philosophy was offered by Pitkin:

To the extent that our concepts and our language are shaped by human nature and the natural human condition, they cannot be justified, and must

133

simply be accepted as given . . . we can become aware of some of our human forms of life. But beyond that we cannot <u>explain</u> those forms of life, cannot give <u>reasons</u> for them. Wittgenstein says that explanations must have an end somewhere.[60]

And in the end what one must say, as Wittgenstein did, is: "This is simply what I do."[61]

Nietzsche never truly accepted this latter Wittgensteinian commandment. He remained with the hope that he could do more for man, and for himself. He sought to craft self-conscious myths which could function as if they were Truths. Wittgenstein resisted this completely. However, the result in Wittgenstein's personal life was an extreme ambivalence toward doing philosophy--he usually counselled his good pupils to go into some other field. His philosophy failed to give him peace. He put philosophy away, but could not leave it.

Schopenhauer said that religious and philosophical systems functioned to console people concerning death. Nietzsche's romantic naturalism functioned to console man without metaphysical Truth. But it wasn't a final revelation and resting place for believers. Everything in the natural realm was not good now that it was no longer evil, that is, the opposite of the metaphysical. The natural, the cultural, the psychological needed to be revaluated. Unlike Schopenhauer, who never changed his philosophy after writing it at an early age, Nietzsche continually struggled with new problems as they arose for him. As he changed, his perspective changed. He only remained true to his affirmation of life. Schopenhauer's (and all metaphysicians') nihilism toward human life was the opposite extreme. As such, Nietzsche transcended the essence of Schopenhauer and much of traditional philosophy.

TO TRANSCEND PHILOSOPHY

Nietzsche considered himself a philosopher, yet he clearly repudiated most of the traditional philosophizing up to his time. He had not studied much philosophy in college, but had read deeply in Greek philosophy and, on his own, mastered Schopenhauer. He read philosophers periodically after his college days. He never wrote any work in a traditional philosophical style, and therefore, his philosophical position must be pieced together from scattered comments.

Conclusions

The mature Nietzsche had one focus for his criticism of traditional philosophers. He indicted them for seeking Truth as "a transcendental solution to life's riddle."[62] Three important philosophical positions were contained in this simple indictment:

> 1. Philosophy should not deal with the "transcendental," that is, metaphysical realms,
>
> 2. Philosophy should not be seen as a solution to the "Why do I exist?" or "Why does anything exist?" questions, and consequently,
>
> 3. Life is an unsolvable riddle only if questioned from a point outside of life, but such a perspective is not attainable.

Philosophy's long standing claim to be the special road to Truth was directly combatted. Such a philosophic quest was driven by the "will to power" in a manner similar to the religious fanatic. The result was ultimately the same, the devaluation of life as it was. Metaphysical realities were used in opposition to everyday actualities. Since Plato, Nietzsche claimed, the metaphysical, the unchanging world of abstract truths, had been brandished against life itself as it was experienced.

Nietzsche pretty much accepted Schopenhauer's definition of "metaphysics":

> By metaphysics I understand all so-called knowledge that goes beyond the possibility of experience, and so beyond nature . . . in order to give information about that by which, in some sense or other, this experience or nature is conditioned, or in popular language, about that which is hidden behind nature, and renders nature possible.[63]

If Nietzsche accepted this definition, then his proclamations about "will to power" and eternal recurrence need to be explained as non-metaphysical. He evidently felt they did not fall under this definition--he felt they were claims about nature. It is easier to accept "will to power" as a hypothesis about nature, but then it is so vague as to be without hope for verification. And undoubtedly, Nietzsche often went too far in claiming "will to power" as a force in all things, even the inorganic. Such claims have the appearance of being metaphysical rather than a generalization based upon experience. "Eternal recurrence" is more of a problem. It is beyond experience and should be classed as metaphysical by Schopenhauer's definition. Nietzsche had toyed with scientific reasonings to support it (as had other contemporary scientists and philosophers), but he left all these thoughts in unpublished materials. One must conclude that Nietzsche was inconsistent in accepting "eternal recurrence"--from the perspective of a philosopher opposed to all metaphysics. Of course, the concept played a moral role in Nietzsche's ethical individualism, and a mythical role in <u>Zarathustra</u>.

This was not Nietzsche's only philosophical inconsistency. He claimed to have freed himself from Schopenhauer, and especially from his metaphysics, yet Schopenhauerian metaphysical comments appear in his mature works, especially in <u>Beyond</u>. Nietzsche's concern with metaphysics was, however, primarily from an ethical perspective. As the earlier citation indicated, it was the use to which metaphysics was put by the traditional philosophers that he objected to most forcefully. He was quite clear about this regarding Kant in his 1886 preface to <u>The Dawn</u>. Therein, he asserted that Kant's creation of his critical philosophy stemmed from his desire for a safe haven for moral truths:

> to create room for his "moral realm" he saw himself obliged to posit an undemonstrable world . . .--it was for precisely that he had need of his critique of pure reason! . . . he would not have had need of it if one thing had not been more vital to him than anything else: to render the "moral realm" unassailable, even better, incomprehensible to reason.[64]

Such philosophers, from Plato through Schopenhauer, used their vision of the Truth as a magical force to compel all to their view. The metaphysician fears claiming his possession as his own and instead dresses it as the absolute truth. Alderman has described this phenomenon:

> through fear we pretend to be what we are not--absolute, certain, eternal. Through fear we insist that our must illusory pretensions be taken as reality itself.[65]

Nietzsche himself may have been guilty of the same in his extended use of "will to power" and his use of "eternal recurrence."

Nietzsche had hoped to cross over from such philosophizing to a stress on experience. As such, he emphasized historical materials and the psychological analysis of man. Philosophy itself, as well as ethics and human activity, had an historical perspective that philosophers loved to ignore. (In the case of philosophers analyzing Nietzsche, they still ignore his history!) Nietzsche also realized that finding the historical origin of something did not exhaust the meaning of that same thing in its current situation. Although at times, he seemed to stray from loyalty to this vision of the limits of the historical perspective.

Well, what should the new philosopher do? He could not reveal reality. He did not have a monopoly on truths. He was a man among others, situated in a cultural environment with a long history. Nietzsche saw the task as one of crafting a new ideal--one to oppose the ascetic priest ideal of Christian culture (and directly descended from the ascetic philosopher ideals of Hellenistic times). Could Nietzsche justify this task and the nature of the ideal he created? Not with old-style philosophy. He presented his ideal in a self-consciously created myth, <u>Zarathustra</u>. Nietzsche seemed to believe this was somehow his "calling." He surrounded his "calling" with romantic naturalism, but the message was one of this-worldly individualism.

Gauged retrospectively, his creation was very provocative--it had effects-- although not those intended by Nietzsche in many instances. However, the new ideal miscarried. Nietzsche was caught within his own new view of philosophy as limited. As one could not accept "will to power", "eternal recurrence", and "the *Übermensch*" as Truths, in the old fashioned sense, the conversion to the new ideal could not be as psychologically compelling. Nietzsche's ethical urgency implied a compelling solution was necessary, but such a solution could only be generated based on a realization that the Truth was at stake. Nietzsche's philosophical perspective eliminated this possibility, and his creations, or symbols, were not designed to play the role of Truths in a quasi-religious way (despite the fact that they eventually played such a role in later cultural appropriations of Nietzsche).

All Nietzsche's creations could do from within his non-transcendental philosophical perspective was to liberate his readers from the old philosophical perspective. As Nietzsche himself said, he gave his way, we have to find our own way. His perspective required the elimination of certain ways, but it did not set a positive goal for all. This ethical vacuity led to numerous interpretations which have been disastrous for Western civilization. Philosophy on Nietzsche's terms is left ethically mute regarding social values. But this may be because Nietzsche really failed to eliminate the metaphysical ground of his individualism. His individualism, as we have seen, had close ties to Hegelian notions of the claim that each individual had some essence which was unique and to be developed. Such an "inner self" is an abstract concept without reference to the normal world of experience. It is a secularized version of Christian metaphysics, and before that, of Platonic metaphysics. The "soul" has merely been replaced by a less clear concept, the "self", the status of which is usually a topic that is avoided.

Nietzsche's view of the self originated in the Lutheran-Christian model, i.e., wherein it was held that the Truth could be isolated, identified and proclaimed. In that same tradition, individual selves were saved by knowledge of the Truth. These selves were seen as complex unities. The true self was immortal and would be rewarded with heaven or hell after its death depending on its religious life. There was no doubt that this true self was:

     1. responsible for its actions,

      2. able to follow religious prescriptions because it had free will, and
      3. known to the individual through self-consciousness.
Nietzsche eventually rejected these three affirmations of mainstream Christianity.

    Belief in Christianity waned and its bedrock about the self also disappeared for Nietzsche. The Christian true self or soul was dropped as an antiquated piece of crass metaphysics. Nietzsche was living in the hey-day of scientific progress and science was not finding souls--was not allowing them into the explanatory frameworks. Philosophy was also getting around to seeing great difficulties with the notion of souls or metaphysical aspects of individuals. Yet grasping the scientific monism of the day seemed obviously wrong to most educated minds. Crass materialism was no more metaphysically sound than "soulism." Kant had offered a solution to this crisis in his minimalist metaphysics of noumenal objects. This move saved free will and responsibility for men's true selves. The cost was in knowledge and certainty. Ewing put it this way: "Kant's answer is that I am real but that what I observe myself in introspection is only appearance."[66] To explain this further one must understand that "appearance" for Kant pertains to all that is not real in itself, but is real in its appearance to man. To the modern reader this probably doesn't help that much. The quandary over what "is real in itself" might mean is not surprising. What is surprising is that late 18th century and early 19th century philosophers could find this language meaningful and satisfying. I will try to shed some light on the metaphysics.

    Kant was forced into such a convoluted metaphysics in order to separate the self, as the causal agent of actions, from the natural, common sense, world of causally connected events. For Kant and his contemporaries, if the human agent was not separated from the natural world in some manner, then human action would be determined by prior causes just like all other physical events. Such determinism was detestable to them because it undermined all morality and Christian doctrine. It also seemed to be counter to common sense intuitions of deliberation and freely chosen actions. The choice for philosophers who saw uniform causality as <u>true</u> for the world was between separating man's causal determination from that of the world or claiming that the perceptions of freedom were erroneous. Kant grasped the former way and developed a metaphysics to support it, while Nietzsche initially grasped the latter and tried to restructure philosophy and morality to be consistent with this choice.

    The ground of Nietzsche's choice was in Kant's philosophy of the self. The self was split into three parts by Kant:

      1. the phenomenal self--what we perceive in consciousness,
      2. the noumenal self--what we believe is real but we know nothing about it except that it is not part of the causal world, and

3. the transcendental unity of apperception--a center of awareness which must be present for experience.

Kant held that the phenomenal self was completely determined while the noumenal self was "outside" of time and space, and therefore, phenomenal causality. Kant defined the phenomenal as the world as it appears, leaving open the possibility of a realm of things-in-themselves, not simply as they appear, that can be thought and believed but not known. Our ordinary concepts were meaningful for science only in relation to the phenomenal world of experience. Kant had secured the concepts of freedom and responsibility--and God--by providing an unknowable realm (the noumenal) for them. Kant rejected all claims to religious or mystical experience which could penetrate to the noumenal realm.

Kant's philosophy was received with Schopenhauerian modifications in Nietzsche's time. Schopenhauer started from the Kantian metaphysical separation of the world into the phenomenal and the noumenal. He went on to flesh out the true noumenal self which he referred to as Will:

> The objective world, the world as idea, is not the only side of the world, but merely its outward side; and it has an entirely different side--the side of its inmost nature--its kernel--the-thing-in-itself . . . calling it after the most immediate of its objective manifestations--will.[67]

Thus Schopenhauer jumped beyond Kant's cautious, minimal characterizations of the noumenal. He gave man knowledge of this reality: "that which is immediately known to everyone, and is signified by the word will."[68] Schopenhauer explained his reasoning:

> Thus if we hold that the material world is something more than merely our idea, we must say that besides being idea, that is, in itself, and according to its inmost nature, it is that which we find immediately in ourselves as will.[69]

Not only the true self but the Kantian unknown "causes" of our perceptions were will: "the will alone is thing in itself."[70] The phenomenal world was not forgotten, and man as a person was intertwined in that world: "the person, is not will as thing-in-itself, but is a phenomenon of will."[71]

The self was also split into parts by Schopenhauer:

1. the empirical character--the individual as manifested in the phenomenal, the desiring ego,

2. the intelligible character--that aspect of Will which determines manifestations of the individual,

3. the subject of knowledge--that aspect of the individual in consciousness which can separate itself from the desiring ego, equated with the traditional soul, and

4. the true self--Will purely and without the characterizations applicable to ego or consciousness.

He definitely set out the separation of the true self from self-consciousness:

> we are accustomed to regard as our real self the subject of knowledge, the knowing I, which wearies in the evening, vanishes in sleep, and in the morning shines brighter with renewed strength. This is, however, the mere function of the brain, not our own self. Our true self, the kernel of our nature, is what is behind that, and really knows nothing but willing and not willing, being content and not content, with all the modifications of this, which are called feelings, emotions, and passions.[72]

And this true self is Will, and is just like Kant's noumenal self: "unchangeable, indestructible, not growing old, not physical, but metaphysical."[73]

Now Nietzsche eliminated the Kantian metaphysics which grounds Kant's and Schopenhauer's positions on a true self. But that Nietzsche retained so much from Schopenhauer is almost unbelievable. Commentators have gone out of their way to track down other influences on Nietzsche--at the expense of showing how many key ideas came directly from his main, self-acknowledged mentors. Nietzsche's problem with his discussions of the self stemmed from his attempt to appropriate all of Schopenhauer he could while yet denying his metaphysical machinery.

When Schopenhauer discussed the empirical character of men he pointed directly to the importance of power concerns--it reads like a draft of Nietzsche's "will to power" position:

> For we experience no real pleasure except in the use and feeling of our own powers . . . we will endeavor to cultivate, employ, and in every way make use of those talents which are naturally prominent in us.[74]

Schopenhauer stressed that these power concerns were only relevant to characterizing the empirical character. But this was all Nietzsche had left after he had jettisoned the metaphysical self! Therefore, the self was driven by the "will to power."

How did Nietzsche flesh out a concept of "self" from the non-metaphysical remains of Schopenhauer's characterizations of the self? Nietzsche never wrote an essay, or even a long series of aphorisms, directed at this explicit problem.

Conclusions

Taking his non-metaphysical desires seriously, we can try to develop his position. Structurally, Nietzsche partitions the self as Kant and Schopenhauer had. Working only in the empirical realm, he had only three sub-realms to specify: the conscious, the social and the "non-conscious." Nietzsche's emphasis on the "non-conscious" paralleled the Kantian emphasis on the metaphysical. Here, then, are the three aspects of Nietzsche's self:

> 1. the self in consciousness--an evolutionary development in the human organism which has social uses,
> 2. the self in society--the person as a social manifestation developed out of the interplay of conscious and "non-conscious" concerns with other persons and their culture, and
> 3. the "non-conscious" self--the "will" in Nietzsche's perspective, the original directive force of the living human organism.

The "non-conscious" self was primary both temporally and logically. Nietzsche, unlike Schopenhauer, gave great importance to a developmental understanding of man, and in this case, of consciousness and social being. It seemed crystal clear to him that organisms had existed before consciousness and cultural groupings. Language was seen as developing at the same time as consciousness. And these two were dependent on a social environment which was interrelated to them. Nietzsche, as a vanguard of modern thought, held that man developed from lower organisms, that is, from organisms without consciousness or culture. In fact, men existed which were not self-conscious, or did not display consciousness and which were not functional as persons in society. But organismic life and its "will" were necessary.

Since the self in consciousness was not primary, it was subservient for Nietzsche. He usually referred to this aspect by stating the instrumental nature of consciousness for the "non-conscious" self. The person being a further development of conscious interaction was also an instrument of "will." These non-primary "selves" expressed the "non-conscious" self in all their manifestations. As "will to power" directs all activity, all empirical manifestations of self manifested "will to power."

The difficulty for man was in learning to see "will to power" as fundamental in his actions. Unlike Schopenhauer's available self-knowledge of one's intelligible character, Nietzschean man started with knowledges which did not expose the reality of self. As such, Nietzsche was revealing new knowledge to man, knowledge not available to introspection or sudden experiences of insight. Self-knowledge had to be won through the study of man.

Nietzsche had ended up with less than Schopenhauer's Will but with more than Kant's cautious agnosticism toward anything other than the world of appearance. The "non-conscious" aspect of self, or "will," was not an experiential item by definition. Nietzsche had held that it was known by its effects. This equated "will" with a scientific hypothesis, or at least an element in such an hypothesis. He claimed that using such an hypothesis of "will to power" as the cause of all events would lead to a better understanding of man and the world. His attempts to persuade others to this new understanding were clear in all his works after <u>Wisdom</u>. But all he had offered was a non-falsifiable perspective for viewing events.

Unless there are arguments which can be generated as to the experiential evidence for and against "will to power," such a sweeping claim is vacuous. Its status would be like that of ether in the 1870's--an element of nature which could not be detected. But ether was abandoned when a series of crucial experiments were agreed to which demonstrated no effects of ether. Nietzsche's "will to power" is worse off than this hypothesis. Not only were there no crucial experiments, but the accumulated wisdom of centuries was ignored. Men have distinguished human actions according to particular motives which do not lend themselves to being reduced to a super-motive such as "will to power." Besides, the implied determinism of "will to power" made no practical sense whatsoever. In pursuit of his new philosophy, Nietzsche had chosen the option of ignoring the cultural wisdom and common sense on man's freedom and responsibility. He failed to re-explain the experiential realities of human action and was forced to a posture of claiming such realities were illusion.

The Nietzschean person was not very similar to the human being which common sense said was real. His reduction of the interaction of persons in society to the epiphenomenon of the struggle of "wills" for dominance was not really helpful. Where common sense identifies individual "will power" as the strenuous effort of an individual to change his habits of action, Nietzsche could only claim the individual was determined to express such "will power" because of "will to power." Change by persons as the result of a complex of factors is really of no interest to the determinist. And this is the primary interest in a moral perspective, in a social world of interpersonal actions. Nietzsche, the theorist, never saw this problem with his position.

The sovereign individual was seen by Nietzsche as a creation of society. He should have stopped at this insight and affirmed the social reality of the person of common sense. Schacht pointed out Nietzsche's viable perspective:

> It is a virtual presupposition of the viability of social life among human beings, he contends, that they regard themselves and each other as accountable for their actions through time; for it is only thus that they may be deemed both liable to imputations of responsibility and guilt for actions

performed in the past, and capable of making promises and undertaking commitments extending into the future.[75]

While Nietzsche was not content with this reality for persons, Schacht was. Rather than turning to a convoluted explanatory hypothesis about a "non-conscious" X, Schacht more clearly refused a quasi-metaphysical move and described persons as "a functional characteristic of a socialized human being."[76]

The "non-conscious" self, or "will," of Nietzsche was, from the least forgiving interpretation, poorly disguised metaphysics. It was similar to a scientism he often decried. From a highly favorable interpretation, his "will" was a starting point for a new image of man, of "soul-less" man. Viewing his "will" as a prophetic insight, it was an early indication of the path that both science and philosophy were going to take in the next 100 years. Science, whether in the Freudian depth psychology or Behaviorist schools, would drive on to attempt to explain human action without recourse to conscious introspection alone. Philosophy would take on the quest of slaying "the ghost in the machine," i.e., of removing "soulism" from understandings of human action.

In a sense, the last 100 years have vindicated the Nietzschean self. It was his use of this self concept in the amalgam of his quasi-metaphysics that has been mostly ignored. The ontological perspective, as Schacht relates it, is gospel in the mainstream of the Western intellectual tradition:

> Human beings, he holds, are fundamentally natural organisms, all of whose faculties are ultimately grounded in physiological structures. The human mind consequently cannot be treated as a thing unto itself, which functions in a completely autonomous manner in relation to the human body in any of its operations. Our perceptual and cognitive abilities, the process of thinking, feeling, evaluating and willing, and the wide range of experiences which constitute our spiritual and social life, all have their basis in our physiological nature.[77]

Schacht, in the tradition of most friendly commentators, goes on to make Nietzsche's position appear clearly as a contemporary anti-realistic non-foundational position. In the name of truth to the sources, however, Nietzsche was never so clearly in any one position. If he would have clearly accepted the social reality of man and his moral concerns, he never would have continued to press for the *Übermensch*, "eternal return," and "will to power." He would have gotten beyond <u>Zarathustra</u>, but there is no indication of this in his final published works.

143

If our experience of life is always in a social setting, then even our concepts of "self" are from within that setting. To abstract from that setting may have its justifications, but the attachment of the "self" to the social world must not be forgotten in the abstraction process. Nietzsche's bizarre reasonings indicating that language was the medium of society, and therefore, not of one's true self demonstrate the quandaries the philosopher can become enmeshed in (and he got this a-linguistic true self from Wagner and Schopenhauer) when abstracting. Nietzsche failed to come to the latter Wittgensteinian perspective that states that all our concepts of the "self" are within language. And Nietzsche failed to see the positive in the fact that language is a social instrument: that the social environment guarantees meaning to our language usage. The new philosopher's limitation to the actual world is the limitation to the world of language and its relation to human activities. This is the bedrock of meaningfulness. Philosophy is not able to step out of this social environment. It cannot transcend the reality of social meanings.

Nietzsche may not have been happy about this limitation for the new philosopher. After all, he was more at home spiritually with artists, and especially musicians. Brandes saw this as early as 1889: "Nietzsche was always heart and soul a musician."[78] Nietzsche himself admitted his addiction to music in a letter to Brandes: "I am afraid I am too much of a musician not to be a romanticist. Without music life to me would be a mistake."[79] And in a final admission of his elevation of the artist over the philosopher he said to Brandes in 1888: "We philosophers are never more grateful than when we are mistaken for artists."[80]

Posterity has labeled Nietzsche a great literary artist. He has had his wish granted. He was also a very creative philosopher. And he was the inspiration to great musical creativity. Zarathustra now lives through the music of Richard Strauss, much as Nietzsche must have felt the man Wagner in his music of deep romantic striving.

NIHILISM AND SUSTAINING ILLUSIONS

Did Nietzsche achieve his destiny, i.e., of providing an alternative to nihilism? An alternative based on the findings of modern science was what he wanted to achieve. Man was another animal species with an evolutionary history. That this fact must be affirmed was clear to Nietzsche. Yet, he stressed a message for individuals--even derided the concept of man in general--, namely, the message of the *Übermensch*. He hoped a few individuals would see the animal reality of man and yet appreciate the cultural image of man as created by man himself. Such individuals would transcend the limits for man as culturally defined. They would seek to understand man's animality and his creativeness. In so doing they would transform all cultural limits, transvaluate the values. Nihilism would thus fall.

But the image of the ideal individual, founded on Nietzsche's understanding of man's animality, was not something to subdue nihilism. "Will to power" as an understanding of man approached a crass reductionism. Recognizing that men seek ends in order to enhance their power is one thing, but claiming that all actions are manifestations of power drives is quite another. Why did Nietzsche propose the later? It seems he should have indicted both the monism and simplification involved in "will to power" given his critiques of other philosophies and science. When Nietzsche tried to employ such a seemingly scientific manner he was at his worst as a philosopher. He seemed to fall into a style similar to his beloved Pre-Socratics. Science remained almost occult in this Nietzschean mode. He was not really familiar with the new scientists of the turn of the century--who were writing of the conventionality of mathematics and the constructions of scientific models (e.g. Henri Ponicare).

Even when one ignores the "will to power" proposals for explanation and zeroes in on his advice for individuals, one does not find nihilism subdued. Hollingdale described Nietzsche's individualist ethics thusly:

> Good means that which is hard but possible, which is attained by "self-overcoming," and the attain-ment of which is attended by the feeling of enhanced power; power over others, power also over oneself.[81]

The interrelation of power over oneself and over others was never made clear. He didn't want to endorse mere power mad conquests of self or others. His love of Greek ideals surely included agreement that hubris, false pride, was a danger for man. The ascetic represented the power mad conquest of self, and he definitely opposed this. He tried to provide a guide to the proper balance in his Zarathustra ideal. Thus he wanted to rule out the ascetic avenue, and the unrestrained egoist. The egoistic self was to be overcome, yet one's self was not to be repressed--but rather expressed with laughter. Nietzsche's ideal: an artistic dancer, Dionysus--a celebrant drunk with the joy of living, yet knowing the human limitations involved in it all. He sought tragic optimism as a replacement for nihilism.

Nietzsche with his ascetic life-style triumphed over his own nihilism. His triumph came in his creations, especially Zarathustra. Like the mythic tales of the great world religions, participation in Zarathustra and in his other works was not designed for the idle spectatorship of reading. Nietzsche described himself and his unresolved quest in his early work on Greek philosophy:

The Philosopher of Tragic Insight. He restrains the uncontrolled drive toward knowledge, but not through a new metaphysic. He does not set up a new faith. He feels the vanishing of the metaphysical ground as a tragic event and cannot find a satisfying compensation for it in the motley spiralling of the sciences . . . One must willingly accept even illusion-- therein lies the tragedy.[82]

He admitted his quest worked for himself and cautioned others that they must find their own way. But for any one who has confronted Western philosophy, the participation in Nietzsche's works will produce a changed searcher after knowledge--especially if one sought other-worldly sanctions for values.

In notes from the 1887-88 period, Nietzsche discussed nihilism as the result of the "Decline of Cosmological Values".[83] This long unpublished note also appears to be very reflective of his own mental development, and the development of Western philosophy as a whole as he saw it. Nihilism is stressed as the result of the realization that long study has been in vain, that is, that what had been thought to be a very meaningful effort is now seen as self-deception and total failure. The wasted effort is realized and the crushing effect is nihilism, or meaninglessness, as it strikes the searcher after meaning.

For Nietzsche, and for man in the West, nihilism represents the loss of a comfortable home in a world which was permeated with meaning. The world was a unity which included man--man had a role and a meaning. This faith in such a world gave meaning to man and the world:

> in consequence of such faith, man rapt in the profound feeling of standing in the network of, and being dependent on, a totality that is infinitely superior to him.[84]

This fulfilling satisfaction was destroyed for Nietzsche: "there is no such universal! At bottom, man has lost faith in his own value when no infinitely valuable totality works through him."[85] The insight this led Nietzsche to was then expressed: "[man] conceived such a totality in order to be able to believe in his own value."[86] With this fresh insight--also the essence of his idea of "will to power" as the will to create such meaning--Nietzsche did not record his own effort at re-establishing a new totality of meaning with the symbol of eternal return, but rather he traced his initial path toward Schopenhauer and other-worldly metaphysics:

> that becoming aims at no goal and that underneath all becoming there is no grand unity . . . one escape remains: to condemn the whole world of

146

becoming as a deception and to invest a world that would lie beyond it, as the true world.[87]

But this path--the path of the ancient Greek philosophers--is found to be no escape in the final realization of the true world as a further self-deception:

> But as soon as man finds out how that world is fabricated, solely out of psychological needs . . . the final form of nihilism emerges: it embraces disbelief in any metaphysical world and thus forbids itself any belief in a true world. . . . one concedes the reality of becoming as the only reality, forbids oneself every kind of clandestine access to afterworlds and false divinities--[88]

Now the psychological power of this deepened nihilism is expressed:

> but one cannot endure this world, which, however, one does not want to deny . . . The categories "purpose", "unity", and "Being", by which we used to invest some value into the world--we withdraw again; and now the world seems valueless.[89]

This represents the state of Nietzsche's ideas after he lost his Schopenhauerian faith: the nihilism of Human which lasted until 1881. Finally a way out was glimpsed with the insight of eternal return--which as a symbol functioned to redirect man to his life. In these late notes, Nietzsche clearly places the cause of nihilism in "faith in reason", i.e., rational metaphysics, and paints the cure in devaluing these methods:

> let us try to see if it is not possible to cancel our faith in them [purpose, unity and Being]! Once we have devalued these three categories, the demonstration that they cannot be applied to the universe is no longer any reason for devaluing the universe.[90]

So Nietzsche's revaluation of values is a devaluing of other-worldly values and a redirection to this world and our lives.

A distinction must be drawn, one that Nietzsche himself seemed unclear about at times, between two meanings of "illusion" that are in Nietzsche's philosophic writings. His original uses of "illusion" were consistent with his quasi-Schopenhauerian thinking. Then he contrasted an illusory world to a metaphysically real world. Our common sense world was then "illusion." But this contrast is not permitted, in the same fashion, once metaphysical worlds are

147

given up. The apparent world is the world in the later Nietzsche. Calling it "apparent", meaning opposed to some more permanent, more real, world he no longer permitted. The first use of "illusion" is thus tied to a metaphysical perspective that Nietzsche disavowed in his later works.

But Nietzsche continued to speak of "illusions" after his Schopenhauerian period, and he therefore must mean something else. And this "something else" is very important in his battle with nihilism. Nietzsche said, in an unpublished note of 1886, that "there is only one world, and this is false, cruel, contradictory, seductive, without meaning. --A world thus constituted is the real world."[91] Man must deal with this real world. Bloom states how the philosopher deals with such nihilism:

> The revelation that philosophy finds nothingness at the end of the quest informs the new philosopher that myth making must be his central concern in order to make a world.[92]

Nietzsche was such a new philosopher, maybe the first such in Western civilization. And his second use of "illusion" was related to myth-making.

Nietzsche never comes out point blank and says we need myths, that is, sustaining illusions, in order to live without being crushed by the meaninglessness resultant from philosophic nihilism. But he saw this and discussed it. His discussion was more open in his early notes and writings. In The Birth, he discussed culture and "illusion": "[The] will finds means to maintain its creatures in life by spreading over existence the blandishments of illusion."[93] He went on to note that "noble natures . . . require special beguilements to make them forget."[94] The philosopher who has been thorough enough and sensitive enough to have completed his intellectual quest and landed in a numbing nihilism surely is "noble", and he needs to forget and get on with living. Then, Nietzsche still hoped for art and metaphysics to co-exist and allow him to live with meaning. In unpublished notes from this time he used "illusions" to make this same point: "one realizes that life requires illusions . . . What life does require is belief in truth, but illusion is sufficient for this."[95] But metaphysical truths were not permitted despite Nietzsche's recognition that "it is the belief in found truth from which the mightiest sources of strength have flowed."[96] The power of permanent truths gave sure meaningfulness, and this was desired by Nietzsche. Art was not able to offer this sustaining power. Only momentary enrapture was possible with art. Once over, nihilism could crowd in again.

At some point Nietzsche made the momentous discovery that it was myth--as illusion and yet with the power of permanent truths--that could sustain man in life. He had hinted that "fable and artifice" might be enough in Wisdom.[97] The

Conclusions

myth, of course, was eternal recurrence as related by <u>Zarathustra</u>. The idea of eternal recurrence came first to Nietzsche, and later the mythical embedding of the idea became his attempt at creating a sustaining illusion. He later grasped Dionysus as a mythic symbol to enforce his mythic stance. (His later uses of Dionysus were not parallel to his early uses in <u>The Birth</u>.)

Nietzsche had glimpsed that the self, the person, was an Apollonian "illusion", or creation, in <u>The Birth</u>.[98] His advance in his later work was to grasp self-consciously this self-creative manifestation, the individual, and create a myth to enhance it. Alderman has described this praise of self-creation in Nietzsche's myth:

> Zarathustra is the teacher who teaches that the source of human creation is not God . . . but only the all-too-human will, the fundamental reality of a free and human mode of being.[99]

And Zarathustra teaches affirmation of life in total. It is a joyous affirmation with no relation to a resignation perspective. Nietzsche put it this way in 1886 as he contrasted Schopenhauer to his mature position: "'Tragedy guides us to the final goal, which is resignation.' Dionysus had told me a very different story; his lesson . . . was anything but defeatist."[100] But Dionysus exists only in a myth! And Zarathustra too!! Is eternal recurrence true? Nietzsche must say no, if a metaphysical claim is meant. Then doesn't the sustaining quality of the myth flounder? I would say so, but Nietzsche hoped for more. He wanted his followers, *Übermenschen*, "to take a hypothesis as hypothesis and yet as regulative."[101] This unpublished note gets at the heart of the problem. Nietzsche believed his *Übermenschen* could sustain themselves with myths they knew were myths, and ultimately as only one perspective from among many. This achievement would truly require a willpower denied to ordinary men. And Nietzsche recognized he had not reached this ideal. Nietzsche accepted this reality and offered a pragmatic, readily available beginning path for nihilistic philosophers in his 1886 Preface to <u>The Birth</u>:

> [to] first . . . teach you how to laugh--if, that is, you really insist on remaining pessimists. And then it may perhaps happen that one fine day you will, with a peal of laughter, send all metaphysical palliatives packing, metaphysics herself leading the great exodus.[102]

Nietzsche continued quoting from Part IV of <u>Zarathustra</u> wherein Zarathustra spoke of the need to dance and laugh. Laughter was referred to as Zarathustra's crown. The philosophical nihilist does not laugh--at least while he is pontificating on philosophic subjects. Laughter is human and life-enhancing. It is a more effective symbol for today than Dionysus or Zarathustra. Nietzsche was the first philosopher who laughed.

INHERITORS OF THE LEGACY

Nietzsche may not have found a way for all to escape from nihilism, but he did a good job of showing that many of the traditional ways of such escape were dead ends. His "heroic and painful way of life"[103] was not in vain. His prescription for philosophers of "an unprecedented knowledge of the preconditions of culture"[104] was adopted by Western science as a whole (although, not by many philosophers to this day). He wanted, as Wagner had, a society's values to be analyzed and understood in their genesis and their function.

If the Zarathustra ideal is pushed aside as not viable for many, where would Nietzsche look for a basis of criticism, a criticism of values and their justifications? He wanted to confront man in his actuality--as an actuality described by science. Science considered man as an animal, as an evolutionary development. Even mind, and its result, cultural life, were evolutionary products. Consciousness, the essence of man in traditional metaphysics, was also an evolutionary product, but merely one product. The necessary conclusion drawn by Nietzsche was revolutionary: through consciousness alone man cannot be known, or understood. An essential corollary followed: if our traditional religious and ethical values were structured on an understanding of man stressing consciousness by itself, they were founded on a false view of man, at least an incomplete view of man. Man overcame his own false self image when he created science which led to the attempt to view man as another animal, i.e., from outside of consciousness. That the complete self was not revealed to consciousness was an early conclusion. It was a holdover of Kant and Schopenhauer, and Nietzsche, in his developmental period, set out his desire to move differently than Schopenhauer, to move non-metaphysically: "to arrive at a thing-in-itself one must start from the natural sciences."[105] In this interpretation, it was a call to the necessity of non-introspective knowledge about man, about individuals. "Will to power" was an attempt to create a workable hypothesis for viewing man in a biological/psychological perspective.

As a hypothesis, "will to power" was not fleshed-out enough to be testable with scientific methods. Freud would attempt an hypothesis along these same lines, and even his has not met the canons of scientific testability. For Nietzsche, science was not the only perspective. He retained a larger awareness won from his study of the ancient Greeks. Man was in a tragic condition for Nietzsche--not because of civilization as Rousseau had, and Freud would, claim--because he was conscious of his fate. The man of the myth of Sisyphus, i.e., one constantly at work on one project after another, but knowing no resolution will be achieved, was man as driven by "will to power." Nietzsche wanted man to be noble, to accept fate's tragic condition, and then to get on with living. Science was a part of that living, but so too were art, music, literature and laughter. Nihilism was too simplistic, so too was "scientism." Nietzsche wanted the individual to confront and affirm the totality of actuality. He may have failed in his own life--the ascetic seemed ingrained in him-- but he hoped to save others.

Nietzsche had not found a worthy disciple to inherit his legacy during his life-time. His correspondence with Brandes was the closest thing to a real intellectual interchange with another person that Nietzsche had in the end of his competent years. It was clear that no ordinary philosopher could take up where he had left off. Nietzsche had murdered traditional philosophy.

Ludwig Wittgenstein was born the year after Brandes offered the first course on Nietzsche in Europe. This Viennese man would become a philosopher (after being an engineer) with a great deal of interest in Freud. Freud never directly confronted his debt to Nietzsche (or Schopenhauer)--he was probably fearful of seeing how much of his libido driven model of man was in Nietzsche's "will to power" and other psychological insights. In addition to the Freudian connection, Wittgentsein read Schopenhauer in his youthful intellectual days. His notebooks display a concern with many of Schopenhauer's ideas. But despite these "close to being Nietzschean influences", Wittgenstein evidently did not study Nietzsche (despite the fact that Nietzsche was very topical during Wittgenstein's formative school years). Yet he developed an attack on traditional philosophy which must be viewed as complementary to Nietzsche's critique.

Although I have been often struck by the similarity of Nietzsche's and Wittgenstein's critiques of philosophic methods, Wittgenstein was not the inheritor of Nietzsche's overall legacy. Both the later Wittgenstein and Nietzsche were philosophic rebels--both had been arch believers earlier in their careers. Both jettisoned metaphysical approaches to philosophy and finally adopted relativistic, anti-absolutist perspectives on philosophy's function. Both attacked the "sacred cows" of philosophy: rationalism and logic. Both needed to redefine "truth" non-metaphysically--and both wanted it tied to actual life. Generally, both demoted philosophy from its esteemed role as "the way" to all truth. Philosophy became merely another cultural tool--one way man dealt with reality.

But they attacked traditional philosophizing for different reasons. Wittgenstein attacked from a method-centered focus. He was a technical philosopher (the engineer as philosopher), or a philosopher's philosopher, and accordingly he attacked the discipline from deep within its way of being. As

151

such, philosophers find his critique of traditional philosophy absolutely telling--or they find it flawed and continue doing philosophy as before. Nietzsche's critique of traditional philosophy was focused from an ethical perspective--Wittgenstein tended to separate ethics from philosophy. It was the rejection of nihilism and its devaluation of human living that Nietzsche wished to combat. He wrote for all, and wanted to use his critique to liberate men for fulfilling lives. Wittgenstein's philosophic activity seemed to alienate himself from fulfilling life--he often recommended to his students that they not pursue philosophy.

Nietzsche's neo-romantic center on life and the inner self was not available to Wittgenstein. The defeat of traditional philosophy was not a victory for Wittgenstein, while it was the great victory for Nietzsche. Life was not to be celebrated by the Wittgensteinian philosopher--or at least, philosophy could not provide a reason for celebration. Wittgenstein could not accept the driving will in man as something to be affirmed. His philosophy ignored the problems of men who do feel such a drive. Such philosophy is of interest only to the philosophical specialists. It fails to inherit the spirit of Nietzsche's quest.

Studying philosophy in a way analogously to searching for religious truths--as Nietzsche did--has been eliminated as a possibility for self-conscious students of philosophy in the Nietzsche/Wittgenstein tradition. Contemporary philosophy cannot grant fulfillment to such quests. Nietzsche, at times, glimpsed just this as he poked fun at the intellectual hubris of Western intellectuals:

> In some remote corner of the universe . . . there was once a star upon which clever animals invented cognition. It was the haughtiest, most mendacious moment in the history of the world, but yet only a moment . . . There were eternities during which this intellect did not exist and when it has once more passed away there will be nothing to show that it existed. For this intellect is not concerned with any further mission transcending the sphere of human life. No, it is purely human.[106]

Philosophy is a human quest, an activity of persons concerned with the realities they confront. Accordingly, one should not expect ultimate values and extra-human truths to result from philosophical quests. Philosophy as an instrument in human problem-solving must put away all religious and metaphysical pretensions. The mature Nietzsche did not pine away because of his new perspective on the limited range of philosophical activity, and in fact, saw the loss of philosophy's claim to dominance as a great liberation. It allowed, demanded a <u>yes</u> to this world, this life. Philosophy produced truths no different from any other human endeavors. A commentator described this viewpoint of Nietzsche:

Conclusions

He says yes to what truth really is--a human interpretation, a perspective, a provisionally acceptable treasure from the depths of man's passions, reason, and experience.[107]

Philosophy is merely a perspective from within man's activities in a pluralistic cultural environment.

Nietzsche, unlike so many twentieth century prophets, whether disguised as philosophers or religious men, accepted the realities of a human world without longing for the old order. In fact, he endeavored to grasp this "barren" reality and reinvest it with significance--or, rather, he showed how one had to do this for oneself. No time was allowed for fruitless searching after a mystical level of reality. No encouragement was given to wallowing in the Existential *angst*. Life was to be "gotten on with." No transcendence was allowed for in Nietzsche's ideal, yet the cold, rational life of science was not his ideal either. Ernest Becker, probably the thinker closest to being an inheritor of Nietzsche's total legacy, said that human life should be viewed as a heroic quest.[108]

Man does feel life. He feels the nonrational forces. He is part of these forces and an object of these forces. Nietzsche's revelation on the innate value of life is stated by Higgins: "the vibrant movement of life, . . . that participation in this movement is fundamentally gratifying in itself."[109] The conscious person is the interchange of life and cultural forces. And Nietzsche wanted man to celebrate this--Dionysus the celebrant is chosen over Jesus the crucified. The choice of the heroic quest is made despite the Existential realities:

> What does it mean to be a self-conscious animal? . . . This is the terror: to have emerged from nothing, to have a name, consciousness of self, deep inner feelings, an excruciating inner yearning for life and self-expression--and with all this yet to die.[110]

Here Becker echoes Nietzsche, and even earlier in The Denial of Death, he expressed a "will to power"-like image of life: "the sense of power and activity have become conscious . . . man's natural yearning for organismic activity, the pleasure of incorporation and expansion."[111] Despite the void that hangs over every human life, the individual is not "healthy" if he is frozen in inaction by this awareness. Rather as John Dewey has preached, stated by Bernstein:

> The primary situations of life are those where there is something to be done, where we manipulate the world in order to achieve desired ends, where we actively transform the situations within which we find ourselves.[112]

153

Becker picked up this same theme and lauded action, not contemplation or meditation:

> The defeat of despair is not mainly an intellectual problem for an active organism, but a problem of self-stimulation via movement. Beyond a given point a man is not helped by more "knowing", but only by living and doing in a partly self-forgetful way. As Goethe put it, we must plunge into experience and then reflect on the meaning of it. All reflection and no plunging drives us mad; all plunging and no reflection, and we are brutes.[113]

Becker here pointed to Goethe, and Kaufmann has recently asserted Nietzsche's great debt to Goethe also:

> To enjoy and explore the passions without becoming their slave, to employ them creatively instead of either being dominated by them or trying to resist them, was the essence of Goethe's autonomy.[114]

William Barrett has also commented on their similarity:

> Faust and Zarathustra are in fact brothers among books. Both attempt to elaborate in symbols the process by which the superior individual--whole, intact, and healthy--is to be formed.[115]

For Nietzsche, as well as Goethe, the challenge of living was to be faced as an artist, as Dionysus, not in resignation as a Christian martyr. While the religious disciple wants "rest, relaxation, peace, calm",[116] the artistic ego glories in change and loves "impressing one's soul on something foreign."[117] The "living want victory, opponents overcome, the overflow of the feeling of power across wider domains than hitherto."[118] These are the relevant insights of the symbol of "will to power". The artist was always Nietzsche's love. It was the artist in himself that threw off the philologist's mask. Finally, the philosopher's role failed also: "in the main, I agree more with the artists than with any philosopher hitherto: they have not lost the scent of life."[119] He saw that art, great art, excites those who participate in it--it brings intoxication similar to that of the creator[120]--and nowhere was this greater in his time than in the music of Wagner. He also said that intoxication results in an exalted feeling of power.[121] This is so very true today with the great medium of the motion picture. Just remember how people say they felt after Star Wars, etc. Nietzsche did not mean to delimit the denotation of "artist" to painters, sculptors and musicians; he put it this way: "he must be above all an <u>artist</u>. And he <u>is</u> one: metaphysics, religion . . . -- all of them only products of his will to art."[122] The "will to power" was manifested in man as "will to create." And the creator was enraptured while his actions serviced this will. The symbol of Dionysus clearly applied: intoxicated activity of great joy is pursued despite the acknowledgement of death as the great limit. As Paul Valadier has said: "This is the decisive difference between Dionysus and Jesus . . . Dionysus confronts death, certain of the overfullness of life and his recreative power."[123] Nietzsche's love of music was also encapsulated in the Dionysus symbol, as Higgins has said:

> The image of Dionysus . . . is an emblem of the vitality of life as we experience it in music . . . The present moment is valued not because it serves as a means to an ultimate assured gratification, but because it is an immediate source of joy in itself.[124]

Now we must pause--step back from the raging affirmation of life which was the intention of the mature Nietzsche. A circumspection about effects on the interaction of men who act as if they were *Übermensch* is called for--a useful step back from the Nietzschean position of individualistic hubris. Unlike Dostoevski's clear sense of the unlimited potential for moral nightmares once the foundation of traditional morality was destroyed, Nietzsche seemed elevated into a world of artists and intellectuals. A nice world where revolutionaries and terrorists were not real options. Nietzsche's world vision was his own: the solitary life of the intellectual artist--the first "drop out". Safeguards are needed only against suicide. Social realities are vague, of no concern. Yet writing itself is social, and makes sense only as a socially directed product. Nietzsche seemed to foresee the evils of modern industrial civilization, socialism and total war, but he didn't prescribe for these. He merely accepted life as tragic. In this respect he was a romantic, in the bad sense of the term, and not a modern thinker. He had not taken in the Marxian insight: to change the world, not merely to understand the world. Here Guyau's vision exceeded Nietzsche's (they were contemporaries-- Nietzsche even read Guyau's works, though with disapproval):

> Science does not reveal to us a universe spontaneously laboring for the realization of what we call goodness: goodness is to be realized, if at all, only by our bending the world to our purposes, by enslaving the gods that we once adored, by replacing the reign of God by the reign of man.[125]

Nietzsche's thoughts represent individualism allowed to get out of control. He critiqued and constructed without regard to the social effects of any of his ideas. The reality of the social embeddedness of all ideas was overlooked in this crucial area. The social needs of man were the clear victim. Man is not merely an animal with power drives nor only a creative individual with self-created projects. Man lives in society and is a reality only as a person in a particular social/cultural environment. Power is not everything--cultural achievements have eliminated this sort of society of brutes. Most men must adapt to their social environment and establish a basic contentment--or face psychological problems as outlined by one of Nietzsche's inheritors, Sigmund Freud.

As others have observed, a creation becomes imperialistic towards its creator. Nietzsche created the "will to power" of the *Übermensch* and then this symbol drew in his own thoughts to elaborate and construct a philosophy for such a creation. Man above morality. Man above social needs and limitations. A transcendent being--as Nietzsche himself said, now that God is dead, the *Übermensch* must live. An exaggeration. A mythic construction. A new source for belief. Yet Nietzsche recognized that he could not offer a justification like that of the world religions. For he had destroyed the metaphysical realm.

How do you begin once the old ground of justification is gone? Self-knowledge, but more empirical than Platonic self-knowledge. The tool of such knowledge? The scientific method. All avenues, not merely physiology, but also ethology, anthropology, psychology and even history and literature. As such, the development of the modern human studies has been the continuation of Nietzsche's project.

Philosophy's role in the project of human self-understanding will be greatly limited in comparison to that envisioned by old-time philosophers. Philosophy in the Wittgensteinian tradition will function as an instrument to clarify human thinking. The open community of philosophers functions much like the community of scientists--it is a forum and proving ground for ideas. The historical record of philosophical development will also function as a brake on new metaphysical urges. If there is any Wittgensteinian rule to guide philosophers who start to venture off toward metaphysical lands, it is surely this statement of Geofrey Vesey's: "Once we allow ourselves to be weaned away just a little from 'our ordinary reckonings' it difficult to draw the line."[126] Our ordinary world is seen by philosophers and everybody else. It is the bedrock of all special enclaves of science, or any other discipline. This real world is where all persons live together. This world with no special seers, and no other realm to be seen, is the world of man living in societies and sharing the earth. These persons share their cultures, their methods of prospering and their ways of coping with the human situation. Sadly, the world has always included societies, or parts thereof, that have acted as though sharing was secondary to dominating. The use of force, or power, in human relationships is a key to understanding in the study of man, but not in the way Nietzsche seemed to mean it most often. In an interdependent world, the exercise of force against humans is the greatest concern possible. Justification is not available from afar (God). Man must confront his use of force and its effects, and take responsibility for all such acts. And, the interactions of men in society display many different manifestations of force through physical, psychological and economic means. It is these power realities that should be the center of a contemporary philosophy with social, moral concerns.

NOTES

1. Thiele, <u>Friedrich Nietzsche</u>, p. 216.
2. Quoted in O'Brien, <u>Son of the Morning</u>, p. 69.
3. <u>Wagner On Music and Drama</u>, p. 74.
4. <u>Wagner</u>, p. 60.
5. <u>The Birth</u>, Fadiman, p. 278.
6. <u>The Birth</u>, Fadiman, p. 180.
7. <u>The Birth</u>, Fadiman, p. 309.
8. <u>Early Greek Philosophy</u>, p. 32.
9. <u>Wagner</u>, p. 138.
10. <u>Gay Science</u>, #278, p. 225.
11. <u>Wagner</u>, p. 72.
12. <u>Will to Power</u>, #1052, p. 543.
13. <u>Wagner</u>, p. 65.
14. <u>Wagner</u>, p. 65.
15. <u>Wagner</u>, pp. 73-4.
16. <u>Wagner</u>, p. 72.
17. <u>Gay Science</u>, #299, p. 240.
18. Jaeger, <u>Paideia</u>, vol. 1, p. 115.
19. <u>Wagner</u>, p. 146.
20. <u>Wagner</u>, p. 146.
21. <u>Wagner</u>, p. 88.
22. <u>Gay Science</u>, #99, p. 154.
23. <u>Untimely</u>, p. 95.
24. Thiele, <u>Friedrich Nietzsche</u>, p. 155.
25. <u>Anti-Christ</u>, Hollingdale, p. 133.
26. Jaeger, <u>Paideia</u>, vol. 1, p. 12.
27. <u>Nietzsche-Wagner</u>, p. 217.
28. <u>Wagner</u>, p. 291.
29. <u>Wagner</u>, p. 291.

30. Quoted in Thiele, <u>Friedrich Nietzsche</u>, p. 204.
31. Thiele, <u>Friedrich Nietzsche</u>, p. 156.
32. <u>Wagner</u>, p. 72.
33. <u>Wagner</u>, p. 74.
34. <u>Gay Science</u>, #99, p. 155.
35. <u>Wagner</u>, p. 96.
36. Feuerbach, <u>The Essence of Christianity</u>, p. 93.
37. Feuerbach, <u>The Essence</u>, p. 87.
38. Feuerbach, <u>The Essence</u>, p. 61.
39. Feuerbach, <u>The Essence</u>, p. 63.
40. Schopenhauer, <u>The World as Will and Representation</u>, vol. 1, p. 324.
41. Schopenhauer, <u>The World</u>, vol. 1, pp. 283-4.
42. <u>The Birth</u>, Golffing, p. 287.
43. <u>The Will to Power</u>, #585, p. 317.
44. <u>Gay Science</u>, #309, pp. 246-7.
45. <u>Philosophy and Truth</u>, p. 63.
46. <u>Philosophy and Truth</u>, p. 65.
47. Quoted in Hollingdale, <u>Nietzsche: The Man and His Philosophy</u>, p. 151.
48. Quoted in Heller, <u>The Importance of Nietzsche</u>, p. 15.
49. Quoted in Heller, <u>The Importance of Nietzsche</u>, p. 16.
50. Alderman, <u>Nietzsche's Gift</u>, p. 104.
51. Quoted in Heller, <u>The Importance of Nietzsche</u>, p. 143.
52. Heller, <u>The Importance of Nietzsche</u>, p. 63.
53. Santayana, <u>The German Mind</u>, p. 136.
54. <u>The Birth</u>, Golffing, p. 4.
55. <u>The Birth</u>, Golffing, p. 93.
56. Santayana, <u>Three Philosophical Poets</u>, p. 175.
57. Scharfstein, <u>The Philosophers</u>, p. 363.
58. Wittgenstein, <u>Philosophical Investigations</u>, #133, p.   51e.
59. Pitkin, <u>Wittgenstein and Justice</u>, pp. 294-5.
60. Pitkin, <u>Wittgenstein and Justice</u>, p. 138.
61. Wittgenstein, <u>Philosophical Investigations</u>, p. 226e.
62. <u>The Birth</u>, Golffing, p. 291. (In a letter of 1887, Nietzsche burst out: "And its all Plato's fault!"[<u>Selected Letters</u>, p. 258.])
63. Schopenhauer, <u>The World</u>, vol. 2, p. 164.
64. <u>Daybreak</u>, p. 3.
65. Alderman, <u>Nietzsche's Gift</u>, p. 54.
66. Ewing, <u>A Short</u>, p. 60.
67. <u>The Works of Schopenhauer</u>, p. 11.
68. <u>The Works of Schopenhauer</u>, p. 26.

69. The Works of Schopenhauer, pp. 30-31.
70. The Works of Schopenhauer, p. 34.
71. The Works of Schopenhauer, p. 37.
72. The Works of Schopenhauer, p. 284.
73. The Works of Schopenhauer, p. 284.
74. The Works of Schopenhauer, p. 191.
75. Schacht, Nietzsche, p. 137.
76. Schacht, Nietzsche, p. 138.
77. Schacht, Nietzsche, p. 33.
78. Brandes, Friedrich Nietzsche, p. 4.
79. Quoted in Brandes, Friedrich Nietzsche, pp. 76-7.
80. Quoted in Brandes, Friedrich Nietzsche, p. 84.
81. Hollingdale, Nietzsche, p. 90.
82. Philosophy in the Tragic Age, p. 16.
83. Quoted in Heidegger, Nietzsche, vol. 4, p. 25.
84. Quoted in Heidegger, Nietzsche, vol. 4, p. 25.
85. Quoted in Heidegger, Nietzsche, vol. 4, p. 25.
86. Quoted in Heidegger, Nietzsche, vol. 4, p. 25.
87. Quoted in Heidegger, Nietzsche, vol. 4, p. 25.
88. Quoted in Heidegger, Nietzsche, vol. 4, p. 25.
89. Quoted in Heidegger, Nietzsche, vol. 4, pp. 25-6.
90. Quoted in Heidegger, Nietzsche, vol. 4, p. 47.
91. Will to Power, #853, p. 451.
92. Bloom, The Closing of the American Mind, p. 208.
93. The Birth, Golffing, p. 108.
94. The Birth, Golffing, p. 109.
95. Philosophy and Truth, pp. 16-7.
96. Human, Faber, #11, p. 19.
97. Gay Science, #290, p. 224.
98. The Birth, Fadiman, p. 339.
99. Alderman, Nietzsche's Gift, p. 172.
100. The Birth, Golffing, p. 12.
101. Quoted in Morgan, What Nietzsche Means, p. 189.
102. The Birth, Golffing, p. 15.
103. Hollingdale, Nietzsche, p. 172.
104. Hollingdale, Nietzsche, p. 172.
105. Philosophy and Truth, p. 151.
106. Early Greek Philosophy, p. 173.
107. Wilcox, Truth and Value, p. 170.
108. Becker, The Denial of Death, p. 283.

109. Higgins, Nietzsche's Zarathustra, p. 200.
110. Becker, The Denial of Death, p. 87.
111. Becker, The Denial of Death, p. 3.
112. Quoted in Bernstein, Praxis and Action, p. 207.
113. Becker, The Denial of Death, p. 199.
114. Kaufmann, Discovering the Mind, vol. 1, p. 22.
115. Barrett, Irrational Man, p. 189.
116. Will to Power, #703, p. 374.
117. Will to Power, #677, p. 359.
118. Will to Power, #703, p. 374.
119. Will to Power, #820, p. 434.
120. Will to Power, #821, p. 434.
121. Will to Power, #800, p. 420.
122. Will to Power, #800, pp. 451-2.
123. Valadier, "Dionysus versus the Crucified," The New Nietzsche, p. 250.
124. Higgins, Nietzsche's Zarathustra, pp. 190-1.
125. Guyau, The Non-Religion of the Future, p. 387.
126. Vesey, Personal Identity, p. 102.

EPILOGUE: THE INTELLECTUAL PENALTY

Ray Monk's recent biography of Wittgenstein was subtitled The Duty of Genius. What is readily apparent in his portrayl of Wittgenstein is the suffering that the duty wrought for the philosopher. Nietzsche's life reveals a similar, harsher suffering garnered from his philosophic thinking. In Nietzsche's case, much of his physical pain may have been directly related to the ups and downs of intellectual pursuits, and his personal relationships connected therewith. J. O. Wisdom has claimed that philosophers generally have difficulties with personal relationships, and often do not have close friends or satisfying relations of a sexual nature.[1] Nietzsche and Wittgenstein truly fit this hypothesis. While Wittgenstein eventually refused to discuss his personal suffering in philosophic ways, Nietzsche confronted the problem of suffering in many ways in his works. Some have said that his whole philosophic effort was a battle against suffering.[2]

Nietzsche, like most philosophers, or even most intellectuals, suffered from being different than the ordinary mensch. As a child, he was a boy among a family unit of women (after the death of his father and little brother). He was a pastor's son, always a mark of difference. He went away to school and saw his childhood friends only on holidays. He excelled at reading the classics of Greece and Rome in their original languages--something most never achieved. Eventually, he developed unique positions on most current events in Europe. And finally, he lived alone physically and geographically when he could.

These surface differences were not the crucial elements in the budding intellectual. It was the perception of difference that led to a constitutional loneliness. The perception arose early in the comparison of his interests with those of his boyhood friends when on holiday from Pforta. The confirmation of the entrenched differentness came at the University in Bonn when Nietzsche tried unsuccessfully to be one of the fraternity fellas. This failure to change his character propelled him into scholarship and intellectual reasoning which generated ideas different from the ordinary. Nietzsche became anti-Christian, anti-modern culture, anti-metaphysical, anti-socialist, anti-scientist and finally, anti-Wagner. He developed a unique interpretation of ancient Greek culture and

161

slowly lost touch with all of his college and Wagnerian acquaintances. Nietzsche commented on his condition of differentness in a letter to his sister on July 8, 1886:

> Where are those old friends of mine. . . . No word, no glance now reaches me. I am silent, for no one understands my words. . . . they have never understood me! . . . It is terrible to be doomed to silence when I have so much to say. . . . This is the most appalling solitude, to be different. . . . Perfect friendship is possible only between equals.[3]

Nietzsche's sister was far from his intellectual equal, as she would prove in her mishandling of his literary estate. Nietzsche continued:

> Between equals: the words are intoxicating. What confidence, what hope, what rendolence of happiness they promise to one who lives always alone of necessity, to a man who is different, who has never met one of his kind. . . . A profound man must have friends, unless he has a God. But I have neither a God nor a single friend![4]

Although events later in 1886 lifted Nietzsche's hopes, again in 1887 he wrote of his absence of an equal to Overbeck:

> If I exclude R. Wagner, so far no one has approached me with a thousandth the passion and suffering that I might come to an "understanding" with him; I was in this way already alone as a child. I am still so today, in my 44th year of life.[5]

No wonder Nietzsche was so ambivalent in his break up with Wagner, and he so appreciated Stendhal who described a type who "knows he he is not like most men; and the knowledge of this difference hurts."[6]

The mature Nietzsche

> had become, in a clearly definable way, "abnormal": he was without some of the characteristics of social man which constitute "normality".[7]

Hollingdale's conclusion is an acceptable perspective, but only one perspective. "What is normal for the intellectual?" should be the focus of another perspective that does not argue with the assertion that all intellectuals are not normal mensch. In fact, it is the response of the intellectual to his abnormality that constitutes his uniqueness, and our interest in his life.

If Freudian psychology has taught us anything, it is that basic psychic needs will be fulfilled in some manner even if the normal channels of satisfaction are blocked. It is of the nature of the intellectual that many of his normal social outlets, or channels, are blocked. This is the essence of the intellectual penalty: to have strong drives for satisfaction, yet to have normal fulfillment mechanisms unavailable. Philosophers represent one way of working out the intellectual penalty. Great philosophers manifest great drives that issue in tremendous compensating output. Philosophers are therefore clearly human, although their life styles appear as inhuman to many.

Because of his difference the intellectual usually finds the ordinary societal avenues of satisfaction unappealing or unavailable. In Nietzsche's case, the Christianity and middle class morality of his environmnet did not provide any solace. But his cultural environment did provide the basic bounds to his search for truth. For the philosopher, the search for truth is the focal point in his search for meaning which has been lifted out of the social context to the intellectual context. Nietzsche's unique role in his intellectual quest was that of the discoverer of the truth of the relativity of truth. Already in <u>Human</u>, he disclosed that the modern Western drive for truth had been an historical development out of the aftermath of Reformation times:

> Incidently, the methodical search for truth itself results from the times when convictions were feuding among themselves. If the individual had not cared about <u>his</u> "truth", that is, about his being right in the end, no method of inquiry would exist at all.[8]

Out of those times, arose modern science, modern philosophy, and modern religious movements all emphasizing the experience of the individual as the basis of truth. Yet, in order to decrease the chaos of self-assertion as the base of truth, scientists and philosophers sought methods to justify their truths. The mainstream Christians justified their faith in history. The new sciences of philology and history, however, destroyed the justification of historic Christianity. By Nietzsche's era, most European intellectuals were looking for a new basis for Christianity and its values, and philosophy and science seemed the only options available. Among a wider spectrum of Europeans, the Classical past and the Romantic appropriation of that past were also available for justifying one's view of the proper values outside of Christianity.

163

Nietzsche: A Philosophical Biography

Nietzsche entered upon this scence as a philologist with strong interests in philosophy, science and romanticism. He also entered alone, closed off from society and without intellectual friends. What did he write about? He wrote about his reasons for not being like everybody else by explaining:

> a) that the Greeks were irrational and not pre-Christian moralists,
>
> b) that Christianity was without solid foundation,
>
> c) that Christian morality was founded on *ressentiment*,
>
> d) that science itself was a tool of the irrational, and
>
> e) that these new prespectives led to nihilism, or the destruction of current values.

But one could not live with such nihilism--with total unfulfillment in an individual life. Nietzsche, the critic of modernity, was merely trying to justify his stance apart from the crowd. If he could persuade others that God was dead, and what that meant, then others would join his quest--he would, therefore, no longer be alone. Others would come to recognize the importance, meaning, of his quest. So despite all Nietzsche's disclaimers, about not seeking disciples, he sought fellow followers at all times--only such could justify his life and the meaning of his suffering for the truth.

What was Nietzsche's solution in the intellectual context? Look to his frustrations for they will reveal the needs fulfilled in his intellectual creations. Nietzsche was apart and alone, without justified meaning for his suffering, and without love. He did not have a metaphysical truth available such that he could play the crucified one, confident in a transcendent justification. He was very clear about this in his final years. He contrasted himself with the "Crucified", as the opposite. He was what he called the "Dionysian". Instead of apart and alone, one merged in participation with the irrational whole that is life. The *Übermensch* was to transcend his loneliness, to achieve participation in life by accepting it totally (eternal recurrence), just as it was, suffering and all. Nietzsche sought to overcome his suffering through the creation of the man who could overcome suffering, namely, the "overman" (*Übermensch*). Only participation in life could bring fulfillment--Nietzsche saw this clearly on the intellectual level despite his complete failure to achieve such on the social level. Only in participation in life was "will to power" revealed to the actor. The passionate man of deeds, not the Socratic questioner, was the man who was fulfilled. Nietzsche's passions generated philosophy, critiques of culture, and Zarathustra. Zarathustra was the friend Nietzsche never had. He loved him, over-estimated his powers as any lover would: Zarathustra's myths were to found Nietzsche's perspective. His perspective was human, tragic, yet joyful, and far from abnormal.

NOTES

1. Wisdom, <u>Philosophy and Its Place in Our Culture</u>, p.   256.
2. Thiele, <u>Nietzsche and the Politics of the Soul</u>, p.   92.
3. O'Brien, <u>Son of the Morning</u>, p. 265.
4. O'Brien, <u>Son of the Morning</u>, p. 265.
5. Thiele, <u>Nietzsche and the Politics of the Soul</u>, p.   175.
6. Harper, <u>Seventh Solitude</u>, p. 5.
7. <u>Human</u>, Faber, #634, p. 264.

APPENDIX

TIMELINE AND HISTORICAL BIBLIOGRAPHY

1844 *Born in Saxony*
1848   Revolution in German states
1849   Father dies from brain damage
                little brother dies
1850   Begins schooling
1852 *Enters gymnasium*
1854   writes poetry and plays piano
1858-59
                Preparatory School Pforta
1859-60
                Preparatory School Pforta
1860-61
                Preparatory School Pforta
                Loves long walks home on breaks
1861-62
                Preparatory School Pforta
                Writing: "Fate and History,"
                        "Free Will and Fate"
                Reads Hölderlin and commends him
                        to friend
                Praises Napoleon III
                Plays Wagner transcriptions for piano
1862-63

      Preparatory School Pforta
      Analyzes "Greatness of Spirit"
      Severe illness in Spring
1863-64
  Preparatory School Pforta
      "Conflict" seen as cultural force
      Theognis as subject of senior essay
1864
OCT   *University Student at Bonn*
      Friendship with Deussen
      Philology under Ritschl
      Reading: Fichte, Hegel, Schelling,
          Feuerbach & "new" materialists
      Tries to be "one of the boys"
          Joins fraternity, duels, etc.
1865
JAN   Depressed with new life & Bonn
          Heros: Bach, Beethoven, Byron
      Reading: Strauss's <u>Life of Jesus</u>(1835)
      Style's himself a disciple of truth
OCT   *University Student at Leipzig*
      Philology under Ritschl
      Idealism renewed
      Reading: Discovers Schopenhauer
1866
      Heros: Schopenhauer, Schumann
      Friendship with Rohde
      States historical Christianity not
          believable
      Publishing: Ritschl recommends
          Theognis paper for publication
      Laments publishing efforts keep him from
          Schopenhauer
SUMMER
      To reanimate Greek spirit of
          Goethe with Rohde
      Hears Liszt's music
      Reading: Hartmann, Dühring,
          Lange, Bahnsen
OCT *University Student at Leipzig*

Philology: Ritschl gets papers of
    Nietzsche published

1867
APR   Begins to polish writing skills
    Models: Lichtenberg, Lessing,
        Schopenhauer
Affirms individualism

Military Service
    Injured severely
    Long recuperation
    Reading: Kuno Fischer, Lange
    Writing: "Kant & Teleology"
        Philosophers' overlook body
        Body = collection
        No intelligence in Nature
        Purpose = forms in Nature

OCT   *University Student at Leipzig*
    Philology under Ritschl

1868
OCT   *University Student at Leipzig*
    Philology under Ritschl
    Hears Wagner's overtures to <u>Tristan</u>
        and <u>Meistersinger</u>
NOV   Meets Wagner
Nietzsche praises "unconscious action"
    lauds self-confidence in Wagner &
    Schopenhauer

1869
APR   Ritschl arranges Basel appointment
    for Nietzsche in Philology
Avows desire to transmit Schopenhauerian
    philosophy to philology

Instructor at Basel
    Lecture on Homer
MAY   Triebschen with the Wagners
OCT   Friendship with Burckhardt
DEC   Christmas with Wagners

1870
    Lectures on "The Greek Music Drama"
    & "Socrates & Tragedy"

APR   *Professor at Basel*
Writing: "The Dionysian Worldview"
SEP   *Volunteer Hospital Corpsman*
Franco-Prussian War
    At front in West
    Contracts illness
  Recuperation
Refuses to talk of war
Idea of Utopian Academy
Writing: notes on Schopenhauer
DEC   "Origin of the Tragic Idea"
    notes on slavery's importance
      to culture
1871
JAN
  Professor at Basel
Lectures on Plato
Writing: begins draft of <u>The Birth</u>
    notes on "Olympian men"
FEB   Illness
MAR   At Lugano
<u>The Birth</u> immersion
Tells Rohde he will abandon
    philology for philosophy
JUN   <u>The Birth</u> completed
    titled "Greek Cheerfulness"
    can't find publisher
SUMMER
    Overbeck moves into Nietzsche's
      apartment building
News that Louvre burned in Parisian
    revolution jars Nietzsche &
    Burckhardt
OCT   *Professor at Basel*
Alters <u>The Birth</u> so Wagner's publisher
    will publish it
DEC   <u>The Birth</u> published
Attends muscial festival with
    Wagner
1872

	Depression from lack of acclaim
	for <u>The Birth</u>
	Lectures on education
APR	Nietzsche offers services to
	Wagner full-time, Wagner
	declines
	Wagners move from Triebschen
	Writing: notes on Pre-Socratics
	Reading: Zöllner
MAY	At Bayreuth for Wagner foundation
	stone ceremonies
	"Blow away" on hearing Beethoven's
	<u>Ninth Symphony</u>
	Meets Frau von Meysenbug
SUMMER	Lectures on Pre-Socratics
	Anti-<u>Birth</u> pamphlet:
	"Philology of the Future"
	jars Nietzsche
	At Munich to hear <u>Tristan</u>
	Refused to go to Bayreuth
	In mountains: writes "The
	Philosopher"
OCT	*Professor at Basel*
	Wagner finishes Ring Cycle
	Wagner visits Nietzsche
	Nietzsche puts aside Pre-
	Socratic studies
	Writing: "On the Pathos of Truth"
	Romundt moves into Nietzsche's building
DEC	Nietzsche refuses Wagner's Christmas
	invitation
1873	
	Reading: Boscovitch on basic elements
	of natural world as non-material atoms
	Writing: "Philosophy in the Tragic Age
	of the Greeks"
	"Philosopher as Cultural
	Physician"
APR	At Bayreuth: movement floundering
	Nietzsche resolves to help with

	writing
	Shelves "Tragic Age"
	Begins <u>Untimely Meditations</u>
MAY	Illness
JUN	<u>UM</u> I completed on Strauss
	Lectures on Pre-Socratics
	Meets Paul Ree
	Writing: "Truth and Lying in an
	Extra Moral Sense"
	<u>UM</u> I published
	A great success with Wagnerites
	plans long series of <u>UM</u>s
SEP	<u>UM</u> II completed on history
OCT	*Professor at Basel*
	Lectures on Plato
	At Bayreuth: Nietzsche's "Summons"
	to Wagnerite cause rejected
	Writing: "Philosophy in Hard Times"
	Reading: A. Spir, <u>Thinking and Actuality</u>
DEC	Writing: "Five Prefaces to Five Unwritten
	Works"
1874	
JAN	Writing: notes critical of Wagner
FEB	<u>UM</u> II published, popular failure
	Depression
	Nietzsche cures self with study
	of Schopenhauer
	<u>UM</u> III completed on Schopenhauer
	Reading: Montaigne, Emerson
	Sister visits Nietzsche
	Hears Brahms at concert
SUMMER	
	At Bayreuth, gives Wagner
	score of Brahms in "jest"
OCT	*Professor at Basel*
	<u>UM</u> III published
	<u>UM</u> IV on philology abandoned
1875	
	Depression
	News of Wagner's <u>Parsifal</u> ideas

	Romundt leaves for priesthood
MAR	Illness, leave of absence
	Sister comes to stay with Nietzsche
At Lucerne & Berne	
	Meditation on father's early death
	Analyzes philosophical positions
	affirms Schopenhauerism
	Reading: Dühring
SUMMER	
	Bayreuth Music Festival rehersals
	Writing: notes on Wagner
	notes on "destroyers" for
	Truth
OCT	*Professor at Basel*
	Perter Gast attends Nietzsche's lectures
	Reading: Stewart on conservation of
	energy
	Buddhist "Sutta Nipata"
NOV	Illness, leave from teaching
	Writing: "The Struggle Between
	Wisdom and Science"

1876

	Illness
MAR	At Lake Geneva
	Reading: Meysenbug's memoirs
	Nietzsche realizes his health
	tied to thoughts & emotions
	UM IV completed on Wagner, from notes
	of Summer '75
SUMMER	
	First Bayreuth Music Festival
	Nietzsche leaves it
	Depression
	Vows to give up music
OCT	*Professor at Basel*
	Depression, Illness
	Leave from teaching
NOV	*At Sorrento, Italy*
	Writing: draft of "Free Spirits"
	to be UM V

	Visits with Wagner in Sorrento (last meeting with Wagner)
	Staying with Ree & Frau Meysenbug
	Reading: French moralists, Burckhardt, Greek histories
	News of Ritschl's death
1877	
	Writing: notes for <u>Human</u>
APR	Ree leaves, but Nietzsche stays on
	Shows <u>Human</u> notes to Meysenbug
SUMMER	At mountains
	Resolves to leave University permanently
	Admits he no longer abides by Schopenhauer's philosophy, espeically his metaphysics
OCT	*Professor at Basel*
	Sister joins him as companion
DEC	<u>Human</u> draft complete: aphoristic style chosen
1878	
JAN	Receives <u>Parsifal</u> from Wagner
MAR	Sends <u>Human</u> to Wagner
MAY	<u>Human</u> published
	No public response
SUMMER	Sister departs
AUG	Wagner's newspaper blasts Nietzsche for <u>Human</u> positions
OCT	*Professor at Basel*
	Writing: reworks Sorrento notes into <u>Mixed Maxims</u>
NOV	Extreme illness
	Sister rejoins Nietzsche
1879	
	Nietzsche requests resignation from University
MAR	*Sils Maria on leave of absence*
	Drafts <u>Wanderer</u>
	Reading: Luther, Janssen, Gogol, Twain, Poe
JUN	Resignation accepted, pension

	granted
SEP	*Naumberg with family*
	<u>Wanderer</u> completed
	Severe illness
	writes of illness
	Ree visits
DEC	Nietzsche's low ebb
1880	
APR	*Venice with Gast*
	Convalescent
	Drafts <u>The Dawn</u>
SUMMER	Spa in Germany
SEP	*Naumberg with family*
OCT	*Basel visit*
NOV	*Lake Maggiore*
DEC	*Genoa, Italy*
1881	
JAN	<u>The Dawn</u> completed
APR	*Venice with Gast*
	Recoaro with Gast
SUMMER	*Sils Maria in solitude*
	Reading: Current Natural Science
	Discovers Spinoza's philosophy
	"Eternal recurrence" idea
	<u>The Dawn</u> published
SEP	*Genoa, Italy*
	No response to <u>The Dawn</u>
	Illness & depression
NOV	Nietzsche perks up
	Writing: notes for <u>Wisdom</u>
	Hears Bizet's <u>Carmen</u>
	(return to music)
	Reading: Mayer's <u>Mechanics of Heat</u>
1882	
JAN	Joyful period
	Writing: 4th book of <u>Wisdom</u>
APR	*To Sicily, where Wagner was*
	Illness on journey, did not meet
	Wagner

MAY   *To Rome at request of Meysenbug*
              Ree there, and meets Lou Salome
SUMMER   Idyllic travels with Lou and
                  without: Triebschen, Berlin,
                  Basel, Leipzig
              Nietzsche does not attend Bayreuth
                  Festival, despite Lou's request
              Ree & Lou depart at end of summer
              Meets Heinrich von Stein
OCT   *Rapollo, Italy*
              Solitude
              Thoughts of suicide, depression
1883
JAN   Drafts Zarathustra Part I
FEB   News of Wagner's death
MAY   *Rome with sister*
SUMMER   *Sils Maria*
              Solitude
              Part I published
                  No public response
              Drafts Part II
SEP   *Naumberg with family*
              Family squables over sister's
                  marriage plans
OCT   *Basel, Genoa visits*
NOV   *Nice, France*
              Drafts Part III
1884
APR   *Venice with Gast*
              Part III published
SUMMER   *Sils Maria*
              Solitude
              Visits of Lanzky & Stein
SEP   *Basel, Zurich visits*
NOV   *Nice, France*
              Drafts Part IV
1885
              Publisher refuses Part IV
              Nietzsche publishes himself

APR	Venice
SUMMER	Sils Maria
SEP	Naumberg
	Good-bye to sister
NOV	Nice
1886	
	Writing: Beyond
	Fifth Book of Wisdom
APR	Venice
MAY	Leipzig with Rohde
JUN	Naumberg
	Nietzsche feels desserted by
	friends
SUMMER	Sils Maria
	Sends Beyond to Taine &
	Brandes
	Publisher agrees to new
	edition of works
SEP	Rapallo
	Writing: new prefaces to works
	Reading: Guyau, Bouget, Zola,
	Baudelaire, Dostoevski
1887	
JAN	Hears prelude to Parsifal
	Writing: notes for Genealogy
	Reading: Renan's Origins of Christianity
APR	Swiss Lakes
	News of von Stein's death
SUMMER	Sils Maria
	drafts Genealogy
SEP	Venice
	Breaks off friendship with Rohde
	Brandes writes of interest
	Reading: Goethe
OCT	Nice
1888	
	Writing: Case of Wagner
APR	Turin, Italy
	Brandes writes of class plans

	Reading: Laws of Manu
SUMMER	*Sils Maria*
	Writing: <u>Twilight</u>,
	<u>Anti-Christ</u>
SEP	*Turin*
	Writing: <u>Ecce Homo</u>,
	<u>Nietzsche Contra Wagner</u>
1889	
JAN	Nietzsche collapses in street
	mental abilities lost
	Overbeck comes to help him,
	takes him to Basel
Basel in nursing home	
	Mother arrives to see him,
	takes him to Germany
Jena in University clinic	
	<u>Twilight</u> published
1890	
JAN	Gast visits, stays for some time
FEB	Overbeck visits
MAR	Mother moves him to her apartment
MAY	*Naumberg in care of mother*
DEC	Sister returns from Paraguay,
	now a widow
1891	
	Sister changes plans from return
	to Paraguay permanently,
	to look after Nietzsche's
	unpublished works
	Sister arranges for Gast to edit
	works
1892	
	<u>Zarathustra</u>, Part IV published
JUL	Sister sails to Paraguay to tie up
	loose ends
1893	
SEP	Sister returns, begins setting up
	Nietzsche Archive
	Sister works with publisher to
	arrange complete works, with

Appendix

a biography by herself
Gast dismissed as editor
Sister changes last name to
    Förster-Nietzsche

1894

Lou Salome publishes <u>Friedrich Nietzsche</u>
    <u>in his Works</u>

SEP   Sister moves to separate apartment
    with Archive

1895   <u>Anti-Christ</u> published
Sister completes vol. I of biography
    (two more volumes through 1904)
Rudolf Steiner completes works on Nietzsche
Sister invites Steiner to join Archive
Steiner teaches sister about Nietzsche's
    thought

DEC   Sister gets mother to give up rights to
    Archive for life pension
Elisabeth Förster-Nietzsche now in complete
    control of Nietzsche materials

1896

AUG   Elisabeth moves to Weimar with Archive

1897

APR   Mother dies
Elisabeth moves Nietzsche to Weimar
    to Villa Silberbeck, donated by
    Meta von Salis
Nietzsche on display to public with Archive

1898

SUMMER   Nietzsche suffers minor stroke

1899

English edition of <u>Genealogy</u>

MAY   Nietzsche suffers severe stroke

1900

AUG   *Nietzsche suffers stroke and dies*

1901

1902

Hans Vaihinger publishes <u>Nietzsche</u>
    <u>as Philosopher</u>

1903

	English edition of <u>The Dawn</u>
1904	
1905	
1906	
	Expanded edition of <u>Will to Power</u> published
1907	
	English edition of <u>Beyond</u>
1908	
	<u>Ecce Homo</u> published
1909	
	English edition of complete works: Oscar Levy edition in 18 vols. through 1911
1910	
1911	
	Vaihinger's <u>Philosophy As If</u> Halevy's <u>The Life of Friedrich Nietzsche</u>
1912	
	English edition of Förster-Nietzsche's biography: <u>The Young Nietzsche</u> and <u>The Lonely Nietzsche</u>
1913	
1914	World War breaks out in Europe Brandes' <u>Friedrich Nietzsche</u>
1915	
	Santayana's <u>Egotism in German Philosophy</u>
1916	
1917	
	Salter's <u>Nietzsche the Thinker</u>
1918	World War I ends
1919	
1920	Musarion edition of complete works in German: 23 vols. through 1929
1921	
	<u>The Nietzsche-Wagner Correspondence</u>, edited by E. Förster-Nietzsche (English edition)
1922	
1923	
1924	

Appendix

	English edition of <u>Philosophy As If</u>
1926	
1927	
1928	
1929	
1930	
	Baeumler's <u>Nietzsche: Philosopher and Politician</u>
1931	
	Foster's <u>Friedrich Nietzsche</u>
	Podach's <u>The Madness of Nietzsche</u>
	(English edition)
1932	
	O'Brien's <u>Son of the Morning</u>
1933	
1934	
	Jung's seminars on Nietzsche's <u>Zarathustra</u>
	(through 1939)
1935	
1936	
	Jaspers' <u>Nietzsche: An Introduction to an</u>
	<u>Understanding of his Philosophic Activity</u>
	Heidegger begins lectures on Nietzsche
	(through 1940)
1937	
1938	
1939	World War II breaks out in Europe
1940	
1941	
	Morgan's <u>What Nietzsche Means</u>
	Brinton's <u>Nietzsche</u>
1942	
1943	
1944	
1945	World War II ends
1946	
1947	
1948	
	Lavrin's <u>Nietzsche: An Approach</u>
1949	
1950	

Kaufmann's <u>Nietzsche: Philosopher,</u>
　　　<u>Psychologist, Anti-Christ</u>

1951
1952

Heller's <u>The Disinherited Mind</u>
Williams' <u>Nietzsche and the French</u>

1953
1954

Schlechta edition of complete works:
　　　3 vols. through 1956
Kaufmann's <u>Portable Nietzsche</u>

1955
1956
1957

Lea's <u>The Tragic Philosopher</u>

1958
1959

Leidecker's <u>Unpublished Letters</u>
Heller's <u>The Artist's Journey into the Interior</u>

1960

Steiner's <u>Friedrich Nietzsche:</u>
　　　<u>Fighter for Freedom</u> (original
　　　pieces from 1895-90)

1961

Heidegger's lectures published in
　　　German
Jaspers' <u>Nietzsche and Christianity</u>
　　　(English edition)

1962
1963
1964
1965

Hollingdale's <u>Nietzsche: the Man and his</u>
　　　<u>Philosophy</u>
Danto's <u>Nietzsche As Philosopher</u>
English edition of Jaspers' <u>Nietzsche:</u>
　　　<u>An Understanding of his Philosophic</u>
　　　<u>Activity</u>

1967

Frenzel's <u>Friedrich Nietzsche: An</u>

Appendix

Illustrated Biography

1968
1969

Middleton's Selected Letters

1970
1971
1972

Stambaugh's Nietzsche's Thought of
    Eternal Return

1973

Hollingdale's Nietzsche
Nietzsche: A Collection of Critical
    Essays, ed. by Solomon

1974

Danhauser's Nietzsche's View of Socrates
Wilcox's Truth and Value in Nietzsche
Hayman's Nietzsche: A Critical Life

1975
1976
1977

Alderman's Nietzsche's Gift
The New Nietzsche, ed. Allison

1978
1979

Breazeale's Philosophy and Truth
English edition of Heidegger's lectures
    (vol. I of 4 vols.)

1980
1981
1982

English edition of Heidegger's lectures
    (vol. IV)

1983

Schacht's Nietzsche

1984

English edition of Heidegger's lectures
    (vol. II)

1985

Nehamas' Nietzsche: Life as Literature
Megill's The Prophets of Extremity

1986

Lampert's <u>Nietzsche's Teaching</u>

1987

Higgins' <u>Nietzsche's Zarathustra</u>
Bloom's <u>The Closing of the American Mind</u>
English edition of Heidegger's lectures
    (vol. III)

1988

Heller's <u>The Importance of Nietzsche</u>

1989

Shapiro's <u>Nietzschean Narratives</u>
<u>Friedrich Nietzsche on Rhetoric and</u>
    <u>Language</u>, ed. Gilman

1990

Thiele's <u>Friedrich Nietzsche and the</u>
    <u>Politics of the Soul</u>

Select Bibliography

Sources of Nietzsche's Writings

Friedrich Nietzsche on Rhetoric and Language, edited and translated with a critical
 introduction by S. L. Gilman, C. Blair, and D. J. Parent. New York.
 Oxford U., 1989.
Nietzsche, F. Also Sprach Zarathustra. München. Goldmann., 1961.
Nietzsche., The Anti-Christ, Thus Spoke Zarathustra, and Twilight of the Idols,
 The Portable Nietzsche, translated, edited, and with an introduction,
 prefaces, and notes by W. Kaufmann. New York. Viking., 1954.
Nietzsche, F. Beyond Good and Evil, translated with an introduction by M.
 Cowan. Chicago. Gateway., 1955.
Nietzsche, F. Beyond Good and Evil: Prelude to a Philosophy of the Future,
 translated, with commentary by W. Kaufmann. New York. Vintage., 1966.
Nietzsche, F. The Birth of Tragedy and the Case of Wagner, translated, with
 commentary, by W. Kaufmann. New York. Vintage., 1967.
Nietzsche, F. The Birth of Tragedy and the Genealogy of Morals, translated by F.
 Golffing. Garden City. Doubleday., 1956; Anchor., 1956.
Nietzsche, F. The Dawn of Day, translated by J. M. Kennedy. volume 9 of The
 Complete Works of Friedrich Nietzsche, edited by O. Levy. London.
 Foulis., 1909; New York. Russell and Russell., 1964.
Nietzsche, F. Daybreak: Thoughts on the prejudices of morality, translated by R.
 J. Hollingdale. New York. Cambridge U., 1982
Nietzsce, F. Early Greek Philosophy and Other Essays, translated by M. A.
 Mügge. volume 2 of The Complete Works of Friedrich Nietzsche, edited
 by O. Levy. London. Foulis., 1909; New York. Russell and Russell., 1964.
Nietzsche, F., Ecce Homo and The Birth of Tragedy, translated by C. Fadiman,
 The Philosophy of Nietzsche, with an introduction by W. H. Wright. New
 York. Modern Library., 1927; 1955.
Nietzsche, F. The Gay Science, With a Prelude in Rhymes and an Appendix of
 Songs, translated, with commentary, by W. Kaufmann. New York.
 Vintage., 1974.
Nietzsche, F. Human, All Too Human, translated by M. Faber, with S. Lehman.
 Lincoln. U. of Nebraska., 1984.

Nietzsche, F. Human, All Too Human, part I, translated by H. Zimmern. volume 7 of The Complete Works of Friedrich Nietzsche, edited by O. Levy. London. Foulis., 1909.

Nietzsche, F. Human, All Too Human, part II, translated by P. V. Cohn. volume 7 of The Complete Works of Friedrich Nietzsche, edited by O. Levy. London. Foulis., 1909; New York. Russell and Russell., 1964.

Nietzsche, F. Joyful Wisdom, translated by T. Common. New York. Ungar., 1960; 1971.

Nietzsche, F. On the Genealogy of Morals and Ecce Homo, translated by W. Kaufmann and R. J. Hollingdale, edited with commentary by W. Kaufmann. New York. Vintage., 1967.

Nietzsche, F. Philosophy in the Tragic Age of the Greeks, translated by M. Cown. Chicago. Regnery., 1962.

Nietzsche, F. Thoughts Out of Season, translated by A. M. Ludovici and A. Collins. volumes 4 and 5 of The Complete Works of Friedrich Nietzsche, edited by O. Levy. London. Foulis., 1909; New York. Russell and Russell., 1964.

Nietzsche, F. Thus Spoke Zarathustra, translated by M. Cowan. New York. Gateway., 1957.

Nietzsche, F. Thus Spoke Zarathustra, translated with an introduction by R. J. Hollingdale. Baltimore. Penguin., 1961.

Nietzsche, F. Twilight of the Idols and The Anti-Christ, translated, with an introduction and commentary, by R. J. Hollingdale. Baltimore. Penguin., 1968.

Nietzsche, F. Untimely Meditations, translated by R. J. Hollingdale. New York. Cambride U., 1983.

Nietzsche, F. The Use and Abuse of History, translated by A. Collins. Indianapolis. Library of Liberal Arts., 1957.

Nietzsche, F. The Will to Power, translated by W. Kaufmann and R. J. Hollingdale, edited with commentary by W. Kaufmann. New York. Vintage., 1967; 1968.

The Nietzsche-Wagner Correspondence, translated by C. V. Kerr, edited by E. Förster-Nietzsche. New York. Liveright., 1921; 1949.

Philosophy and Truth: Selections from Nietzsche's Notebooks of the Early 1870's, translated and edited with an introduction and notes by D. Breazeale. Atlantic Highlands. Humanities., 1979.

The Philosophy of Nietzsche, edited with an introduction by J. Clive. New York. Mentor., 1965.

Selected Letters of Friedrich Nietzsche, edited and translated by C. Middleton. Chicago. U. of Chicago., 1969.

Unpublished Letters, translated and edited by K. F. Leidecker. New York. Philosophical Library., 1959.

Studies of Nietzsche

Alderman, H. Nietzsche's Gift. Athens. Ohio U., 1977.

Brandes, G. Friedrich Nietzsche. New York. Haskell., 1972.

Brinton, C. Nietzsche. Cambridge. Harvard U., 1941; New York. Harper., 1965.

Danhauser, W. J. Nietzsche's View of Socrates. Ithaca. Cornell U., 1974.

Danto, A. Nietzsche as a Philosopher. New York. MacMillan., 1965.

Foster, G. B. Friedrich Nietzsche. New York. MacMillan., 1931.

Frenzel, I. Nietzsche: An Illustrated Biography, translated by J. Neugroschel. New York. Pegasus., 1967.

Halvey, D. The Life of Friedrich Nietzsche, translated by J. M. Home. London. Unwin., 1914.

Harper, R. The Seventh Solitude. Baltimore. Johns Hopkins U., 1965.

Hayman, R. Nietzsche: A Critical Life. New York. Oxford U., 1980; New York. Penguin., 1987.

Heidegger, M. Nietzsche. 4 volumes. New York. Harper., 1979-1987.

Heller, E. The Disinherited Mind. London. Bowes & Bowes., 1952; Hammondsworth. Penguin., 1961.

Heller, E. The Importance of Nietzsche. Chicago. U. of Chicago., 1988.

Higgins, K. M. Nietzsche's Zarathustra. Philadelphia. Temple U., 1987.

Hollingdale, R. J. Nietzsche. Boston. Routledge., 1973.

Hollingdale, R. J. Nietzsche: The Man and His Philosophy. Baton Rouge. Lousianna State U., 1965.

Jaspers, K. Nietzsche: An Understanding of His Philosophical Activity, translated Wallraff and Schmitz. Chicago. Regnery., 1965.

Jung, C. G. Nietzsche's Zarathustra: Notes of the Seminar Given in 1934-1939, edited by J. L. Jarrett. 2 volumes. Princeton. Princeton U., 1988.

Kaufmann, W. Nietzsche: Philosopher, Psychologist, Anti-Christ. New York. Vintage., 1950; 1968.

Lavrin, J. Nietzsche: An Approach. London. Methuen., 1948.

Lea, F. A. The Tragic Philosopher. London. Methuen., 1957.

Megill, A. The Prophets of Extremity. Berkeley. U. of California., 1985.

Morgan, G. A. What Nietzsche Means. Cambridge. Harvard U., 1941; New York. Harper., 1965.

Nehamas, A. Nietzsche: Life as Literature. Cambridge. Harvard U., 1985.

O'Brien, E. J. Son of the Morning: A Portrait of Friedrich Nietzsche. New York. Ballou., 1932.

Peters, H. P. Zarathustra's Sister. New York. Crown., 1977.

Salter, W. M. Nietzsche the Thinker. New York. Ungar., 1917; 1968.

Schacht, R. Nietzsche. London. Routledge., 1983.
Shapiro, G. Nietzschean Narratives. Bloomington, Indianna U., 1989.
Stambaugh, J. Nietzsche's Thought of Eternal Return. Baltimore. Johns Hopkins
    U., 1972; Lanham. Univeristy Press of America., 1988.
Steiner, R. Friedrich Nietzsche: Fighter for Freedom, translated M. I. de Ris.
    Englewood. Steiner Publications., 1960.
Thiele, L. P. Friedrich Nietzsche and the Politics of the Soul. Princeton. Princeton
    U., 1990.
Wilcox, J. T. Truth and Value in Nietzsche. Ann Arbor. U. of Michigan., 1974.
Williams, B. Nietzsche and the French. Oxford. Blackwell., 1952.

Nietzsche Collections

Nietzsche: A Collection of Critical Essays, edited by R. C. Solomon. Garden
    City. Anchor., 1973.
The New Nietzsche: Contemporary Styles of Interpretation, edited by D. B.
    Allison. New York. Delta., 1977.

Other Sources

An Anthology of German Poetry from Hölderlin to Rilke in English Translation,
    edited by A. Flores. Garden City. Anchor., 1960.
Barrett, W. Irrational Man. Garden City. Anchor., 1962.
Barzun, J. Darwin, Marx and Wagner. New York. Little Brown., 1941; Garden
    City. Anchor., 1958.
Becker, E. The Denial of Death. New York. Free Press., 1973; 1975.
Bernstein, R. J. Praxis and Action. Philadelphia. U. of Pennsylvania., 1971.
Bloom, A. The Closing of the American Mind. New York. Simon and Schuster.,
    1987.
Dodds, E. R. The Greeks and the Irrational. Berkeley. U. of California., 1951;
    1966.
Donadio, S. Nietzsche, Henry James, and the Artistic Will. New York. Oxford U.,
    1978.
The Essential Schopenhauer. New York. Barnes and Noble, 1962.
Ewing, A. C. A Short Commentary on Kant's Critique of Pure Reason. Chicago.
    U. of Chicago., 1938.
Feuerbach, L. The Essence of Christianity, translated by G. Elliot. New York.
    Harper., 1957.
Force and Freedom: An Interpretation of History by Jacob Burckhardt, edited by
    J. H. Nichols. New York. Meridian., 1955.
Friedrich Hölderlin: An Early Modern, edited by E. E. George. Ann Arbor. U. of
    Michigan., 1972.

Gutman, R. W. <u>Richard Wagner: The Man, His Mind and His Thought</u>. New York. Harcourt., 1968.

Guyau, M. <u>The Non-Religion of the Future</u>. New York. Schocken., 1962.

Heine, H. <u>Religion and Philosophy in Germany</u>, translated by J. Snodgrass. Boston. Beacon., 1959.

Jaeger, W. <u>Paideia</u>, translated by G. Highet. 3 volumes. New York. Oxford U., 1939; 1965.

Kant, I. <u>Critique of Judgement</u>, translated by J. H. Bernard. New York. Hafner., 1951.

Kant, I. <u>Critique of Pure Reason</u>, translated by N. K. Smith. New York. MacMillan., 1929; St. Martin's., 1965.

Kaufmann, W. <u>Discovering the Mind</u>. 3 volumes. New York. McGraw-Hill., 1980.

Kaufmann, W. <u>From Shakespeare to Existentialism</u>. Boston. Beacon., 1959; Garden City. Anchor., 1960.

Kaufmann, W. <u>Hegel: A Reinterpretation</u>. New York. Doubleday., 1965; Garden City. Anchor., 1966.

Kaufmann, W. <u>Tragedy and Philosophy</u>. New York. Doubleday., 1968; Garden City. Anchor., 1969.

Lange, F. A. <u>The History of Materialism and Criticism of Its Present Importance</u>, translated by E. C. Thomas. London. Routledge., 1957.

Magee, B. <u>Aspects of Wagner</u>. New York. Oxford U., 1988.

Magee, B. <u>The Philosophy of Schopenhauer</u>. New York. Oxford U., 1983

Mertz, J. T. <u>A History of European Thought in the Nineteenth Century</u>. volume II. New York. Blackwood., 1904-12; Dover., 1965.

Millington, B. <u>Wagner</u>. London. Dent & Sons., 1986.

Pitkin, H. F. <u>Wittgenstein and Justice</u>. Berkeley. U. of California., 1972.

Santayana, G. <u>The German Mind</u>. New York. Crowell., 1939; 1968.

Santayana, G. <u>Three Philosophical Poets: Lucretius, Dante & Goethe</u>. Cambridge. Harvard U., 1910; Garden City. Anchor., 1953.

Scharfstein, B. <u>The Philosophers: Their Lives and the Nature of Their Thought</u>. New York. Oxford U., 1980.

Schopenhauer, A. <u>The World as Will and Representation</u>, translated by E. F. Payne. 2 volumes. New York. Dover., 1969.

Schwegler, A. <u>A History of Philosophy in Epitome</u>, translated by J. H. Seelye. New York. Appleton., 1877.

Silz, W. <u>Hölderlin's Hyperion: A Critical Reading</u>. Philadelphia. U. of Pennsylvania., 1969.

Snell, B. <u>The Discovery of the Mind</u>. Cambridge. Harvard U., 1953.

Taylor, R. <u>Richard Wagner: His Life, Art and Thought</u>. New York. Toplinger., 1979.

Vesey, G. <u>Personal Identity: A Philosophical Analysis</u>. Ithaca. Cornell U., 1977.

Wagner, R. The Ring of the Nibelung, translated by A. Porter. New York. Norton., 1977.

Wagner On Music and Drama: A Compendium of Richard Wagner's Prose Writings, translated by H. A. Ellis, edited by A. Goldman and E. Sprinchorn. New York. Dutton., 1964.

Willey, T. E. Back to Kant. Detroit. Wayne State U., 1978.

Wisdom, J. O. Philosophy and Its Place in our Culture. New York. Gordon & Beach., 1975.

Wittgenstein, L. Philosophical Investigations, translated by G. E. M. Anscombe. New York. MacMillan., 1953; 1968.

The Works of Schopenhauer, translated by Haldane & Kemp, edited by W. Durant. Garden City. Garden City Publishing., 1928.

INDEX

affirmation, 36, 51, 64, 69, 75-76, 77-79, 81
109, 112-13, 118, 127, 130, 134, 149, 155
Alderman (Harold), 132, 136, 149
amour fati, 63, 118, 127
animal will, 45, 64
Apollo, 74
Apollonian theme, 8-9
arete, 127
Aristotle, 89
ascetic ideal, 45, 69, 100-03, 108, 117-18

Barrett (William), 154
Barzun (Jacques), 15
Basel, 31-32, 37-38, 50, 70, 76, 80
Bayreuth, 12, 30, 33, 37, 70
Becker (Ernest), 153-54
Berkeley (Bishop), 27
Berlin, 70
Bernstein (Richard), 153
Bible, 116
"blond beast," 111
Bloom (Allan), 148
Boltzmann (Ludwig), 5
Bonn, 6-7, 161
Brandes (George), 93, 103, 144, 151
Breazeale (Daniel), 29-30
Buddhism, 13, 52, 88, 90
Burckhardt (Jacob), 31-33, 36, 38, 50, 129
Byron (Lord), 6, 124

Christianity, 6, 12-14, 16, 19, 29, 47, 88, 90, 94, 96, 110, 112-15, 117-18, 123-25, 138, 163-64
conscience, 48-49, 90, 116-17
consciousness, 52, 55, 95, 101, 126, 130, 132, 139-41, 150-51, 154
conversion, 12-13, 20
Crucified (the), 118, 164

death, 14, 61, 69, 81, 103, 108, 128, 133, 155
decadence, 32-33, 108-11, 113-14, 117
democracy, 32, 40
Democritus, 42
depression, 20, 37-38, 50, 56, 63, 76, 81, 85
determinism, 55, 58, 62, 87, 99, 109, 138, 142
Dewey (John), 153
Dionysian theme, 8-9
Dionysus, 74, 93, 111, 118, 125, 130, 146, 149-50, 154-55

ego, 20, 38, 75, 101, 140
egoism, 49, 62, 69, 75, 91, 101
Emerson (Ralph), 124
Engels, 5
Epicurus, 47
Euripides, 10

191

eternal recurrence, 62-63, 69, 73-74, 77-79, 81-82, 86, 89, 111-12, 118, 124, 127, 130, 135-37, 144, 149, 164

eternal return, 74, 143
Ewing (A. C.), 138

fate, 15, 36, 110
feeling of power, 52, 56, 101, 115, 126-27, 155
Feuerbach (Ludwig), 129-30
Franco-Prussian War, 33
free spirits, 37-41, 45, 47, 50-51, 54, 56, 64-69, 73-74, 88, 90-92, 94, 96-97, 101-02, 115-17, 126, 131
free will, 38-39, 42, 55, 62, 67-68, 87, 110, 138
Freud (Sigmund), 48, 151, 156

Gast (Peter), 93
Genoa, 62-63, 78
genius, 14, 16, 18, 20-21, 30, 33, 45, 66
Germania, 6
Germany, 12, 124
God, 13-14, 53-54, 67, 76, 81, 86, 89, 93, 97, 99, 110, 112-13, 115-17, 124-25, 128, 130, 133, 139, 149, 155-57, 162, 164
god, 10, 21, 114
Goethe, 6, 20, 89, 103-04, 110-11, 124, 154-55
Greek culture, 7-8, 15-17, 22, 26, 34, 123-24, 162
Greek philosophy, 7, 28-29, 34, 134, 142, 145
Guyau, 155

Hegel, 116, 129
Heller (Eric), 133
Heraclitus, 22, 26
higher men, 64-65, 69, 74, 88
Higgins (Kathleen), 153
Hobbes, 94
Hölderlin, 6, 124
Hollingdale (R. J.), 91, 112, 145
Homer, 16
hubris, 2, 96, 145, 152, 155

illusion, 8-11, 17, 26, 28, 30, 34-36,

39-40, 45, 74, 108, 127-28, 147-49
immoralist, 110, 117, 131
individualism, 91, 116, 126, 128, 136-37, 155
innocence, 50, 56, 69, 75, 78-79, 93-94, 100, 110, 115

Jesus Christ, 17, 77, 94, 115-16, 125, 154-55

Kant, 11, 16-17, 27, 35, 42, 49, 55, 95, 129, 136, 138-39, 141
Kaufmann (Walter), 82, 116, 154
Lange (F. A.), 29
Lanzky (Paul), 81
laughter, 146, 149-50
Lea (Frank), 14
Leipzig, 7, 15, 31, 70, 93
Lessing, 6
logic, 152
loneliness, 18, 31, 85, 97, 103, 161, 164
Luther, 116

madness, 50, 65-66
marriage, 70
Marx, 5, 48
master, 90-92, 99
mathematics, 5
Megill (Allan), 86
metaphysics, 9-10, 13-14, 26, 29, 35, 38, 41-42, 46, 48, 51, 62, 66, 80, 86, 103, 115, 119, 123, 129, 135-38, 143, 146, 149-50, 155
Meysenbug, 69-70
morality, 7, 18, 38, 42, 45, 47-49, 51-52, 54, 57, 64, 66-68, 88-89, 92, 94, 96, 99, 109, 114, 117-18, 138, 156, 163-64
music drama, 22
myth, 9, 11, 17, 26, 28, 34, 39, 61, 69, 87, 94, 101, 134, 137, 148-50, 165

naturalism, 91, 110, 115, 134, 137
Naumberg, 6, 32, 50, 78
Nazi, 40, 90
Neo-Kantianism, 7, 66, 123
Nice, 78, 81, 86
Nietzsche; ealry life, 5-8; & philology, 7-12; Birth of Tragedy, 8-12, 14-16, 25, 28,

192

Nietzsche (cont'd)
8-12, 14-16, 25, 28, 32-34, 39, 46,
51, 67, 74, 96, 107, 125, 133, 148-
50; Untimely Meditations, 17-22, 29,
37-38, 46, 66, 79, 85, 93; Tragic Age,
25-30, 37; "Philosophers' Book," 29-
31; "The Philosopher as Cultural Physician," 35; Human, 36-43, 45-46, 50,
54, 61, 64, 69, 73, 81, 85, 94, 96-
98, 108, 119, 163; Mixed Maxims, 46-
47, 50; Wanderer, 46-50; Dawn, 51-56,
62-63, 132, 136; Wisdom, 8, 61, 63-
71, 73-74, 85, 93-96, 108, 116, 126,
128, 131, 142, 149; Zarathustra, 2,
61, 63-64, 67, 69, 73-82, 85-86, 93,
96, 98, 103, 107-08, 109, 114, 117-
18, 118, 132, 136-37, 143, 145, 149-
50, 155; Beyond, 61, 63, 85-93, 98,
136; Genealogy, 61, 85, 98-103, 117,
131; Twilight, 61, 107-12; Anti-
Christ, 61-62, 107, 112-16, 127;
Ecce Homo, 61, 107, 112, 116-19;
Wagner Case, 61, 107, Nietzsche
Contra, 107; "Will to Power," 61,
112; influence of Wagner, 33, 36-
37, 64, 69, 73, 107, 123-29; influence of Schopenhauer, 7-9, 11-
21, 30, 32-36, 42-43, 46-47, 64,
66, 76-77, 96-98, 111, 114, 123,
128-36, 139-41

O'Brien (E. J.), 46
Overbeck, 70, 76, 162
overman, 38, 75, 131, 164

Parmenides, 28
Paul (Saint), 115
perspectivalism, 97
pessimism, 28, 34, 42, 81, 93, 95,
97, 101, 124-25, 129, 133
Pforta, 6-7, 32, 161
philology, 7-8, 12, 15-17, 25, 33,
41, 115, 123, 163
Pindar, 116
Pitkin (Hannah), 133-34
Plato, 2, 10, 16, 28-29, 51, 76,
135-36
Poincare (Henri), 145
Pre-Socratics, 25, 27, 31, 145

Rapallo, 70, 73, 93
Ree (Paul), 37-38, 50, 69-70, 76, 98
Renaissance, 111, 114
revaluation, 89, 112, 148
Ritschl, 7, 25, 31, 33
Rohde, 93, 104
Romaticism, 6, 11, 64, 66, 69, 95, 111
Rome, 69, 76
Rousseau, 20, 32, 151

Salome (Lou), 63, 70, 76, 80
Salter (W. M.), 49
Santayana, 133
scepticism, 30, 51
Schacht (Richard), 142-43
Scharfstein (B.), 133
Schiller, 6
Schopenhauer, 7, 9, 11-21, 26, 29-30, 32-
36, 39, 42-43, 46, 49, 51, 62, 66, 76-77,
80, 95, 98, 114, 116, 123-24, 126, 128-
31, 134-36, 139-40, 144, 146, 149, 151
science, 11, 14, 17-18, 27, 35-36, 39, 42,
45, 47, 51, 53-54, 62, 64-65, 68, 70,
86, 94-96, 99, 102, 109, 115, 119, 124,
138-39, 143, 144, 150-51, 153, 155-56,
163-64
self-affirmation, 99, 113
self-consciousness, 95, 101, 116, 138, 140
self-overcoming, 22, 78, 145
sexuality, 112
Sicily, 69
Siegfried, 16, 127-28, 131
Sils Maria, 50, 62, 76, 80, 86, 93, 104,
107
skepticism, 34
slave morality, 99
socialism, 40, 90
Socrates, 10, 57, 108, 117
Sorrento, 37
soul, 19, 26-27, 35, 47, 52, 55, 66, 68,
78-79, 87, 101, 115, 138
Spinoza, 62, 89
Stein (Heinrich von), 80, 98
Stendhal, 162
Stoics, 89
Strauss (David), 12, 17, 115
Strauss (Richard), 144
suffering, 11, 13, 20, 42, 47, 56, 77,
79-80, 91, 95, 130, 161, 164

superman, 38, 113
Sysiphus, 151

Taine, 93
Thales, 43
Theognis, 25, 28
tragedy, 8-9, 14, 16, 21, 25,
  36, 64, 74, 124-25
transvaluation, 112, 117
Tribschen, 70
Truth, 11-12, 19, 40, 65, 67, 96,
  101-03, 128, 134-35, 137-38
Turin, 103-04, 107

Übermensch, 38, 74-82, 90-92,
  98, 112-13, 117, 124, 126,
  137, 143-44, 149, 155-56, 164

Valadier, 155
Venice, 80, 85, 93, 104

Wagner, 7-8, 11-19, 21-22, 29-
  34, 36-38, 42, 46, 69-70, 73,
  76, 107, 123-129, 144, 150,
  155, 162
Williams (Bernard), 46
will to create, 131, 147, 155
will to health, 97, 118
will to power, 74-75, 77-80, 87-
  92, 94, 98-103, 113, 117, 124,
  126, 131, 135-37, 140-44, 147,
  150-51, 153, 155-56, 164
will to truth, 48, 90, 97, 103,
  126, 129, 131
wisdom, 18, 63, 67, 69, 77, 82,
  95
Wisdom (J. O.), 161
Wittgenstein, 5, 65, 133-34,
  151-52, 161

Zarathustra ideal, 103, 103, 111-
  16, 130, 146, 150
Zeus, 28